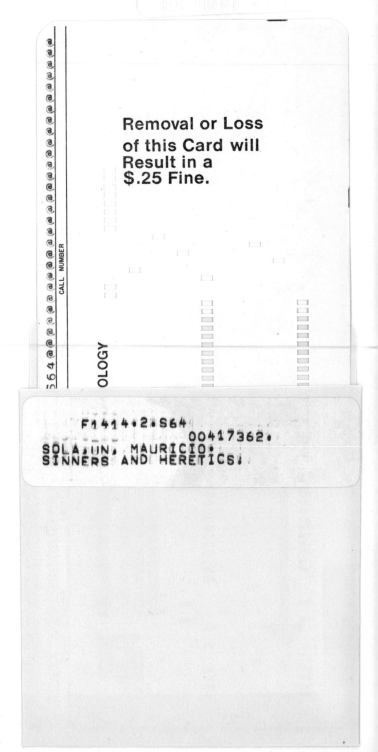

CALL NUMBER

564

OLOGY

**Removal or Loss
of this Card will
Result in a
$.25 Fine.**

SINNERS AND HERETICS

SINNERS AND HERETICS

The Politics of Military
Intervention in Latin America

MAURICIO SOLAÚN and MICHAEL A. QUINN

58
ILLINOIS STUDIES IN THE SOCIAL SCIENCES

UNIVERSITY OF ILLINOIS PRESS
Urbana Chicago London

TO ROBERT E. SCOTT

© 1973 by The Board of Trustees of the University of Illinois
Manufactured in the United States of America
Library of Congress Catalog Card No. 72-78402

ISBN 0-252-00284-9

PREFACE

This study offers a comparative exploration of the causes of coups d'état in Latin America during the post–World War II period. Based in large part on an analysis of approximately one-half of the number of successful coups in the area between 1943 and 1967, the study describes their main processes and provides an explanatory framework which facilitates understanding of the coups.

In the presentation of our analysis we hope to overcome some of the weaknesses of the literature on Latin American coups. First of all, studies often generalize their findings on the basis of an inspection of a few specific cases or an analysis of several unidentified coups. In contrast, the present study is explicitly founded on the analysis of thirty cases in the post–World War II period, a period chosen for its relevance to readers in the light of contemporary problems. The thirty coups and our findings with respect to each are enumerated for those who might be interested in the interpretation of specific cases.

Another shortcoming evident in some of the literature refers to the matter of oversimplified analysis. Usually, no distinction is drawn between those factors which provide a relatively enduring structural and cultural basis for coup activity and those which act as mere triggering agents in situations already conducive to some form of political breakdown. As we develop them in the text, the relatively enduring causes of the coups furnish the parameters within which the triggering factors operate. For example, the persistent weakness of political party organization provides the structural context in which a particularly strife-torn election may trigger a military takeover.

Some studies of military intervention in Latin America, particularly those which rely almost exclusively on statistical techniques, fail to provide a general perspective that can help the reader gain insight into the complex logic of the coup process. This weakness can be accounted for in part by the fact that it is very costly and difficult to operationalize most of the relevant macrosociological variables with which comparative political theorists have concerned themselves. In addition, the low incidence of some critical macrosociological variables does not favor sophisticated statistical analysis. For our part, we feel that the difficulties are more than compensated for by the understanding that can come from working with such variables, which are fertile sources for generating hypotheses concerning political stability and breakdown in the Latin American context.

In establishing an analytical perspective for the book we have drawn primarily from the structural-functional current of comparative political theory. However, those parts of the analysis that make explicit use of the concept of equilibrium reflect the logic of economic theory. As we shall see, from this equilibrium perspective coups appear as the product of relatively severe imbalances between the dimensions of political participation and political organization in given societies. We have also drawn on certain elements of legal theory which enable us to establish requirements for regime stability and the long-term absence of coups d'état.

A final criticism which can be made of the literature on Latin American coups and, we might add, of broader comparative studies as well, is that the nature of the actual processes which lead up to and define the coup d'état are seldom given any systematic examination. Many studies designed to explore hypotheses relating to political violence have simply lumped together the most diverse kinds of violence — nonpolitical violence, coup d'état, and revolution. We feel rather strongly that it is a mistake to confuse the kind of violence associated, let us say, with the change of government in Panama in 1949 with that which brought about the Castro regime in Cuba in 1959. Our study begins by introducing the important distinction between coup d'état and revolution, and the study as a whole offers a systematic consideration of the nature of the various processes which lead up to and define the coup d'état. As in some other investigations of political violence, we explore the factors that contribute to both the breakdown and the resilience of political systems. However, our study emphasizes the nature of coup processes and it links them to the various cultural and structural characteristics that are prevalent in Latin America. In this respect, we have emphasized the qualitative dimensions of Latin American coups.

It is our hope that the concepts, hypotheses, and categories that are established in the text will be of help to future researchers. In the final analysis, the formulations presented in our study cannot be refined until systematic country-by-country studies are undertaken. In our view, these studies should constitute the foremost priority of researchers interested in furthering understanding of the complexities of the coup d'état.

At this point it might be helpful to present a few comments on the organization of our study. Chapters 1 and 2 are devoted largely to preliminary matters of definition and analytical perspective. In addition to providing a necessary basis for the discussion in subsequent chapters, the first two chapters also serve to introduce the reader to some of the prior research that has been directed at questions of political breakdown generally and Latin American coups in particular. Chapters 3 and 4 make use of our data on the thirty post-war coups for the purpose of getting at the nature of the processes that triggered them during the period in question. The data presented in these middle chapters enable us to offer some judgments concerning the relative utility of the explanations commonly adduced to account for Latin American coups. Chapters 5 and 6 deal with some of the relatively enduring structural and cultural characteristics that furnish the parameters within which the coup processes operate. Socioeconomic and political structures, as well as the character of the political culture found throughout much of the area, are prominent topics of discussion in these final two chapters of the book. Chapter 6 concludes with a paradigm that attempts to integrate the materials of the study by bringing together some of the factors that are necessary to an understanding of coups d'état in Latin America.

In the preparation of this study we have benefitted much from the suggestions of numerous friends and colleagues. In particular, we would like to thank Robert Byars, Fernando Cepeda, Raymond Duncan, Harry Johnson, Juan Linz, Joseph Love, Martin Needler, and Alejandro Portes, all of whom read and commented on the manuscript at different points in time during the preparation and revision of the study. We are also grateful to the Graduate College Research Board, the Center for Latin American Studies, and the Department of Sociology at the University of Illinois for providing the financial support necessary for execution of the study. We also owe many thanks to Deborah Danby and Ann Wendell for their assistance with the many research and administrative tasks that were needed to get the study into final form. Finally, special thanks are due our wives, Joan and Margaret, who provided the moral support and understanding so necessary to completion of the work. Naturally, all of these wonderful people helped to shape the strengths of the book, but only the authors can be held responsible for any shortcomings that it may contain.

Urbana, Illinois
May, 1972

CONTENTS

1

DEFINITIONS AND APPROACHES

This chapter is designed to establish a foundation for our analysis of the principal characteristics and causes of Latin American military coups, or *golpes de estado,* as they are called throughout the area. The initial concern here is with the definition of key concepts. In the second section of the chapter the focus centers on two analytical interpretations that provide a basis for consideration of the various explanations which have been used to account for Latin American coups. But first we turn to a few remarks about the general nature of the coup d'état.

Coup d'État Defined

For purposes of this study, a coup is defined as the unlawful removal and replacement of the chief executive of a country by a force that is predominantly military in character. As such, coups are a form of political violence that involves the breakdown of existing regimes. In the remainder of the present section the several components that comprise our basic definition are considered in some detail, with examples drawn from the Latin American experience for illustrative purposes.

A fuller appreciation of our definition can be achieved by comparing coups with another kind of political violence with which they are often contrasted — revolutions. In general terms, both *golpes* and revolutions are forms of political violence which result in the forcible removal of established governments.[1] At the same time, coups can be distinguished from revolutions in terms of the character of their participants. In the

[1] This similarity leads Martin Needler to consider coups a form of "revolutionary" violence. See Martin C. Needler, *Political Development in Latin America: Instability, Violence, and Evolutionary Change* (New York, 1968), p. 49.

latter case, the executive is toppled by a force composed primarily of civilian participants, whereas elements from the country's military establishment play the leading role in coup situations. In Latin American coups the principal actors are members of the armed forces or the police. Normally the army emerges as the source of the coup, thereby reflecting its predominant position vis-à-vis the other services.

Of course it is true that some coups involve the cooperation of civilians with military elements in the preparation and execution of the attempt to bring down the government. It is also true that large-scale revolutions ultimately involve the creation of popular armies from among the civilian population. This does not negate the essential difference between revolution and coup d'état — revolution is primarily a civilian phenomenon, while coup d'état is predominantly military in character. The lower the level of civilian participation, the more the phenomenon can be classified as a "pure" coup and vice versa.

Another criterion often used to distinguish between coups and revolutions is the intensity of violence. Revolutions involve a good deal more bloodshed than coups. Taking the number of lives lost as a rough indicator of the level of violence, there can be no doubt that history's bona fide revolutions — the French, the Russian, and the Mexican, for example — have been far more violent than Latin American *golpes*. While coup deaths seldom exceed a hundred,[2] loss of life due to revolutions is ordinarily estimated in the tens of thousands, and sometimes much higher estimates are found.[3] This difference is not difficult to understand, given the fact of civilian participation in revolutions. For one thing, the sheer magnitude of numbers directly involved is far greater in revolutions. Moreover, the loose organization and ignorance of the professional skills necessary for the efficient use of violence that are characteristic of civilian participation tend to produce a great deal of "wasted" blood. Also, revolutions are stretched over much longer periods of time. A coup d'état seldom extends more than two or three days at the most, while revolutions commonly endure over a period of several years. Each of these factors contributes to the fact that revolutions are more violent than coups.

At the same time, it would be a mistake to assume that all coups are bloodless because, in fact, they vary in intensity of violence. Some coups may be executed without any bloodshed worthy of mention. This is the

[2] See William S. Stokes, "Violence as a Power Factor in Latin American Politics," *Western Political Quarterly,* 5 (1952), 445-468.

[3] For example, Charles C. Cumberland estimates that almost two million lives were lost as a result of the Mexican Revolution! See his *Mexico: The Struggle for Modernity* (New York, 1968), pp. 245-246, 336.

coup generally popularized in the literature. A case in point occurred in November, 1948, when the Venezuelan army removed President Gallegos without having to fire a single shot. In this instance and others like it, the mere demonstration of the capability for violence is sufficient to make the threat of its use credible, the normal result being the flight of the deposed executive.[4] At times, however, the situation escalates, and the safety of the deposed president is jeopardized. An example is the Bolivian coup of July, 1946, when President Gualberto Villarroel was not only removed from office, but brutally assassinated as well. According to one account, "the junta's assassins cornered President Villarroel in his own offices and shot him, then threw him, still alive, from the second-story window where a mob seized the body and hanged it from a lamp post...."[5] In some other instances, violence is even broader in scope — furious fighting and substantial loss of life occur. This is particularly likely to be the case when the army splits on the issue of the *golpe,* for then the probability that two or more units will do battle against one another is quite high. For example, the combat that led to the 1945 ouster of the Venezuelan president, Isaías Medina, involved thousands of troops and police, and tanks and airplanes were utilized. The violence occasionally results in hundreds of fatalities. In short, revolutions are more violent than coups, yet some *golpes* are anything but bloodless, and coups in general exhibit some variation with respect to accompanying levels of violence.

Coups and revolutions also differ with respect to the extent of political and socioeconomic change that takes place subsequent to the forcible overthrow of the government. Revolution is usually defined in terms of fundamental changes in political and socioeconomic organization. George Blanksten, for example, defines revolution as "a vast and impersonal movement of considerable proportions. [The revolution] may recast the entire social order, bringing far-reaching changes affecting virtually all sectors of society."[6] In comparison, *golpes* — Blanksten calls them "typical Latin American revolutions" — "do not normally bring fundamental social and political changes...."[7] The point is often made

[4] For a discussion of the potential for violence as an important political resource in Latin America, see Charles W. Anderson, *Politics and Economic Change in Latin America* (Princeton, N.J., 1967), chap. 4.

[5] Stokes, "Violence in Latin American Politics," p. 458.

[6] George I. Blanksten, "Revolutions," in *Government and Politics in Latin America,* ed. Harold E. Davis (New York, 1958), p. 120. See also Walter Laqueur, "Revolution," in *International Encyclopedia of the Social Sciences* (New York, 1968), XIII, 501-507.

[7] Blanksten, "Revolutions," p. 141.

that coups involve little more than changes in top governmental personnel — the "ins" and the "outs" switch places, and control over the spoils of office passes from the deposed executive and his entourage to the *golpistas*.[8]

While it is undoubtedly correct that revolutions generally produce political and socioeconomic changes of greater magnitude than coups, this distinction must be qualified carefully because many Latin American *golpes* have brought about substantial changes in their own right. Most coups involve a good deal more than a simple reshuffling of top government personnel. In some instances — mainly those which have been accompanied by bloodshed and a measure of civilian participation — Latin American coups have produced a degree of socioeconomic change. Social class relationships may even be affected.[9] The coups that took place in Guatemala in October, 1944, and in Venezuela in October, 1945, are cases in point. The former case ushered in the moderately leftist regime of Juan José Arévalo, who initiated substantial labor and agrarian reforms. In the latter case, civilian reformers of *Acción Democrática* joined with junior army officers to remove the president. During the following three years of *Acción Democrática*'s ascendancy, land reform projects, labor unions, and peasant organizations were actively promoted. Indeed, the reformist zeal of the party leadership eventually led it to support policies hostile to the same military officers who had helped it to power in 1945. The rather far-reaching character of the reforms that led the military to remove Rómulo Gallegos' government in November, 1948, is concisely described by Harry Bernstein:

> The army officers' cooperation with Acción Democrática had been deceptive. They could not accept the promises, made in public, to socialize the land for the Venezuelan peasants or to lead the workers towards Venezuelan socialism. Even more dangerous to them — as members of a profession rather than a social class — was the new proposal . . . that the army and its officers be reduced in size and influence and replaced by workers' and peasants' militias. The idea of trade union battalions and *campesino* rifles was . . . antimilitary . . . in itself. It was stopped.[10]

Similar fears led the Peruvian military to conduct a preemptive coup

---

[8] See, for example, *ibid.* Similar interpretations are offered by Laqueur, "Revolution," and Merle Kling, "Towards a Theory of Power and Political Instability in Latin America," *Western Political Quarterly*, 9 (1956), 21-35.

[9] According to Needler's data, the class dimension is increasingly apparent in contemporary Latin American coups. Needler, *Political Development in Latin America*, chap. 4.

[10] Harry Bernstein, *Venezuela and Colombia* (Englewood Cliffs, N.J., 1964), p. 61.

in 1948, when it blocked the accession to power of Víctor Raul Haya de la Torre and his left-wing APRA movement. In short, some Latin American *golpes* have produced a measure of socioeconomic change, while others have been conducted in order to ensure that such change would not be carried out. Both types of coups will be analyzed at greater length in subsequent chapters of this study.

From a slightly different perspective, coups are significant to the extent that they bear on efforts designed to achieve a higher level of socioeconomic development. In one sense, *golpes* can be particularly damaging to such efforts. Governments threatened by coups tend to be ineffective; excessive preoccupation with their own preservation leaves governments with little energy to direct toward socioeconomic programming and related growth goals. Moreover, the turnover of top governmental personnel that a high frequency of coups produces makes it exceedingly difficult to achieve sustained developmental efforts. Undoubtedly, Honduras' current low level of socioeconomic development can be understood partly in terms of the fact that it had 116 presidents in the space of 126 years.[11] On the other hand, *golpes* are sometimes justified as necessary to remove governments opposed to significant changes in the status quo. Occasionally, coups may even install a technocratic regime committed to the pursuit of economic development. The 1964 Brazilian coup appears to be a case in point.[12] In short, the relationship that exists between socioeconomic change and coups d'état is a complex one that will receive more attention later. For now, suffice it to note that many coups have appreciable socioeconomic consequences.

Even in those numerous cases where the forcible overthrow of government by the military has had no appreciable effect on social class relationships, the impact of the *golpe* often has gone beyond a mere reshuffling of top government personnel. Some coups have resulted in important changes of political structure. For example, when Juan Vicente Gómez seized power from Venezuelan president Cipriano Castro in 1908 with the aid of the army, the *golpe* ushered in a highly repressive

[11] William S. Stokes, *Honduras: An Area Study in Government* (Madison, Wis., 1950), p. 181.

[12] The technocratic elements characteristic of the military government of Marshal Humberto Alencar de Castelo Branco (1964-67) are described in Cândido Mendes de Almeida, "Sistema Político e Modelos de Poder no Brasil," *Dados,* no. 1, 2nd semester, 1966, 7-41. It should be noted that authoritarian regimes committed to economic modernization along capitalist lines are not new to Latin America. In this sense see the remarks on "enlightened unifying dictatorships" in Gino Germani and Kalman Silvert, "Politics, Social Structure and Military Intervention in Latin America," *European Journal of Sociology,* 2 (1961), 62-81.

dictatorship which was to last until the mid-1930s. Gómez, who came to be known as the "tyrant of the Andes," introduced important political changes: "The political terms . . . laid down were indeed harsh, one-sided, and not open to debate. After a century's struggle over federalism, liberty, and greater regional expression, there emerged just the opposite: a strong, central power and one-man rule."[13] In other instances, significant political changes have followed coups executed against authoritarian regimes. For example, the personalistic, military rule of the Colombian dictator, Gustavo Rojas Pinilla, was terminated by a coup in 1957. In the period which followed, political parties were reactivated, elections were held, and the country again enjoyed freedom of the press. This *golpe* initiated a period of civilian rule which has continued without interruptions to the present time. Both authoritarian and "liberalizing" coups can produce significant changes in political structure, with effects that are felt over relatively long periods of time.

In summary, revolutions generally produce political and socioeconomic consequences of greater magnitude than coups d'état. At the same time, Latin American *golpes* exhibit substantial variability with respect to their consequences. *Golpes* tend to have effects that go well beyond a simple reshuffling of top government personnel.

Up to this point we have attempted to clarify our basic definition of *golpe de estado* by providing some comparisons with revolutions. In so doing, we discussed the participants, the intensity of violence, and the character of the political and socioeconomic consequences produced by the forcible overthrow of government. Two additional features of the coup phenomenon must be discussed before concluding this section: (1) *golpes* are illegal, and (2) they result in breakdown of the formally constituted regime.

An adequate definition of coups depends in part on recognition of their unlawful character. *Golpes* are illegal because they violate the laws of presidential tenure found in the constitution. The *golpistas* ordinarily break laws of executive succession as well by departing from the constitutionally established line of succession in selecting a replacement for the deposed president. In most types of regimes, authoritarian as well as democratic, the constitution calls for subordination of the military to the chief executive; the armed forces are not empowered to remove the president. Thus coups are a rebellion against constituted authority.[14]

---

[13] Bernstein, *Venezuela and Colombia*, p. 51.

[14] Most Latin American constitutions specifically charge the military with upholding the constitution. Some sources have suggested that constitutional clauses of this nature qualify the principle of military subordination to the chief

The wide gap between law and action that characterizes coup situations points to a central problem experienced by coup-ridden Latin American societies. This gap defines an unstable situation in which political crises create irresistible pressures toward forcible military intervention. In the absence of a strong, effective legal system, political competition often leads to escalated conflict and coup d'état.

By stressing the unlawful character of coups we do not mean to say that they take place in a normative vacuum. *Golpes* normally occur in the context of a set of informal ground rules that are no less effective for being unwritten. In a sense, these unwritten rules constitute a code of etiquette for the *golpistas*. For example, this traditional code specifies that the deposed president shall not be subjected to unnecessary physical discomfort; exile, not the firing squad, is the lot that commonly falls to forcibly unemployed chief executives. The violation of this code produces a sense of shock, as witnessed by the reactions to the assassination of President Villarroel during the 1946 Bolivian coup d'état. In sum, coups are illegal, but they ordinarily take place within the context of a set of time-honored, informal expectations that exercise a normative force over the participants and thereby serve to limit the violence surrounding the conflict.

Finally, it is important to emphasize the relationship of *golpes* to the formally constituted regime — the basic laws and structures of government. As noted previously, it is often suggested that the change of top government personnel is virtually the only significant consequence of coups. Actually, this focus on the change of personnel tends to obscure the impact of coups on the legal and structural frameworks that define society's central governmental institutions. Although the actual extent to which *golpes* alter the regime varies from one case to another, in no case does a regime emerge totally unaffected. At a minimum, *golpes* forcibly alter the regime by causing a breach in the formal chain of command between the executive and the military. All coups bring about a reorganization of formal government structures by producing a *struc-*

---

executive by allowing the armed forces to disobey presidential orders that are deemed unlawful. In Brazil, for example, the military is instructed to obey the chief executive, but only "within the limits of the law." In this regard see Alfred C. Stepan, *The Military in Politics: Changing Patterns in Brazil* (Princeton, N.J., 1971), pp. 75-79. Although clauses of this kind may contribute to debates about the legality of coups, the fact is that they do not empower the military to remove the chief executive. *Golpes* are unlawful. According to constitutional principles, disputes surrounding the legality of actions taken by the chief executive should be resolved through formally instituted legal procedures, such as impeachment or resorts to higher judicial authority.

tural fusion between the executive and the military. At the moment of
the coup, the military widens its formal sphere of competence, taking
the selection of the executive upon itself.[15] In addition, Latin American
golpes frequently have broader effects on formal government organization. For example, they often produce a cycle characterized by the alternating of democratic and authoritarian regimes, and in doing so they
reorganize various formal agencies of the state, such as the congress
and the judiciary. All of this means that coups involve the breakdown
of existing regimes. In effect, coup-ridden Latin American polities have
been incapable of institutionalizing effective regimes. In the words of
Federico Gil, "the problem of Latin America has been the primary one
of getting along in an orderly or semi-orderly way under *any* political
system."[16]

These comments on the nature of Latin American coups are intro-
ductory in character. As we proceed they will be expanded and the usefulness of our conceptual formulations will become clearer. For present
purposes, we merely wish to dispel any doubts about our use of the term.
A coup d'état is the illegal removal and replacement of the chief executive of a country by a predominantly military force. Usually involving
some violence, the *golpe* is a product of escalated political conflict that
results in the breakdown of existing regimes.

General Approaches to Latin American Coups

Before moving on to a detailed consideration of the specific factors
that lead to coups d'état in Latin America, it would be useful to elaborate two general interpretations that can help us orient our thinking
with respect to the various explanations that have been adduced to
account for *golpes*. Much of the prior scholarship on Latin American
coups intersects with the two approaches. For this reason, in addition
to the relevance of the two interpretations for the analysis to be presented in subsequent chapters, both will be sketched briefly at this point.
Before beginning, however, two caveats need to be made. First, the following remarks are not intended as a substitute for a review of the liter-

[15] Frequently, intervention results in the creation of a provisional government
charged with preparing for presidential elections within a limited period of time.
At other times, the military may take over indefinitely. Needler suggests that the
former pattern has predominated in recent years. See Needler, *Political Development in Latin America*, p. 28.

[16] Federico Gil, "Comments," in "Pathology of Democracy in Latin America:
A Symposium," ed. W. W. Pierson, *American Political Science Review*, 44
(1950), 149. Our emphasis.

ature on Latin American coups. For such a review the reader must look elsewhere.[17] Second, the two interpretations will be set forth in highly explicit fashion, as ideal types. In presenting the two approaches in this way, it is our intention to establish a basis for analysis, not to cram the work of others into our types in a Procrustean manner. While many scholars have emphasized one of the interpretations at the expense of the other, the two are not mutually exclusive, and some authors have dealt with the problems raised by both approaches. Keeping these remarks in mind, we may proceed with our discussion of the two interpretations. For lack of better terms, they will be referred to as the "participation-problem" and "organization-problem" interpretations.

The participation-problem interpretation views the coup d'état as a response to the mounting pressures brought to bear when traditionally deprived groups begin to demand a greater role in deciding how goods and services are allocated in their society. Historically, these deprived elements have had little or no voice in such decisions, and their share of the goods and services produced in the society has been correspondingly insignificant. Today, however, these groups, often led by members of the urban lower middle class, are growing steadily more dissatisfied with their traditional nonparticipant status on the periphery of society. They are undergoing the so-called "revolution of rising expectations" and, increasingly, they are demanding a role in the political decision-making process that allocates goods and services within the society. This desire to take part in the decision-making process is motivated in large part by the hope of gaining a significant share of those benefits that are allocated as a result of that process. Violence enters the picture when the swelling pressures for participation on the part of traditionally deprived groups encounter opposition from the established groups of the upper and upper middle classes. The paucity of material production and the frequently low rates of economic growth characteristic of societies that have not attained high levels of socioeconomic development engender a sense of psychological insecurity and a belief that there simply is not enough to allow everyone to live in relative comfort. These attitudes are prevalent throughout Latin America, and they lay the foundation for conflict between the traditionally deprived and the established groups. The ensuing conflict between "haves" and "have-nots" is interclass in character and is reflected in conflicting ideologies about the ideal society. As participatory pressures mount, political activity tends to become

[17] See the thorough review by Lyle N. McAlister, "Recent Research and Writings on the Role of the Military in Latin America," *Latin American Research Review*, 2 (1966), 5-36.

highly radicalized and the likelihood of violence increases, thereby creating a tense crisis atmosphere that pervades the society. In the final analysis, the military may conduct a coup d'état for the purpose of mediating the acute interclass conflict or to impose either leftist or rightist solutions.

This interpretation of military intervention sees *golpes* as typical of developing societies undergoing unbalanced growth. Coups are viewed as a distinctive product of countries in a state of "transition," where high rates of social mobilization encourage the so-called "revolution of rising expectations" and the subsequent emergence of traditionally nonparticipant groups as politically relevant entities.[18] Against this background of social dynamism, the sluggish rates of economic growth that frequently plague emerging countries are incapable of expanding the economic base fast enough to accommodate the newcomers without threatening the society's already established groups. The mounting pressures brought to bear by the newcomers are sure to encounter defensive resistance from the established groups. The acute conflict and political crisis created by this type of situation may often lead to a coup d'état. This is almost precisely the interpretation of coups that is offered by Martin Needler, who indicates that "there is an inverse relationship between mass participation and constitutional stability" in most Latin American countries: "One is thus presented with a dialectical tension: if mass participation rises faster than the level of economic development, then constitutional functioning breaks down, usually with the imposition of a military regime...."[19] A similar interpretation of Latin American *golpes* has been offered by Germani and Silvert.[20]

Many other observers of the coup phenomenon in Latin America have pointed to causes that rely indirectly on the participation-problem interpretation. As these causes will be treated in detail in subsequent chapters, they only need to be introduced briefly at this point, with the intent of showing where they intersect with the general interpretation of coup activity that we have described. In so doing, we show how a variety of specific causes can be subsumed in part under the more general interpretation, though it is of course necessary to avoid the temptation of forcing the causal explanations into our ideal types.

---

[18] Karl Deutsch's treatment of social mobilization exemplifies the participation-problem interpretation of coup activity. See his article, "Social Mobilization and Political Development," *American Political Science Review*, 55 (1961), 493-514. For a treatment of transitional politics in Latin America, see Robert E. Scott, "Political Elites and Political Modernization," in *Elites in Latin America*, ed. Seymour M. Lipset and Aldo Solari (New York, 1967), pp. 117-145.

[19] Needler, *Political Development in Latin America*, p. 95.

[20] Germani and Silvert, "Military Intervention."

First, those who attempt to explain coups explicitly in terms of inter-class conflict overlap greatly with the interpretative scheme presented above — mounting levels of participation from below encounter resis-tance that produces interclass conflict and the subsequent possibility of military intervention. The noted Argentine social scientist José Nun offers an interclass explanation for Latin America *golpes* that conforms in part with the participation-problem interpretation. Adding a novel twist, Nun describes what he calls the "middle-class military coup": "... in many cases, Latin American middle classes are threatened by the ... working classes. ... Therefore, the army — that in the majority of the countries represents the middle classes ... — comes to the defense of the threatened sectors [via coup d'état]. ..."[21] Other more tradi-tional explanations view coups as a product of military conservatism that accrues to the interests of the dominant classes while discouraging social change.[22] Many Latin American Marxists share this view — the armed forces are seen as a repressive instrument at the service of an exploitative oligarchy.

Another explanation sometimes offered to account for Latin Amer-ican coups that relies indirectly on the participation-problem interpre-tation makes reference to imperialism, especially U.S. imperialism. In this context the United States is seen both interfering more or less directly in the domestic affairs of Latin American countries and sup-porting their military establishments with weapons and technical assis-tance for the purpose of insuring that the increasing participatory pres-sures do not lead to left-wing governments hostile to U.S. interests in the area.[23]

In summary, one general explanation of Latin American coups points to the destabilizing effects of the mounting participatory pressures that are brought to bear by traditionally deprived groups no longer content to remain passive. In discussing this interpretation, it has been shown that coup explanations involving interclass conflict and U.S. interference intersect with this participation-problem interpretation to some extent. We now turn to the second major interpretation of the *golpes*.

The organization-problem interpretation of Latin American *golpes*

[21] José Nun, "A Latin American Phenomenon: The Middle-Class Military Coup," in *Latin America: Reform or Revolution?*, ed. James Petras and Maurice Zeitlin (Greenwich, Conn., 1968), p. 147.

[22] See, for example, Edwin Lieuwen, *Generals vs. Presidents: Neomilitarism in Latin America*, rev. ed. (New York, 1964), p. 104.

[23] See, for instance, Irving L. Horowitz, *Three Worlds of Development: The Theory and Practice of International Stratification* (New York, 1966), pp. 272-290.

points to organizational weaknesses as prime determinants of coups d'état. In an immediate sense, coups can be seen as both cause and effect of ineffective government organization. *Golpes* often are brought about by inadequate government functioning, and a high frequency of coups produces a relatively amorphous situation in which the institutionalization of effective governmental structures is virtually impossible. Weak government organization also can be related to specific organizational weaknesses in political parties and the military establishment, as well as to the destabilizing effects of certain general cultural orientations and economic organization. As we shall see, all of these factors tend to produce a lack of cohesion or coordination that is felt at the very heart of the political system.

Although some sources have related these factors to problems of participation and interclass conflict, the literature concerned with the destabilizing effects of organizational problems in Latin America has tended to stress the role of intraelite conflict in coups d'état. Unlike the participation-problem approach, this interpretation underplays the pressures for participation that originate on the periphery of the society. The emphasis here is on elites and intraclass conflict, on confrontation between "ins" and "outs" for control of government and the opportunities for gain that such control carries with it. While ideological differences are seldom involved here, the incessant squabbling characteristic of escalated intraclass conflict often produces a rapid turnover of chief executives. As suggested by Merle Kling, "In Honduras, from 1824 to 1950 . . . the executive office changed hands 126 times. During the nine-year interval ending in 1940, Ecuador had no less than fourteen presidents, four of them during [a] single month. . . ."[24] Needless to say, the political instability reflected in these cases is considered to be confined to the body politic and its personnel; the organization-problem approach characteristically devotes little attention to coups that have some effect on social class structure. This selective focus suggests the basis for Kling's sardonic description of Latin American *golpes* — "*plus ça change, plus c'est la même chose.*"[25]

The organization-problem interpretation is accompanied by an emphasis on the static or chronic, as opposed to the more dynamic or "transitional," sources of coups. Thus, for example, some authors have pointed out that certain deeply ingrained, traditional cultural patterns

[24] Kling, "Political Instability," p. 22. Payne also deals with high turnover of governmental personnel and intraclass conflict. See James L. Payne, *Patterns of Conflict in Colombia* (New Haven, Conn., 1968).

[25] Kling, "Political Instability," p. 34.

are important impediments to coordinated, harmonious action. Excessive pride, a low propensity to compromise, and the tendency to stress personal charisma over more impersonal or legal forms of social organization are of great significance, according to this line of thinking, when it comes to explaining the sources of the intraelite conflict that often leads to military intervention.[26]

As suggested above, the organization-problem approach stresses the weaknesses of various structures as a likely cause of coup activity in Latin America. Kling, for example, focuses on static economic organization as an important source of coups. According to him, the stagnant, closed character of economic structures in Latin America induces violent competition for control of government as an alternative path to wealth and power. In effect, a stagnant economy tends to produce an oversupply of politicians, thereby increasing the intensity of political conflict, weakening government structures, and leading to the possibility of a high frequency of coups.[27]

Another theme of the organization-problem interpretation singles out weak political party organization as an important cause of coups in Latin America.[28] The highly particularistic character of most Latin American parties is reflected in their excessive multiplicity and tendency toward fragmentation or splintering. This particularism and the subsequent weakness of party organization encourage *golpes* by making it exceedingly difficult for the parties to perform one of their principal functions — the aggregation or reconciliation of diverse interests.[29] As a result of the ensuing bitter conflict that frequently prevails both within and between the parties, consensus falls dangerously low and the military may be forced to step in to prevent the dissolution of society.

Approached from another perspective, weak, fragmented political parties cannot serve as effective mechanisms for the orderly transfer of power through the electoral process. The frequent *golpes* that accompany electoral strife and attempts at *continuismo* (i.e., the illegal continuation of the president in office) can be at least partly accounted for

[26] See, for instance, John P. Gillin, "Some Signposts for Policy," in *Social Change in Latin America Today: Its Implications for United States Policy,* ed. Richard N. Adams *et al.* (New York, 1960), pp. 14-62. A similar argument is presented by Payne, *Conflict in Colombia.*

[27] Kling, "Political Instability."

[28] In this sense see Payne, *Conflict in Colombia,* especially chap. 7.

[29] For a good treatment of this subject, see Robert E. Scott, "Political Parties and Policy-Making in Latin America," in *Political Parties and Political Development,* ed. Joseph LaPalombara and Myron Weiner (Princeton, N.J., 1966), pp. 331-367.

by the fact that the parties are not effective vehicles for the peaceful transfer of political power.[30] Looked at from this point of view, the military is seen reacting to problems in the civilian sector, rather than instigating coups for its own purposes. In the words of one observer of the Latin American military, "*The coup is, ultimately, a product of the political activity in the civilian sector.* . . . The military role is not autonomous or self-contained; it is reactive, dependent upon the movements of civilian political forces."[31]

Another variation of the organization-problem interpretation emphasizes organizational weaknesses within the military as a significant cause of coups. It has often been pointed out that low levels of military professionalism are conducive to intervention of the armed forces in the political process.[32] In this view, lax or sporadic attention to specific military duties can encourage a series of internal organizational problems — acute politicization, insubordination, and disunity — which increase the probability of coups d'état. Presumably, the achievement of high levels of military professionalism would significantly decrease the frequency of forcible military intervention by virtue of its salutary impact on these internal organizational problems. A dissenting view suggests that increasing levels of training and occupational expertise within the military need not result in the relegation of the troops to the barracks.[33] In a similar vein, some authors have suggested that high levels of technical competence suit the military for roles as nation-builders.[34] This competence, particularly when considered in light of the weakness of civilian institutions, may encourage the armed forces to conduct a *golpe* with modernizing goals in view.[35] This revisionist position can be criticized in its own right. In effect, the pressures of the nation-building role may serve to politicize and fragment the armed forces, thereby encouraging continued political instability and the possibility of additional

[30] For the role of *continuismo* in coups, see Stokes, "Violence in Latin American Politics."

[31] Payne, *Conflict in Colombia*, p. 143. The emphasis is Payne's.

[32] See, for example, Edwin Lieuwen, *Arms and Politics in Latin America*, rev. ed. (New York, 1961), pp. 151-153.

[33] Nun, "Middle-Class Military Coup," p. 148.

[34] For a general statement of this position, see Lucian W. Pye, "Armies in the Process of Political Modernization," *European Journal of Sociology*, 2 (1961), 82-92.

[35] As lucidly discussed by Stepan, the Brazilian military's conception of national security has focused on problems of internal subversion as of recent years, and these problems have encouraged the military to concern itself with the whole matrix of questions relating to socioeconomic development. This enlarged conception of national security has contributed to the politicization of the armed forces in that country. See Stepan, *Military in Politics*, chap. 8.

coups d'état beyond the one that brought the nation-builders to power.[36] Though they differ in important ways, these contrasting views suggest the importance of military organizational problems in leading to situations favorable to *golpes*.

The concept of military corporate interests designates a final theme that intersects with the organization-problem interpretation of Latin American *golpes*. From this perspective, coups are interpreted as a product of military efforts to defend their organizational interests. Conceptually, these interests derive from membership in the military establishment as distinct from membership in a particular social class. At times, the corporate interests explanation suggests that *golpes* are a reflection of military desires for material aggrandizement. In this view, coup activity is seen as a product of the armed forces' efforts either to maintain or to improve their equipment, salaries, and related fringe benefits by gaining control of the national budget.[37] From a slightly different perspective, it is sometimes argued that the military may find it necessary to conduct a coup in order to protect its corporate interests from what it sees as a serious threat posed to its continued existence or unity by certain political groups.[38]

In summary, the organization-problem interpretation views Latin American *golpes* as a product of organizational weaknesses that undermine coordinated, harmonious action in government and politics. This analytical construct emphasizes the role of intraclass conflict in producing a variety of structural weaknesses that culminate in ineffective government organization and coups d'état. In setting forth the basic themes that cluster around this view, four variations have been described — those referring to cultural orientations, economic organization, political parties, and the military establishment itself.

Before closing this section, it would be well to elaborate a bit on the relationship that exists between our two general interpretations of coup violence. As we suggested at the outset, the two interpretations need not be considered mutually exclusive. Indeed, the two are complementary to some extent, as participation and organization are, in a sense, two sides of the same coin. One can even look at some of the specific coup explanations presented in the foregoing through the perspectives offered by both interpretations. For example, although the military corporate interests explanation ordinarily is treated by the literature as an organi-

[36] *Ibid.*, especially part 4.

[37] In this sense see John J. Johnson, *The Military and Society in Latin America* (Stanford, Calif., 1964), p. 73.

[38] For example, see Stepan, *Military in Politics,* pp. 153-171, 204-209.

zational problem, it also intersects with the participation-problem approach. There is a clear difference between the concepts of social class and military corporate interests, yet, historically, the group interests of the Latin American armed forces have been threatened most often by groups that have attempted to extend political participation to lower class sectors on the margins of society. Cases in point are the Venezuelan and Brazilian *golpes* of 1948 and 1964 respectively.[39] In these cases and others like them the corporate interests of the military are similar to those of the upper socioeconomic strata in their mutual opposition to the emerging marginal sectors. In this sense, the military corporate interests phenomenon intersects in part with the participation-problem interpretation. In effect, the corporate interests explanation suggests the complementary character of our two general interpretations by showing how a single factor can be usefully perceived from the vantage point of the two contrasting perspectives. This theme of complementariness is dealt with at length in the next chapter; but first we may finish out this section by showing how the contrasting aspects of our two interpretations can help to account for some of the conflicting views that characterize the literature on Latin American coups.

One could offer several explanations for the conflicting interpretations of Latin American *golpes* that appear in the literature on the subject. One possibility, of course, is that no real contradiction exists in those particular cases in which scholars have studied different coups. It is quite possible that one *golpe* may be primarily the product of intraclass conflict, for example, while a different one may be predominantly interclass in origin. For this reason, one should not expect agreement among studies involving analysis of different cases. It should be noted, however, that even studies that employ sampling techniques can reach contradictory conclusions as to the nature of the coups. Failure to take into account either the somewhat cyclical nature of Latin American coups or the fact that the predominant type of *golpe* varies from time to time can result in conflicting findings. For example, a sampling of coups drawn from the period 1949-54 would produce an analysis that stressed the conservative character of Latin American *golpes*, while a sampling from the period 1943-47 would result in a far brighter, reformist interpretation.[40] In short, the variability of the coup phenomena must

[39] *Ibid.* and John D. Martz, *Acción Democrática: Evolution of a Modern Political Party in Venezuela* (Princeton, N.J., 1966), p. 308.

[40] For an interesting discussion of these points, see Needler, *Political Development in Latin America,* chaps. 2, 4. According to Needler, Latin American coups have become increasingly interclass-conservative in character. As we shall

be kept in mind when reviewing the different accounts found in the literature.

Turning to those cases in which real contradictions exist, some understanding can be gathered by referring to the character of our two general interpretations. As we have seen, each of the two interpretations holds a distinctive perspective on the nature of the escalated conflict that leads to coups — the participation-problem interpretation stresses interclass conflict, as a by-product of dynamic, so-called transitional periods; the organization-problem approach, on the other hand, emphasizes the long-established, chronic patterns of intraclass conflict that result from certain enduring cultural and structural factors. It is apparent that some of the contradictions in the literature can be understood at least partly in terms of the emphasis given to these two contrasting perspectives on the origins of coups d'état. An example can be found in comparing the studies of Germani and Silvert and James Payne.[41] Germani and Silvert stress the relationship between *golpes* and processes of socioeconomic change and make explicit reference to interclass conflict, an important feature of transitional periods. Payne, on the other hand, thoroughly rejects the relevance of rates of social change and categories formulated in terms of reform.[42] From Payne's analysis, it is obvious that he conceives of Latin American coups solely in terms of the traditional, intraclass squabbling between "ins" and "outs."

The point that should be made here is that by emphasizing the dynamic sources of coups (i.e., their links to social change), Germani and Silvert end up viewing the *golpes* as a predominantly interclass phenomenon. Payne, on the other hand, interprets coups as chronic phenomena resulting from long-established patterns of intraclass conflict. This interpretation is at least partly a result of his emphasis on the constant, enduring causes of the *golpes* (e.g., deeply ingrained cultural patterns). In short, commitment to one framework more or less exclusive of the other can produce a rather one-sided analysis that runs the danger of twisting data to fit a preconceived mold.

One might conjecture that commitment to contrasting analytical approaches is a reflection of deeper ideological differences. This would help account for some of the inflexibility with which the proponents of

see, however, intraclass conflict remains a source of *golpes* in the area. In addition, some recent coup-emergent regimes (e.g., Peru, post-1968) have pursued a left-wing course.

[41] Germani and Silvert, "Military Intervention," and Payne, *Conflict in Colombia.*

[42] Payne, *Conflict in Colombia,* pp. 71-72, 155-158.

various conflicting interpretations have confronted one another. For example, the totally opposing views on the relevance of U.S. interference in Latin American *golpes* might be understood at least partly in these terms.[43] The question of American interference never fails to bring out high emotion, and this is true not only of the Latin American scholars, but of some of their North American counterparts as well.

At any rate, the one-sidedness that results from adhering too closely to either one of the two general interpretations, exclusive of the other, is an undesirable state of affairs that must be surmounted in any comprehensive treatment of Latin American coups d'état: both general interpretations are necessary to a full understanding of the *golpes*. Although the contrasting points of view associated with the two have resulted in contradictory accounts at times, in certain important respects the two interpretations are complementary. In fact, a degree of synthesis can be achieved by exploring the relationship that exists between the levels of participation and political organization in any given society. The following chapter is devoted to a discussion of this important relationship.

[43] Horowitz presents the case for U.S. interference in his *Three Worlds*, pp. 272-290. Charles Wolf argues against this view in his article, "Political Effects of Military Programs: Some Indications from Latin America," *Orbis*, 8 (1965), 871-893.

2

ANALYTICAL PERSPECTIVE

We have already discussed the definition and two basic interpretations of the Latin American *golpe*. In this chapter, with the aid of an equilibrium framework that relates political participation and organization in societies, we will first establish some analytical relationships between types of political breakdown and political imbalance. In the second section of the chapter, the model is employed to organize a discussion of political development, which is often considered a determinant of the capacity of regimes to avoid coups d'état during the process of socio political change. In the third and final section of the chapter, the three types of regimes found in Latin America — the democratic, the authoritarian, and the totalitarian — are analyzed in view of their prospects for sustained political development or breakdown. Before proceeding with our discussion, however, we must deal briefly with two preliminary matters relating to the nature of equilibrium models and our key concepts.

Equilibrium models have been systematically developed in the field of economic theory. In contrast, and even though many propositions in comparative politics presuppose a notion of equilibrium, this concept has seldom been employed explicitly in the theoretical literature in this area in view of certain limitations perceived to be inherent in the process of conceptual formalization. First, the concept of equilibrium imposes on the theorist the difficult task of forging systematic interrelationships among the variables with which he chooses to work. Given the complexity of most politically relevant variables, it becomes extremely difficult to work effectively with more than a few variables within the context of an equilibrium model. In addition, many of the variables dealt with by comparative political theorists are very costly and difficult to operationalize, and equilibrium models are restricted to variables that are quantifiable to some extent.[1] It has also frequently been suggested that formulations in terms of equilibrium are conservatively biased and that they are therefore of little use in studying problems of conflict and sociopolitical change.[2]

From our point of view, none of these limitations outweighs the utility of formalizing much of our analysis in this chapter in terms of the equilibrium concept. Although strictly speaking our framework includes only two variables, we attempt to maximize by taking advantage of the analytical rigor of model-building without becoming insensitive to the role of other related factors. In other words, our discussion here relies on the equilibrium framework to the extent that it can contribute to the analysis of political breakdown and stability, but complementary factors are introduced where appropriate. Finally, there is no logically necessary reason why equilibrium models have to be considered conservatively biased. As we use them, the concepts of political participation and organization are useful in accounting for various forms of system breakdown as well as stability. On the whole, we find the equilibrium framework of value in sharpening our conceptual formulations and, above all, in generating hypotheses concerning political change — political breakdown and development.

Political participation and political organization are the key variables in our equilibrium framework. Both concepts are highly complex. While one can compare societies in terms of relative levels or degrees of participation and organization, these concepts manifest certain qualitative aspects that are extremely difficult to discuss in these terms. Some of these aspects are introduced in the course of our discussion, but first we can establish a point of departure for considering the analytical framework by presenting basic definitions for the two concepts.

The first variable, political participation, refers to forms of demand-making vis-à-vis government. The greater the frequency and scope of demand-making activity, the higher the level of political participation

[1] There are various levels of quantification. In economics, the most advanced of the social sciences, equilibrium models employ concepts that are amenable to numerical expression (i.e., measurement in terms of interval scales). In contrast, the nature of most of the macrosociological variables employed by comparative political theorists precludes quantification in this sense. At best, an equilibrium framework like our own talks in terms of "more" or "less" (i.e., measurement in terms of ordinal scales).

[2] In this sense see the critique by Orlando Fals-Borda, "The Ideological Biases of North Americans Studying Latin America," paper presented at a conference organized by the University Christian Movement, Columbia University, December 2, 1966. (Mimeograph.)

and vice versa. By way of example, the greater the proportion of the population taking part in politically active groups, and the broader the scope of their demands, the higher the level of participation. In contrast to participation, organization refers to the notion of political control. A polity which has a highly developed capacity for control exhibits a high level of political organization and vice versa.[3] In this context, the level of structural differentiation or complexity of the regime may be taken as a rough indicator of the level of organization in the polity.[4] Taking these definitions as a point of departure, we may now begin our discussion of the interrelationships between the participation and organization variables in the context of our equilibrium framework.

Political Equilibrium and Political Breakdown

Political systems are in equilibrium when there is balance between levels of participation and organization in the system. Perfect equilibrium is exemplified by any of the points along the 45° line in Figure 1. In effect, any point on this line describes an ideal situation in which all the political activity (participation) in the society is perfectly coordinated (organized). Points A and B are examples of this condition. This ideal equilibrium, never attained in the real world, represents a utopia in which there are absolutely no pressures for altering the sociopolitical order. In other words, points along this line are indicative of those ideal instances in which all activity in the political system is perfectly coordinated, without creating pressures for altering the existing level of participation.

In the real world, however, all societies find themselves in states of disequilibrium or conflict if for no other reason than the fact that re-

[3] The capacity for control of the polity and, especially, its governmental institutions refers to their ability to convert political activity into support for the regime. In part this capacity is similar to Almond and Powell's discussion of the regulative capability of political systems. See Gabriel A. Almond and G. Bingham Powell, *Comparative Politics: A Developmental Approach* (Boston, 1966), pp. 196-197. Both terms refer to the dimension of political order. However, our formulation differs from theirs in that we view control as relatively neutral vis-à-vis the means used to shore up the regime. As we shall see, political control can become repressive, depending on the character of the participation-organization imbalance prevailing in society, but it can also refer to situations of high consensus in which a relatively harmonious coordination of political actors with the regime is attained.

[4] Structural differentiation or complexity is employed in definitions of organizational development by many sources. See, for instance, Samuel P. Huntington, *Political Order in Changing Societies* (New Haven, Conn., 1968), pp. 17-20.

FIGURE 1. The Basic Equilibrium Framework

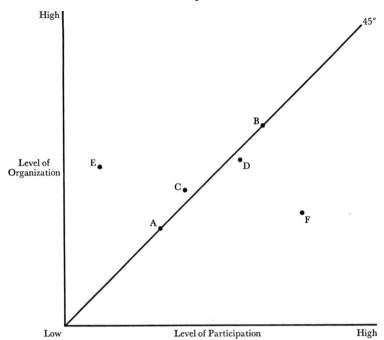

quirements of effective organization and the demands for participation exist in a state of mutual tension. At any single point in time, the requirements of coordination inevitably curtail participation to some degree, while changes in participation demand subsequent adjustments in organization.[5] Nevertheless, some societies are able to withstand this tension better than others. Societies which are able to maintain themselves fairly close to the equilibrium line in Figure 1 — for example, at points C or D — increase the likelihood that they will be able to incorporate pressures for change without experiencing either coups or revolutions. These societies are characterized by political institutionalization — by well-established, relatively permanent, formal political organizations.[6] The regimes in these societies are stable; changes tend to occur

[5] For a statement of this problem in organization theory, see Peter M. Blau and W. Richard Scott, *Formal Organizations: A Comparative Approach* (San Francisco, Calif., 1962), pp. 242-244.

[6] In part we are drawing from Huntington's discussion of political institutionalization: "... the process by which organizations and procedures acquire

within the established legal framework. Stability is promoted by virtue of the fact that participation and organization are never very far out of balance. In addition, the kinds of political participation found in institutionalized polities tend to be nondisruptive of the established order. The scope of political demand-making activity tends to be restricted to relatively manageable demands for the implementation of specific policies.[7]

As we shall see in subsequent chapters, Latin America's unstable polities deviate markedly from this pattern. In most countries throughout the area, the scope of political demand-making broadens periodically to include disruptive pressures for changes in the very nature of the regime. Nonsecular elements present in the political culture found throughout much of the area contribute to the moralization and ideologization of political conflict. In an atmosphere in which opponents are viewed as "sinners" and "heretics," lack of consensus and disruptive, uncompromising types of political activity are common. This kind of setting tends to produce a high degree of imbalance between the participation and organization dimensions. In terms of Figure 1, most Latin American societies tend to find themselves far from the 45° line — at points E and F, for instance — where the possibilities of political breakdown are great.

Point E on the graph describes a situation in which the level of political organization exceeds the level of participation. There is a lag in participation and sharing in the goods and services allocated by a political system which is "overorganized." In situations of this kind, pressures for change in the direction of the 45° equilibrium line are created. On the one hand, demands for increased participation and sharing will be fed into the political system in an effort to redress a situation of per-

value and stability." See Huntington, *Political Order*, p. 12. Unlike Huntington, however, we do not define institutionalization in terms of the characteristics of organizational development (e.g., complexity) that are generally viewed as encouraging stability. As our later discussion reveals, some Latin American regimes (e.g., Nicaragua) have achieved a fairly high degree of political stability over long periods of time in the absence of highly differentiated political organizations. For this reason, we define political institutionalization exclusively in terms of the stability of the regime (i.e., its record in avoiding breakdown). In this way, the relationship between stability and the characteristics of political organization remains a matter for empirical verification in specific cases.

[7] Almond and Powell describe the emergence of relatively specific and pragmatic political orientations as characteristic of the process of secularization of political culture — one of the basic components of their definition of political development. See Almond and Powell, *Comparative Politics*, pp. 57-63.

ceived "underparticipation."[8] At the same time, the society's highly centralized political institutions may not be flexible enough to process and act on these demands in an effective fashion. Overcentralization produces ossification, a factor which makes it increasingly difficult for organizations to get enough accurate information from their environment and to generate sufficient energy to confront effectively a participatory crisis without undergoing some sort of political discontinuity.[9] Instead of allowing greater expression to demands for increased participation, overorganized regimes often artificially restrict participation through the application of repressive measures in an effort to curtail what appear to be serious threats to their existence.[10] Repressive measures result in a self-fulfilling prophecy of sorts — overcentralized governments deny room for the autonomous articulation of demands through legal channels, thereby encouraging disruptive increases in demand-making activity (e.g., violence and revolutionary movements) that are hostile to the stability of the regime. In the final analysis, the confluence of developments in both the participation and organization sectors creates a stress that tends to propel the society back in the direction of the 45° line. If and when the situation becomes acute, some form of political breakdown, whether revolution or coup d'état, is likely to occur, thus moving the society in the equilibrium direction.

There is, of course, no assurance that the society thus moved will come to rest on or near the 45° line. Government often finds it very difficult to coordinate sharp increases in participation. It often happens that the society overshoots the 45° line by a considerable amount, moving in the direction of point F. (More will be said of this erratic type of fluctuation later.) Point F represents the converse of point E. It describes a situation of relative "overparticipation" and "underorganization." The organizational framework of the polity is too fragmented to

[8] As participation and organization are but two sides of the same coin in the context of our equilibrium framework, overorganization and underparticipation are terms that refer to the same general phenomenon from complementary points of view. Specifically, societies that fall above the 45° line in Figure 1 are to some degree characterized by both terms.

[9] The relationship between overcentralization and political breakdown is a frequent theme in the literature. See, for instance, Almond and Powell, *Comparative Politics,* p. 101. For a relevant discussion from the perspective of communications theory, see Karl Deutsch, *The Nerves of Government* (New York, 1963), part 3.

[10] The role of repression in the maintenance of regimes is seldom systematically explored in the comparative politics literature. As suggested by Schmitter, the study of the organizational or control dimension of the polity usually stresses consensus. See Philippe C. Schmitter, *Interest Conflict and Political Change in Brazil* (Stanford, Calif., 1971), pp. 4-5.

convert participatory pressures into a substantial level of support for the regime. Conflict and violence are usual in such cases, and ultimately (at the lower far right side of Figure 1) major social disintegration or revolution tends to result. However, the situation ordinarily does not proceed that far before a reaction sets in, again moving the society back in the direction of the 45° line. In this case, the most powerful force in the society, ordinarily the military, will intervene via coup d'état to curtail levels of participation by imposing order (i.e., organization or control). In short, a society at point F is under stress that tends to move it back in the equilibrium direction.

The discussion up until now has suggested that some form of political breakdown is increasingly probable as one moves away from the 45° equilibrium line in either direction. At this point we can be more explicit about the probable relationship that prevails between distance from the line and various kinds of political breakdown. As previously noted, the literature on Latin American coups has stressed either the role of participation problems in the occurrence of interclass coups or the role of organization problems in intraclass *golpes*. From the perspective of our equilibrium framework, however, all coups can be seen as the product of disequilibrium between participation and organization. It seems reasonable to suggest that the nature of breakdown depends upon the degree of imbalance between these two dimensions of the political system. The greater the distance from the 45° equilibrium line, the broader and more abrupt will be the changes in the regime. If this hypothesis is correct, revolutions would occur at points farthest from the line, intraclass coups at points closest to the line, and interclass coups at intermediate points of imbalance.[11] These relationships suggest not only the more violent nature of revolution, but also the fact that revolutions seldom occur because societies rarely deviate so extremely from a situation of equilibrium. The tendency is for a coup rather than a revolution to occur, moving the society back to a state of greater balance.[12]

It is important to note that the character of political breakdown is not determined merely by the degree of imbalance between levels of participation and organization. The overall character or quality of participation and organizational forms also plays a part in determining the

[11] Some support for this hypothesis is presented in our analysis in Chapter 4. The higher incidence of civilian participation and violence characteristic of interclass as opposed to intraelite *golpes* suggests the greater degree of imbalance present in interclass conflict situations.

[12] It is in this sense that a case can be made for the contention that many "small revolutions" (coups) can prevent a "big" one (a real revolution). See Huntington, *Political Order*, p. 362.

type of breakdown that may result from imbalance within the equilibrium framework. In effect, it can be hypothesized that the type of *golpe* depends on the characteristics of the particular sector of Figure 1 in which the society happens to find itself. The portion of the graph that lies to the left of the 45° equilibrium line describes a situation in which participation is curtailed. If relatively severe, underparticipation tends to produce a left-wing interclass coup, such as the Venezuelan *golpe* of 1945. At other times, however, underparticipation — generally when it is less severe — may result in an intraclass coup which merely reorganizes power among the ruling elite. Brazil's October, 1969, "coup within a coup" is a case in point.[13]

In contrast to these coups of underparticipation, the sector of Figure 1 that falls to the right of the equilibrium line denotes situations in which political organizations are relatively fragmented and the regime is unable to coordinate effectively the prevailing level of political activity. Overparticipation in this kind of situation tends to assume disruptive, escalated forms, such as violent street demonstrations and working-class strikes. These disruptive pressures tend to produce right-wing interclass coups, such as the one that took place in Brazil in April, 1964. However, as we shall see in Chapter 4, the pressures produced by situations of overparticipation do not always lead to interclass coups. At times, particularly when levels of imbalance between participation and organization are less severe than they were in Brazil prior to the 1964 *golpe,* regimes that lie to the right of the 45° equilibrium line may experience intraclass coups that allegedly are designed to restore order, morality, and efficiency to government. An example would be the 1952 Cuban coup that removed the relatively fragmented and corrupt democratic government of Carlos Prío Socarrás.

In summary, the Latin American *golpe* is a complex phenomenon whose character is determined by the overall situational context in which the polity finds itself;[14] both the degree and the quality of the participation-organization imbalance are important determinants of the type of coup. In closing this section, it is worthwhile to note that political actors often have divergent perceptions as to the situation prevailing in the society at the moment of the coup. While conservative factions tend to believe that the society is experiencing too much participation,

---

[13] "Coup within a coup" is Schneider's phrase. See Ronald M. Schneider, *The Political System of Brazil: Emergence of a "Modernizing" Authoritarian Regime, 1964-1970* (New York, 1971), *passim.*

[14] In this sense see the discussion of Brazilian *golpes* by Stepan, *Military in Politics,* p. 53.

leftist groups will claim that there is too little participation. A parallel case of divergence will be found between pro- and anti-government cliques in situations of intraclass conflict. The clashing ideologies or mentalities manifested by key political actors are one of the factors that determine the scope of the conflict and, consequently, the character of the imbalance that exists in any given situation. In addition, conflicting perceptions are indicative of the basic lack of consensus which leads to the coup d'état.

Political Development and Political Breakdown

Thus far we have been discussing the relationship between imbalance and political breakdown, a relationship represented by sharp movements to the left- and right-hand sides of the 45° equilibrium line. Our discussion now turns to the theme of political development, the dynamic process by which societies increase their levels of political participation and organization. In terms of Figure 1, development occurs as societies move from the lower left- to the upper right-hand side of the graph. In this context it is important to note that gains in political development can only be consolidated effectively if there are increases in both of the developmental variables. Significant increases in participation (e.g., the entrance of new class groups into the political process) must be accompanied sooner or later by modifications in the organizational structure of the regime (i.e., increases in its capacity for control and structural differentiation). Otherwise, participatory gains will not be effectively consolidated, and a situation of "decay" rather than development will result.[15] As we shall see, participatory increases in the Latin American context often have not been consolidated effectively; regimes have frequently found it very difficult to make the coordinative adjustments in organization that are necessary to accommodate emerging groups without breakdown.[16]

[15] See Samuel P. Huntington, "Political Development and Political Decay," *World Politics*, 17 (1965), 386-430.

[16] Considering the polity as a whole, the emergence of new, relatively autonomous interests is one type of structural differentiation. In dealing with political development, however, this kind of differentiation can be highly disruptive if it is not accompanied by concomitant increases in differentiation of the regime (i.e., the formal-legal institutions of government). In effect, the key variable for consolidating participatory increases and gains in political development is this latter kind of differentiation. Increases in the control capacity of regimes occur with the emergence of new, specialized sets of regulative norms and governmental organizations to institutionalize the changes in participation.

FIGURE 2. Political Development of the United States, 1928-68

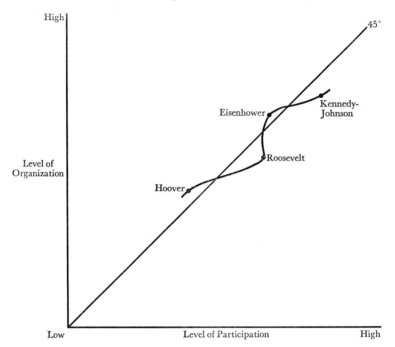

While consolidation of gains in development requires a substantial measure of mutual adjustment between political activity and political structure, this does not mean that political development occurs in the absence of imbalance between the participation and organization dimensions. Indeed, lags or imbalances are a typical feature of the development process. In addition, political development is not a unilinear process. There is more than one path toward higher levels of both participation and organization, and a period of development can be ushered in by political breakdown in some instances.

A few countries have attained a relatively high level of political development without experiencing much in the way of breakdown. Excepting the Civil War, the United States provides a case in point. Figure 2 represents our interpretation of the character of American political development over a forty-year period during the present century.

The most notable thing about this figure for our purposes is the gradual evolutionary character of American political development during the forty-year period in question. The society never deviates far from the 45° equilibrium line in the process of achieving higher levels of development. Levels of participation and political organization are never very far out of balance. Interesting is the mildly cyclical development line that distinguishes Republican and Democratic administrations in terms of where they strike a balance between levels of participation and political organization. The former tend toward a bias in the organization direction; the latter in the participation direction. In social policy terms, this difference may be translated as a general preference for consolidation as opposed to innovation, with Republicans adhering to the former and Democrats to the latter.

This evolutionary pattern of development is characterized by the absence of coups or revolutions. This does not imply, however, a total absence of situations of imbalance in the process of political change. Even in politically institutionalized societies such as the United States, substantial changes in political participation and organization tend to be accompanied by a degree of violence and strife. During transitional periods of political change there are overt pressures to alter power relationships and increase the participation of marginal groups. In Figure 2, for example, the New Deal period shows a marked increase along the horizontal axis of participation. In essence, periods of transition tend to be turbulent because modifications of the regime are needed in order to accommodate the broadened scope of demands produced by groups that had previously been marginal to the political process. These pressures for change in the regime involve a challenge to basic norms and constitutional principles, and society tends to become increasingly politicized and polarized into hostile camps. Political conflict during periods of transition is ideologized, and support for the regime diminishes.

Despite this tendency toward increases in conflict and violence during transitional periods, American society does not deviate far from the equilibrium line. The adaptive capacity of the American system has permitted organizational and participatory adjustments without breakdown. For example, the demands for the incorporation of labor into the political system during the New Deal period were met by increases in structural differentiation. The legal principles regulating the employment contract were modified to permit collective bargaining. This, in turn, was accompanied by the emergence of more complex relationships between management and labor, and ultimately the materialization of more differentiated structures. Thus the simple hierarchical relationships between management and employee were transformed by the development of labor unions into an additional unit within the structure of the firm. Furthermore, government also experienced differentiation with

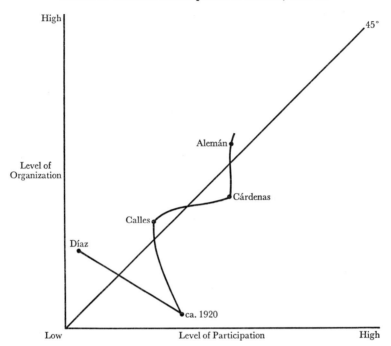

FIGURE 3. Political Development of Mexico, 1910-52

the enactment of specialized labor legislation to regulate interclass conflict and the creation of specialized mediating agencies. As indicated by Figure 2, large participation gains followed by consolidation of these gains is indicative of the successful passage of a transitional period. Of course a successful transition, such as that of the New Deal era, does not exclude the occurrence of new and different pressures to alter the power structure of the society. As witnessed by developments in race relations in the United States during the 1960s, transitional periods are recurrent.

In contrast to the United States, Mexican political development presents an alternative path toward higher levels of participation and political organization. Figure 3 offers a rough sketch of Mexico's political development between 1910 and 1952.

Most notable about this figure is the fact that Mexican political development was ushered in by a period of revolutionary breakdown. The violent turmoil of the revolutionary period of transition — represented in the graph by the severe overshooting of the 45° line after Díaz —

held sway from Díaz' fall at the hand of the revolution in 1910, through several years of anarchy, until almost 1930. Only after the establishment of the National Revolutionary party (the PRI today) by Calles in 1929 did Mexico's development line begin to approximate the relatively evolutionary, cyclical pattern that was observed in Figure 2, with Cárdenas increasing participation in the PRI and extending material benefits, followed by a period of consolidation under Alemán. In effect, party rule in Mexico has led the country away from the personalistic type of leadership with limited participation, such as that of Díaz, to a more differentiated system with broader participation.[17]

Examples from both the United States and Mexico indicate that more than one path toward political development exists. Higher levels of participation and political organization may come about in evolutionary fashion at times, while at others political development may be ushered in by revolutionary breakdown. In a sense, these two cases represent extremes that might lead one to think that political development can be deemed compatible with virtually any kind of violence. If development can follow revolution, why not coup d'état as well? Although our discussion in the previous chapter suggested that the immediate consequence of *golpes* is structural fusion, not differentiation, some coups have eventually been followed by political development. The experience of Chile — coups during the 1930s, followed by political development and stability through the 1960s — indicates that this may happen at times. Still, for reasons that we shall explore, as a general rule a high frequency of coups tends to frustrate sustained development. Latin America offers numerous examples to support this contention.

In Figure 4, Argentina is used to illustrate a pattern that is observed in many Latin American countries. This figure indicates that political development is not an inevitable process. The erratic development line — the sizable overshooting or fluctuations it traces about the 45° equilibrium line — depicts a pattern of political stagnation or even decay. When Castillo was removed from power by a military coup in 1943, Argentina was suffering from a severe participation lag. During Perón's subsequent years in power, important steps were taken toward the incorporation of the urban masses (Perón's *descamisados*) into Argentine political life. However, Perón's transitional politics were not consolidated. His overthrow in 1955 has been followed by more than a decade of alternating retrenchment and indecision. Under Onganía's repressive

[17] For the role of the PRI in this respect, see Robert E. Scott, *Mexican Government in Transition,* rev. ed. (Urbana, Ill., 1964).

FIGURE 4. Political Development of Argentina, 1943-70

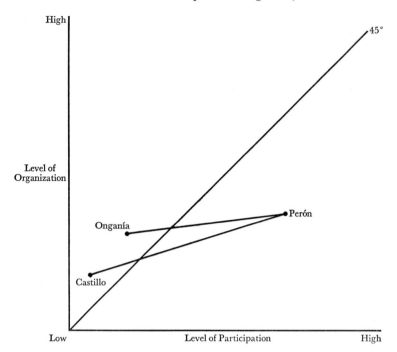

regime (1966-70), levels of participation were curtailed and structural differentiation was somewhat reduced when the general ordered all political parties abolished, the congress closed, and several unions placed under political interdict. Since the forcible removal of Onganía, yet another coup has occurred, thus confirming the erratic, nonevolutionary pattern of the Argentine situation.[18]

This erratic pattern of frequent, coup-studded oscillations about the 45° line, a pattern that results in political stagnation or decay rather than development, is a common one in Latin America. In subsequent chapters the politically debilitating effects of a high frequency of coups d'état will be investigated in detail. For now it is enough to reiterate that there is nothing inevitable about political development, nor do all societies follow identical paths if and when they achieve relatively high levels of both participation and political organization.

[18] It is worth noting (by contrasting Figures 2 and 4) that democratic and authoritarian regimes can occur on both sides of the 45° line, depending on their specific policy orientations and characteristics.

Political Development, Breakdown, and
Latin American System Types

Political development need not be conceptualized only as a dynamic process of change. The same criteria that define it as a process can also be utilized to characterize political systems at a given point in time. By way of contrast, relatively developed polities manifest higher levels of participation and structural differentiation than do less developed ones. In terms of Figure 1, relatively developed systems will be found toward the upper right-hand side of the graph, and less developed ones toward the lower left-hand side. Thus point B exemplifies a higher level of political development than does point A. The importance of dealing with this static conception of political development lies in that it has been hypothesized that whether or not societies experience breakdown in the process of change depends to some extent upon the stage of political development that they have attained.[19] In this view, political systems whose level of development places them in the upper right-hand portion of the graph seldom deviate far from the 45° line of equilibrium, and their chances for avoiding breakdown are thereby enhanced. In this respect, some sources have defined political development as the capacity of a system to absorb change and reach higher levels of development within the legal framework of the society or while maintaining equilibrium.[20]

As the level of political development may affect the ability of any given regime to avoid breakdown, we should undertake a brief technical discussion of the developmental characteristics of the three basic types of political systems found in Latin America — the democratic, the authoritarian, and the totalitarian.[21] We will first describe the basic

[19] For a forceful presentation of this point of view, see S. N. Eisenstadt, *Modernization: Protest and Change* (Englewood Cliffs, N.J., 1966). The organization-problem interpretation outlined in Chapter 1 concurs with this hypothesis — political breakdown is considered a function of chronic, enduring properties of "underdevelopment."

[20] See, for instance, Needler, *Political Development in Latin America,* p. 5. In terms of Figure 1, this definition of development can be exemplified as the propensity to move along the 45° line from point A to point B. Of course, as noted earlier, even the most developed societies experience some turbulence during periods of transition, when increases in participation tend to produce deviations from the 45° line. In this context, it is possible to view political development as a capacity to maintain an imperfect or dynamic equilibrium in the face of pressures for change.

[21] For an extensive general treatment of regime types, see Almond and Powell, *Comparative Politics,* chaps. 10-11. Our discussion also draws from Huntington, *Political Order,* especially pp. 24-32.

generic properties of each type of system and then present some variations and qualifications on the main themes.

As an ideal type, democratic systems are characterized by very high
levels of political development. These systems manifest an effectively
differentiated formal-constitutional structure which is in turn differentiated from political organizations, such as parties and interest groups.[22]
The best example of differentiation of the formal-constitutional structure is the autonomy of the judiciary from the executive institutions of
government.[23] The rule of law, which expresses the autonomous character of the society's constitutional and legal institutions, is an example
of the differentiation that separates the regime from partisan groups in
democratic systems. In other words, formal-legal governmental roles exhibit a high degree of autonomy from their incumbent office holders; the
state is autonomous of the ruling groups. Were this not the case, competitive elections (a fundamental democratic prerequisite) would not
be possible, and constitutional rule (another feature of democratic systems) would be replaced by the will of "the Leader" or "the Party."
In sum, the basic legal and governmental framework of society (i.e.,
the regime) is highly differentiated and autonomous of partisan groups
in the democratic ideal type.

In addition to this differentiation between the formal-legal sphere of
government and the political sphere, the democratic ideal type presupposes differentiation between socioeconomic and political structures.
The party system cannot be the exclusive domain of a particular social
or economic group if it is to function effectively as a coordinative
mechanism for linking the regime with societal groups. The party system in a viable democracy must be autonomous of particular groups in
order to aggregate the interests of society's many competing interests.[24]
If this were not the case, formal government would be exposed to cap-
ture by particular interests and other groups would suffer exclusion,

[22] Employing Schmitter's terms, democracy requires differentiation between
"authority groups" and "political associations." See Schmitter, *Interest Conflict*,
p. 6.

[23] In presidential democracies there is also a large measure of autonomy between the executive and legislative powers. In parliamentary democracies, however, this autonomy is reduced by virtue of the close relationship that exists
between the chief executive and parliament.

[24] Of course this does not mean that social and economic interests must remain aloof from the parties. Indeed, we shall see later on that a measure of
participation by socioeconomic elites in the parties can be a stabilizing force.
The point we are making here is that the party system cannot become the
exclusive preserve of particular social or economic groups if democracy is to
prove viable in the long run.

thereby undermining the legitimacy of the regime and increasing the probability of breakdown.

Finally, the democratic ideal type requires a multiplicity of specialized interest groups to serve the function of articulating various social interests and to countervail the particularistic tendencies that would prevail in the absence of a substantial number of groups. This characteristic suggests an obvious corollary of the democratic system — the presence of a high level of political participation. The high level of structural differentiation characteristic of the democratic ideal type promotes stability by fostering the legitimacy of the regime and allowing for effective coordination of the high level of participation.

In contrast to the democratic system, the ideal type of the authoritarian dictatorship is characterized by lower levels of both structural differentiation and political participation.[25] First, these dictatorships, which constitute the most common type of nondemocratic system found in Latin America, are typified by the absence of an effectively differentiated formal-constitutional structure. Ordinarily the executive is controlled by a dictator who has broad legislative powers, and the judiciary lacks political autonomy. In addition, there is little differentiation between the formal-legal structures of government (the regime) and political structures; there is a fusion between the offices of government and the incumbents. This fusion results in the absence of competitive elections and the prolonged continuation of successful *caudillos* in power. In other words, the executive office has no autonomy apart from "the Leader"; the office belongs to the dictator.[26]

The authoritarian ideal type is also characterized by the existence of a large gap between political theory and practice. While they are in fact dictatorships, authoritarian governments often affect a democratic posture in legal texts and public rhetoric.[27] At times, authoritarian gov-

[25] The following discussion draws on the fundamental essay by Juan Linz, "An Authoritarian Regime: Spain," in *Cleavages, Ideologies and Party Systems: Contributions to Comparative Political Sociology*, ed. Erik Allardt and Yrjö Littunen (Helsinki, 1964), pp. 291-341.

[26] While the extent to which Latin American authoritarian governments are personalistic is subject to variation, they have most often adopted a unipersonal type of chief executive. The most significant exception to this pattern is found in the generally short-lived juntas that often serve the function of dismantling authoritarian regimes.

[27] See, for instance, the tract by Fulgencio Batista y Zaldívar, *Respuesta* (Mexico, D.F., 1960). It should be noted that no regime is wholly immune to the problems raised by the incongruity between ideology and political practice. However, the gap tends to be much wider for the authoritarian type than it is for either the democratic or the totalitarian ones, in which ideologies tend to

ernments even attempt to justify themselves as necessary to cure the so-called "pathologies" of democracy. Whatever the case, the ideological support for authoritarian rule is weak as a result of the sharp incongruity between theory and political reality.

The weakness of political party organization is another hallmark of the authoritarian ideal type. Authoritarian governments either ban parties altogether or, alternatively, the "official" parties that do exist tend to be relatively impotent. This weakness of political parties suggests the relatively low level of political participation that typifies authoritarian dictatorships, which tend to present themselves as "apolitical" (i.e., anti-politician). As parties are relatively weak or nonexistent, authoritarian regimes must look to the military for their primary base of support.[28]

This combination of a strong military base and weak political parties lends authoritarian governments a highly bureaucratic appearance. In fact, however, these regimes suffer from a weakness of bureaucratic organization at the highest level. As conceived by Weber, bureaucracy is characterized by the autonomy of offices and limited authority — "the essence of bureaucracy is circumscribed authority."[29] Seen in this light, the fusion of the office of the chief executive with the incumbent and the concentration of power in the hands of the dictator underscore the weakness of bureaucratic organization at the summit of authoritarian systems. By way of contrast, the presidency of the United States is a highly bureaucratic role.

Finally, while authoritarian systems manifest relatively low levels of structural differentiation in comparison with democracies, they nevertheless exhibit a kind of limited pluralism in that some interest groups — particularly those of the business community and in some cases those of the labor sector as well — are allowed a measure of autonomy as long as they do not threaten top government authorities.[30] Though not rival-

provide support for the ideal-type political characteristics of the respective systems.

[28] One of the major functions of the party system is the mobilization of the civilian population for the purpose of determining or supporting governments. In the absence of strong parties, the level of political participation will be relatively low and governments must look elsewhere for support. Authoritarian dictatorships tend to rely primarily (though not exclusively) on the military for support. For pertinent comments on the nature of parties, see Huntington, *Political Order,* especially chap. 7.

[29] Blau and Scott, *Formal Organizations,* p. 61.

[30] As suggested by Schmitter, group autonomy under authoritarian forms of government is less than that characteristic of democratic systems, yet greater than that allowed by totalitarian ones. Schmitter, *Interest Conflict,* p. 383.

ing the military in importance, some authoritarian governments rely on corporate interests such as these for a measure of support.[31]

Authoritarian dictatorships share certain elements in common with a third basic ideal type — the totalitarian dictatorship. Neither has an effectively differentiated formal-constitutional structure, and in neither type is there substantial differentiation between the state and the ruling groups.[32] At the same time, totalitarian systems differ from authoritarian ones in several important respects. First, totalitarian systems have a strong, official political party that mobilizes the civilian populace in support of government. In addition, these systems benefit from the presence of a powerful ideology which legitimizes the dictatorship. Also, totalitarian systems are typified by lower levels of subsystem autonomy in comparison with authoritarian ones; greater control is exercised over the functioning of interest groups and other institutions, including the military. In totalitarian systems the party rather than the military or any corporate interest group furnishes the main source of support for the regime. Recognized social forces are co-opted into the ruling party.[33] Finally, the totalitarian ideal type has a highly complex governmental structure that penetrates the entire social fabric. Particular emphasis is placed on the incorporation of the lower classes into the polity. This combination of party strength and complex governmental organization suggests higher levels of structural differentiation and capacity for control in these systems than is the case in authoritarian dictatorships. In other words, totalitarian systems are more developed in the organizational sense than are authoritarian ones. Totalitarian systems also exhibit higher levels of participation as a result of their attempts to mobilize the population by means of the official ruling party, something authoritarian regimes seldom do.[34]

Our discussion of the organizational and participatory characteristics of the three ideal types indicates that the democratic system is the most

[31] The authoritarian dictatorships of Getúlio Vargas in Brazil and Juan Perón in Argentina provide conspicuous examples of this corporatist tendency. Both relied to some extent on organized functional interests for support.

[32] Though there is not complete fusion between the party and the governmental bureaucracy in the totalitarian ideal type, the party rather than the formal-legal structure of government is the principal integrating force.

[33] In general terms, parties are a more complex or developed type of organization than interest groups are because they transcend particular interests in the attempt to mobilize broad sectors of the population.

[34] Indeed, most Latin American authoritarian governments arise in response to crises of overparticipation, and in this context they attempt to demobilize civilian participants by force.

politically developed of the three, followed by the totalitarian and authoritarian types in that order. Calling to mind the presentation of the preceding section, the discussion with respect to the development characteristics of the ideal types suggests a similar ordering of regimes along the political stability dimension. The analysis of the regime types suggests that democratic regimes are most resistant to breakdown; authoritarian ones are least resistant; and totalitarian systems are intermediate with respect to their chances for avoiding breakdown.

The democratic ideal type is the most stable of the three systems. The high level of political institutionalization characteristic of the democratic type is a product of its organizational and participatory characteristics. Given the high levels of structural differentiation that separate the state from its incumbents, the democratic system possesses a strong electoral organization which makes it possible to resolve political crises within the limits of the law by effecting periodic changes of top government personnel. Furthermore, democratic systems have a highly differentiated formal-legal organization characterized by a multiplicity of normative levels. This normative differentiation lends flexibility to the regime by allowing it to incorporate pressures for change during transitional periods without having to alter the basic elements of the legal system. That is, change can be incorporated within the law by effecting partial normative changes that do not alter the basic principles of the highest law (i.e., the constitution). As discussed at length in the final chapter, this sort of flexibility is notably absent in those Latin American systems that lack an effectively differentiated formal-legal organization. Finally, democratic systems tend to be more stable than alternative regime types because of the high costs of military intervention in a system that exhibits high levels of political participation. With the strong party system characteristic of the democratic ideal type, the military would find it difficult to gather support for intervention because majoritarian groups will attempt to gain power via elections.[35]

In contrast to democracy, the authoritarian ideal type is relatively prone toward instability. As the authoritarian dictatorship is charac-

---

[35] As we shall see in Chapter 4, most Latin American coups involve a degree of civilian support as one of the factors triggering breakdown. Conversely, and as suggested by Allende's Chile, a high level of participation in civilian political institutions, especially the party system, tends to discourage forcible military intervention. In such cases, the armed forces fear that their involvement might be ineffective and that intervention might even lead to civil war. Indeed, post-Perón Argentina suggests that *golpes* which occur in situations of high civilian participation in political life tend to be unsuccessful at institutionalizing regimes. In such cases, frequent successive *golpes* may result.

terized by fusion between the formal governmental structure and the incumbents, free elections are not possible. As noted previously, authoritarian governments tend to be led by *caudillos* who seek to remain in power indefinitely with the aid of military support. This combination of weak electoral organization and the primacy of military support leads to situations in which military intervention is very likely during times of political crisis. In other words, political crisis under authoritarian dictatorship provides fertile ground for coups d'état.

There are other reasons why authoritarian governments are quite susceptible to *golpes*. First, they tend to rely on interest groups rather than political parties for their civilian support. In contrast to political parties, interest groups tend to be highly particularistic proponents of specific interests and they are therefore of little use for mobilizing broadbased support among the population. The gathering of such support is a prime function of political parties, and the fact that they tend to be weak or nonexistent in authoritarian dictatorships points to a major organizational weakness of this type of system. In addition, the sharp incongruity between democratic ideology and dictatorial practice that characterizes authoritarian governments spawns frequent crises of legitimacy. The wide gap between law and political practice has a similar effect. All of these factors help account for the frequent instability and coups that typify the authoritarian dictatorship.

Although there is only one case of a totalitarian system in Latin America — Castro's Cuba — a note on the lower coup propensity of this ideal type relative to the authoritarian one is in order. While totalitarian systems lack the structurally differentiated electoral organization needed to insure the changeover of top executive leadership without some form of violence, they nevertheless exhibit a low propensity toward coups.[36] The reasons for this fact are not difficult to understand. As noted earlier, totalitarian systems are typified by a strong official party which mobilizes the support of various segments of the population and controls the activities of interest groups. Within this system the party rather than the military is counted on as the prime source of support for the regime. Consequently, crises in totalitarian systems are not charac-

[36] The existence of a strong, autonomous electoral organization is one of the key factors that distinguishes the democratic system type from its totalitarian counterpart. The democratic ideal type manifests a higher degree of structural complexity and subsystem autonomy than does the totalitarian one. Furthermore, this higher level of organizational development suggests a potential for higher levels of participation in the democratic setting. As noted, the organizational and participatory characteristics of the democratic system type mark it as the most politically developed of the three regime types dealt with here.

terized by a predominance of military violence or coups d'état. In addition, the totalitarian dictatorship is less likely to experience frequent crises than is its authoritarian counterpart. The strong ideological support typical of totalitarian dictatorship lends the regime a degree of resilience lacking in the authoritarian system type where, as we shall see, there is marked tendency toward the dismantling of the regime in favor of democratic forms of government.

In summary, our discussion of the three ideal types suggests that democratic regimes are the most politically developed and stable, followed by totalitarian and authoritarian systems in that order. In fact, however, this statement is in need of some qualification because political systems do not exist in the rarefied atmosphere characteristic of ideal-type formulations. Rather, all polities operate within a complex matrix of cultural, historical, and socioeconomic factors that have a decisive effect on the character of political behavior. Specifically, these contextual factors have a bearing on both the level of political development of the political system and its ability to avoid breakdown.

In the Latin American context, for example, democratic regimes have varied with respect to levels of both structural differentiation and participation, two criteria central to our definition of political development. Germani and Silvert have compared democratic systems with "limited participation," "enlarged participation," and "total [or mass] participation."[37] The first two types may be exemplified by the middle-class democratic regimes of pre-1930 Argentina (limited participation) and the Chilean regime under Christian Democratic government, which exhibited some working-class participation and expansion of government services (enlarged participation). The Allende government in Chile, which is presently attempting a fuller incorporation of marginal and working-class groups into the polity, could be cited as an example of a democratic regime with mass participation in the making.[38]

As with democratic systems, authoritarian ones also have had different levels of political development. At the lower extreme, we find highly personalistic, patrimonial, and quasi-monarchical systems, as was the case in the Dominican Republic under Trujillo. The extent to which the personal patrimony of the dictator and the state were indistinguishable during Trujillo's rule is suggested by the fact that he was able to

[37] Germani and Silvert, "Military Intervention."
[38] Whether or not this experiment will succeed is open to doubt. Germani and Silvert interpret Latin American *golpes* as a product of the difficulties encountered in attempting to create mass democracies in the area. *Ibid*. More will be said on this topic in later chapters.

commission one of his sons into the army at age three and raise him to the rank of colonel at age six![39] At the opposite extreme, some authoritarian governments, particularly those found in the socioeconomically more developed countries, although generally personalistic,[40] are characterized by higher levels of bureaucratization and the incorporation of differentiated social forces into the polity. For example, Perón's Argentine dictatorship was typified by a relatively high level of interest group participation in politics and, as a consequence, the patrimonial factor was less in evidence. In fact, the level of political mobilization achieved such heights under Perón that his regime clearly departed from our authoritarian ideal type in this respect.

The fact that both democratic and authoritarian systems in Latin America exhibit substantial variation with respect to levels of political development suggests that some authoritarian regimes might attain higher levels of development than some democratic ones.[41] For example, it could be argued that Brazil's present authoritarian regime exhibits higher levels of both participation and organization than did the limited democracies of the Old Republic. Obviously, differences in historical period have an important impact on the nature of regimes.

The discussion of ideal types also requires qualification in that many Latin American coups are a product of the so-called "pathology of democracy." As we shall detail in later chapters, many *golpes* are a result of aborted attempts to institutionalize democracy under adverse cultural and socioeconomic conditions. That is, nonsecular elements in political culture and low levels of socioeconomic development have proven highly inimical to efforts to institutionalize the highly complex, differentiated democratic forms. Under these adverse conditions increases in political participation tend to be highly disruptive, and the

[39] *The New York Times,* December 29, 1969, p. 29. In this respect, this type of regime can be considered "pre-modern." For an interesting study of the Trujillo regime, see Robert D. Crassweller, *Trujillo: The Life and Times of a Caribbean Dictator* (New York, 1966). The Duvalier regime in Haiti provides the most recent example of a highly patrimonial system in Latin America.

[40] Not counting the temporary juntas, the most conspicuous exception to the generally personalistic character of Latin American authoritarian regimes is provided by Brazil since 1964. For a detailed treatment of this case, see Schneider, *Political System of Brazil, 1964-1970.*

[41] In the opinion of Almond and Powell, some totalitarian and authoritarian regimes have been more developed than democratic ones. They also hold that no authoritarian regime has been more developed than any totalitarian one and that this latter system type has only approximated the high levels of political development achieved by the stable mass democracies of the West. See Almond and Powell, *Comparative Politics,* p. 308.

regime finds it extremely difficult to maintain a degree of structural differentiation sufficient to produce the levels of control that are needed for sustained political development. In the pathology of democracy syndrome the scope of political demand-making escalates, and "rational" forms of political action are replaced by violence and repression. Support for the established order declines precipitously, and political breakdown is likely in this atmosphere. In terms of our equilibrium framework, the pathology of democracy is described by erratic oscillation or overshooting of the 45° line. Instead of the relatively incremental adjustments in participation and organization that characterize most sustained developmental efforts, the wide departures from the 45° equilibrium line that typify the pathology of democracy describe a situation of political stagnation or even decay rather than development.

The preceding remarks suggest the need for empirical qualification of the three ideal types presented at the outset of this section. In the Latin American context, many democratic experiments have ended via coup d'état, while there have been some cases of politically underdeveloped authoritarian regimes which have endured over relatively long periods of time. At the same time, the ideal types retain usefulness and validity as general analytical constructs for suggesting propensities toward breakdown. As we will see in later chapters, the only three Latin American countries that have avoided coups or revolutions since World War II — Chile, Mexico, and Uruguay — are relatively democratic countries.[42] In addition, authoritarian governments generally have ended via *golpe de estado*.

In concluding our discussion in this chapter, we should emphasize the need for investigation of the interrelationships between political institutionalization or stability on the one hand and the socioeconomic dimensions of politics on the other. As suggested in the preceding paragraph, there is no simple, one-to-one relationship between political development and stability. The Latin American experience presents cases in which a relatively high degree of political institutionalization or stability has been achieved in the absence of high levels of structural

---

[42] Of course it is possible to argue the extent to which these countries are democratic. For the Latin American context, however, these countries exhibit a good number of democratic characteristics, such as constitutional continuity, civilian rule, periodic changes of the chief executive by way of scheduled elections, and the fact that they show a measure of respect for individual freedoms under all but the most serious crisis conditions. In support of this interpretation, see Martin C. Needler, "Political Development and Socioeconomic Development: The Case of Latin America," *American Political Science Review*, 62 (1968), 889-897.

differentiation and participation, the main criteria of political development. Nicaragua under the Somozas and Trujillo's Dominican Republic are cases in point. In instances such as these, one must transcend the notion of political development in order to understand the phenomenon of political institutionalization in the Latin American context. This can best be done by introducing the notion of balanced sociopolitical development, which focuses on the congruity or "fit" between political and socioeconomic structures. As elaborated later on, the concept of balanced sociopolitical development helps account for cases like Nicaragua which have achieved a relatively high degree of stability in the absence of high levels of structural differentiation and participation. Seen in this light, the low frequency of coups in Nicaragua since World War II can be understood in terms of the congruity that exists between the country's authoritarian, quasi-monarchical polity and its relatively underdeveloped socioeconomic structures.[43] Conversely, Batista's attempt to impose a highly personalistic authoritarian system in relatively socioeconomically developed Cuba produced a severe incongruity which led to a major breakdown — the 1959 revolution.[44] In a similar vein, the high coup frequency of post-Perón Argentina can be viewed as a product of authoritarian attempts to demobilize political participants in a society characterized by a relatively high level of socioeconomic development. The theme of balanced sociopolitical development is pursued at greater length in later chapters. For now suffice it to note that greater understanding of political stability in Latin America can be achieved by examining the complex interrelationships between political and socioeconomic structures.

[43] The notion of socioeconomic development and its relationship to political structure are treated in Chapter 5.

[44] In this sense see Mauricio Solaún, "El Fracaso de la Democracia en Cuba: Un Régimen 'Patrimonial' Autoritario (1952)," *Aportes*, July, 1969, pp. 57-80.

3

SOME EXPLANATIONS

Preceding chapters have presented some preliminary comments on the nature of the Latin American coup phenomenon. This chapter focuses on some of the causes that led to *golpes* in the area between 1943 and 1967. In particular, eight different explanations will be presented at this point:

1. Interclass conflict
2. Intraclass conflict
3. Personal interests of a leader
4. U.S. interference
5. Military corporate interests
6. Low levels of military professionalism
7. Weakness of electoral mechanisms
8. Governmental ineffectiveness and illegitimacy

Three other factors — the character of Latin American culture, levels and rates of socioeconomic development, and political party structure — can be treated more conveniently in later chapters.

Before presenting these eight explanations, a few remarks about the nature of our research procedures are necessary. At the outset of the research the first objective was to become familiar with the various explanations that have been used by Latin American specialists to account for the relatively high frequency of *golpes* in the area. Once acquainted with the different explanations, we wanted to find out how valid the various explanations are. In other words, we wanted to know to what extent they can be used to account for the Latin American coups. To this end, we took a sample of thirty *golpes*.[1] A variety of sources were then consulted in an attempt to ascertain the relative frequency with which the various explanations can be employed to account for the occurrence of the *golpes*.[2] In so doing it was not possible to attack the frequency problem directly because the definitions of the scholars are not always precise, and some of the sources relied upon for gathering the data, especially newspapers and periodicals, do not present their accounts in the relatively abstract manner employed by scholars. For this reason it was necessary to operationalize the various explanations by establishing descriptive indicators for them. Based on a search of the sources, selected coup characteristics were established as indicators for the eight explanations to be presented in this chapter, and a review of the sources then enabled us to ascertain frequencies for these explanations. For example, a *golpe* that occurs in conjunction with elections (a coup characteristic) is established as an indicator of the weakness of electoral mechanisms (an explanation often found in the literature). After counting the number of times that coups take place in connection with elections, it is possible to speak objectively about the applicability of its related explanation. By following this procedure with each of the eight explanations we achieve our goal: bringing empirical evidence to bear on the relative utility of the various explanations.

In this chapter the different explanations and their related indicators will be set forth, leaving to the following chapter a more detailed discussion of the coup processes subsumed under these explanations and the results of our analysis of source materials. Table 1 summarizes our findings.

Interclass Conflict

Latin American coups have often been explained as the product of intense interclass conflict. As noted in Chapter 1, the participation-problem interpretation of *golpes* ordinarily refers to factors of interclass strife common to dynamic, transitional periods. In the intense competition for scarce resources, the confrontation between the deprived classes and the "establishment" often becomes acute. In the end, the military may step in to mediate the conflict or to impose either rightist or leftist solutions. As we have already seen, this explanation of forceful military

[1] For comments on sampling and a listing of the thirty coups selected for study, see Appendix A.
[2] The primary and secondary sources consulted are listed in Appendix B and in the Bibliography.

TABLE 1. Data Gathered from Sources on Coup Characteristics

	I		II	III	IV	V
Explanations	Interclass Conflict		Intraclass Conflict	Personal Interests of a Leader	U.S. Interference	Military Corporate Interests
Indicators (coup characteristics)	Oppose Left	Make Reforms	Coups Not in 1 or 2	Acute Personalism	U.S. Personnel Involvement	Fear of Group
	1	2	3	4	5	6
	El Sal. 1944 Bol. 1946 Peru 1948 Vene. 1948 Bol. 1951 Pana. 1951 Vene. 1952 Col. 1957 Braz. 1964 D.R. 1965 Arg. 1966	Bol. 1943 Ecua. 1944 Guat. 1944-O Vene. 1945 Haiti 1946 El Sal. 1948 Vene. 1958	Guat. 1944-J Braz. 1945 Ecua. 1947-A Ecua. 1947-S Nica. 1947 El Sal. 1949 Pana. 1949 Haiti 1950 Cuba 1952 Col. 1953 Peru 1962 Bol. 1964	Nica. 1947 Pana. 1949	Vene. 1948 Bol. 1951 Pana. 1951 Braz. 1964 D.R. 1965	El Sal. 1944 Peru 1948 Vene. 1948 Bol. 1951 Pana. 1951 Vene. 1952 Peru 1962 Braz. 1964
Number of coups by indicator	11	7	12	2	5	8
Percentage of 30 coups by indicator	36.7	23.3	40.0	6.7	16.7	26.7
Number of coups by explanation	18		12	2	5	8
Percentage of 30 coups by explanation	60.0		40.0	6.7	16.7	26.7

	VI Low Levels of Military Professionalism			VII Weakness of Electoral Mechanisms		VIII Governmental Ineffectiveness and Illegitimacy		
Explanations								
Indicators (coup characteristics)	Substitution of Personnel	Promotion	Physical Clashes	Elections	Continuismo	President-Congress Conflict	Civilian Violence and Direct Action	Overt Civilian-Military Coalition
	7	8	9	10	11	12	13	14
	El Sal. 1944	Bol. 1943	El Sal. 1944	Ecua. 1944	El Sal. 1944	Ecua. 1947-A	Bol. 1943	Bol. 1943
	Guat. 1944-O	Ecua. 1944	Guat. 1944-O	Vene. 1945	Guat. 1944-J	Peru 1948	El Sal. 1944	Ecua. 1944
	Ecua. 1947-S	Guat. 1944-O	Vene. 1945	El Sal. 1948	Braz. 1945	Haiti 1950	Guat. 1944-J	El Sal. 1944
	El Sal. 1948	Vene. 1945	Bol. 1946	Bol. 1951	El Sal. 1948	Pana. 1951	Guat. 1944-O	Guat. 1944-O
	Braz. 1964	Ecua. 1947-S	Ecua. 1947-S	Cuba 1952	Haiti 1950		Braz. 1945	Braz. 1945
	D.R. 1965	El Sal. 1948	Peru 1948	Vene. 1952	Pana. 1951		Bol. 1946	Vene. 1945
	Arg. 1966	El Sal. 1949	Vene. 1958	Vene. 1958	Vene. 1952		Haiti 1946	Bol. 1946
		Cuba 1952	D.R. 1965	Peru 1962	Col. 1953		Peru 1948	Ecua. 1947-A
		Braz. 1964		Bol. 1964	Col. 1957		Haiti 1950	Peru 1948
		D.R. 1965			Vene. 1958		Pana. 1951	Haiti 1950
					Bol. 1964		Col. 1957	Pana. 1951
					D.R. 1965		Peru 1962	Col. 1953
							Bol. 1964	Col. 1957
							Braz. 1964	Bol. 1964
							D.R. 1965	Braz. 1964
							Arg. 1966	D.R. 1965
Number of coups by indicator	7	10	8	9	12	4	17	16
Percentage of 30 coups by indicator	23.3	33.3	26.7	30.0	40.0	13.3	56.7	53.3
Number of coups by explanation	15			17		20		
Percentage of 30 coups by explanation	50.0			56.7		66.7		

Sources: See Appendix B and Bibliography.

intervention in the political processes of Latin American countries appears quite clearly in the works by Germani and Silvert and (with a novel twist) José Nun.[3]

In the attempt to establish indicators for this interclass conflict explanation of coups, a review of the sources suggested two characteristics which seemed especially well suited to the task. As military intervention in cases of interclass conflict ordinarily takes on either right-wing or leftist overtones, the following two coup characteristics may be used as indicators of the presence of escalated interclass conflict: (1) opposition to egalitarian or leftist groups, or (2) support for substantial socioeconomic reforms.

A coup is characterized by opposition to egalitarian or leftist groups when the military intervenes for the purpose of subduing any group which attempts to carry out programs aimed at substantial socioeconomic reforms. For example, the 1964 Brazilian coup was conducted in part because President João Goulart's policies of agrarian reform and nationalization of private oil refineries were interpreted as threats by the country's established interests.[4] Anti-reform coups may also be preventive in nature when they are executed to prevent the accession to power by groups espousing leftist programs which are perceived as threats by the dominant classes. Peru's 1948 anti-*Aprista* coup was of this nature. In saying that any given coup is anti-egalitarian or anti-reformist in character it is important to be sure that the *golpe* results in the repression of forces which the "establishment" perceives as a serious threat to its interests. It is necessary to make this distinction because some Latin American coups, in the absence of more apparent arguments, have been justified as a means to combat an alleged Marxist threat, even in those cases in which such threats are generally considered to be fictional by the nation's elite. In this sense, it is important to distinguish the actual perceptions of the coup's actors from after-the-fact rhetoric, which may mislead more than it enlightens. At any rate, coups executed in opposition to reform groups are right-wing in character.

On the other hand, coups may also be leftist or reformist in nature.

[3] Germani and Silvert, "Military Intervention," and Nun, "Middle-Class Military Coup."

[4] In this sense see Thomas E. Skidmore, *Politics in Brazil, 1930-1964: An Experiment in Democracy* (New York, 1967), chap. 8. In this context we should emphasize that our definition of socioeconomic reform refers exclusively to actions designed to alter social class relationships in the short run. Thus the Brazilian military's post-1964 emphasis on economic modernization within the capitalist mold does not qualify as reformist. Rather, the 1964 *golpe* was anti-reformist in our sense of the word.

A coup conducted in the interests of substantial socioeconomic reform is an indicator of the presence of interclass conflict in the *golpe* situation. In such cases the military sides with deprived sectors of the population in opposition to the oligarchy and its fellow travelers. This was the case in 1945, for example, when the Venezuelan army overthrew the incumbent conservative regime in favor of young reformists. Of course, one must again be sure to distinguish the facts from mere political rhetoric. A coup can be considered reformist only when some honest efforts are made to back up "revolutionary" rhetoric with policy measures designed to produce some significant change in the country's social class structures.

One point should be emphasized in this context. Both of our indicators of escalated interclass conflict require the presence of action designed either to forestall or promote a redistribution of wealth and power among social classes. This point is important because there have been cases of Latin American coups that have produced dictatorial regimes headed by personnel with a lower class background who have had no serious intentions of promoting significant socioeconomic change. Such regimes, termed *condottieri* by Lambert,[5] are highly patrimonial in character. They lead to the private enrichment of the dictator and his entourage — to personal upward mobility rather than changes in the social class relationships that permeate the entire society.[6] Such regimes at times have taken strong action against some upper class families, but without the intent of implementing broad social change. According to Bourricaud, for example, this was the case with Augusto Leguía's Peruvian dictatorship: "During [his] eleven-year reign from 1919 to 1930 [Leguía] severely punished the opposition by the great families, which were exiled, silenced, and cut off from sources of public patronage, for the purpose of insuring the economic well-being of those who had just achieved power by virtue of their complete loyalty to Leguía's person."[7] *Golpes* that result in the accession to power of this patrimonial type of regime cannot be considered the product of acute

[5] Historically, this term refers to leaders of private bands of mercenary soldiers in Italy during the fourteenth and fifteenth centuries whose object was to carve out a state for themselves on which they could grow fat. See Jacques Lambert, *Latin America: Social Structure and Political Institutions,* tr. Helen Katel (Berkeley, Calif., 1967), p. 154.

[6] There are some historical cases in Latin America where the frequency of this phenomenon has led to a collective myth that politics is the road "from rags to riches." For pre-Castro Cuba, see Mauricio Solaún, "Democracia en Cuba."

[7] François Bourricaud *et al., La Oligarquía en el Perú* (Lima, 1969), p. 39.

interclass conflict because the lower class character of the regime's leadership is not accompanied by policies designed to alter social class relationships. For purposes of this study, coups that bring this type of regime to power are better viewed as products of the escalated conflict that is common among members of the dominant social strata. This type of conflict will be discussed in the next section of this chapter.

In conclusion, the presence of either a right-wing or a reformist orientation in a coup situation provides us with useful indicators of escalated interclass conflict. These indicators are, however, restrictive in nature; that is, they are not sensitive to subtler forms of interclass conflict in coup situations. For example, a coup intended to mediate between divergent class interests, as opposed to one that sides either for or against change, is not registered by either of our indicators. In such a case it is difficult to detect any class bias in our source materials, either in terms of the class composition of the groups repressed by the coup or in the character of the policies imposed by the military subsequent to the takeover. As a result, we cannot establish an indicator to tap such a subtle interclass dimension. Nonetheless, the right-wing and reformist criteria that we have chosen are good restrictive indicators. They effectively detect cases of escalated interclass conflict.

Intraclass Conflict

Latin American *golpes* often are interpreted as the result of intense conflict that is restricted to the society's dominant groups. Conflict in these instances is of the more traditional, intraclass variety. As noted in our discussion of the organization-problem interpretation, the intraclass conflict that produces coups results from vigorous competition between "ins" and "outs" for the control of government and the opportunities for prestige and power that such control brings with it. The issues are in this sense purely political in character. They do not involve questions of socioeconomic reform or change in social class relationships, as do the *golpes* that result from escalated interclass conflict. The patterns of intraclass conflict — deeply rooted in the structures of virtually every Latin American society — are nonetheless very costly to political stability. High levels of intraclass strife militate against stability by undermining the ability of political organizations and governmental institutions to coordinate those activities necessary to the maintenance of a viable order. In the end, acute conflict of this sort can produce *golpes*, as the military is placed under strong pressures to take sides in the confrontation between "ins" and "outs." As we have seen, both Merle Kling and

James Payne offer coup explanations that conform in all basic respects with the intraclass conflict one.[8]

In the attempt to specify indicators for this explanation of the *golpes* it is best to establish a residual category in connection with the two indicators employed under the interclass conflict explanation. The residual indicator specifies that in order to qualify under the intraclass explanation, the coup d'état in question cannot fall under either of the indicators of the interclass explanation. The logic is quite simple. All coups are the product of escalated political conflict which is predominantly interclass or intraclass in nature. If not the former, then intraclass conflict can be specified as the source of the *golpe*. Often the sources employed in gathering the data make the intraclass character of the coup quite clear. It may be explained as a showdown between "ins" and "outs"; it may be called a "typical Latin American revolution" or "palace revolt"; or the elite status of all the participants may be indicated in some other fashion. Still, in terms both of the logic of explanation and the diversity of possible descriptions, the absence of interclass conflict best defines the intraclass variety. In sum, a coup not falling under indicators 1 or 2 (interclass conflict) defines indicator 3 (intraclass conflict). For example, the coup that removed Panamanian President Daniel Chanis, Jr., in November, 1949, is a case of a *golpe* induced by intraclass conflict.

Our residual indicator, of course, shares the imperfection of the two indicators of interclass conflict. As the two are not sensitive to milder, more latent forms of interclass conflict, it is quite possible that the residual indicator of intraclass conflict might be detecting at times what are in fact instances of the milder interclass variety. At times, both types of conflict are present in the coup situation. In effect, a case can be made that the probability that a coup will succeed increases when both types of escalated conflict are present.[9] However, for the sake of economy our indicators register the type of conflict that predominates in the *golpe* situation and classify the coup accordingly.

Personal Interests of a Leader

Latin American coups have been interpreted as the result of a single individual's desire for executive power and the material benefits to

---

[8] Kling, "Political Instability," and Payne, *Conflict in Colombia.*

[9] As suggested by Linz, division within the ruling group is a basic factor in political breakdown. See Juan Linz, "The Breakdown of Democratic Regimes," paper prepared for the Seventh World Congress of Sociology, Varna, Bulgaria, September, 1970.

which the presidential office provides access. This interpretation of coups is one with which North Americans are quite familiar. News of coups in Latin America never fails to evoke colorful images of Generalissimo Fulano de Tal, standing in review of his banana republic's semi-comic armed forces. This sort of explanation for the *golpe* is appropriate in those instances in which "a single individual, generally but not always a military man, uses [an] army to make himself master of the state. . . ."[10] The *caudillo* (literally, "the leader") rules in his own self-interest. In contrast to those explanations which adduce military corporate or group interests as a cause of coup activity, this explanation emphasizes the *personal* interests of the leader. In coups where the personal interests of the leader predominate, one usually finds that the *golpe*'s top man held a personal grudge against the president (e.g., Panama in 1949), or that he felt threatened by him (e.g., Nicaragua in 1947). Kurt Arnade offers a vivid description of a Bolivian coup attempt in 1939 that clearly depicts the presence of personal interest in coup situations:

> In Cochabamba, Bolivia, I was once witness to a revolt instigated by Colonel Peño y Lillo, Commander of an influential officers' training school. The revolt was entirely without political significance. The motivating factor was a personal one. Colonel Peño y Lillo had served in the Chaco war against Paraguay. His record was that of an efficient officer, competent organizer, and a gentleman. But since his organizing ability had been utilized almost exclusively for supply rather than combat activities, rumors — in my opinion completely unjustified — were circulated to the effect that he was a coward. It was Colonel Peño y Lillo's belief that his commanding officer, General Quintanilla, was responsible for the rumors. When, after the War, General Quintanilla became President of Bolivia, Colonel Peño y Lillo sought revenge. The revolt was the expression of his sense of personal injury.[11]

In those coups where personal interests predominate, the victorious *caudillo* can have himself installed as chief executive in place of the deposed president. At other times, as in the case of Nicaragua in 1947, the leader may prefer to replace the removed executive with one of his faithful followers. In that way public opinion can be placated while the leader still maintains control through his puppet president.

When the personal interests of a single leader are predominant in the

[10] Lyle N. McAlister, "Civil-Military Relations in Latin America," *Journal of Inter-American Studies,* 3 (1961), 344.

[11] Kurt C. Arnade, "The Technique of the Coup d'État in Latin America," in *The Evolution of Latin American Government,* ed. Asher N. Christensen (New York, 1951), pp. 310-311.

coup situation, evidence of acute *personalismo* is apparent. That is, the force of personal charisma is overwhelmingly present. In the words of John Gillin, "In [Latin American] politics, a man is not commonly elected or acclaimed to office because he represents the social, economic and political positions of his followers, but *because he embodies in his own personality those inner qualities that they feel in themselves* and they would like to manifest, had they but the talent to do so, in their own actions."[12] By construing *personalismo* as an emphasis on the personal qualities of the single leader, its presence to a high degree in coup situations can be used as an indicator for the personal-interests-of-a-leader explanation. Whenever a single personality thoroughly dominates the situation, acute *personalismo* is present. Alexander's description of the 1947 Nicaraguan *golpe* provides a case in point:

> Nicaragua has been controlled by its army since General Anastasio Somoza seized power soon after the withdrawal of the United States Marines from that country in the early 1930's. He maintained control, though he was not always officially in office, until his assassination late in 1956. The power of the army (the National Guard) was demonstrated in 1947 when an elected civilian president, Leonardo Argüello, sought to undermine the position of General Somoza. The result was that the general who had been careful to retain this position as commander-in-chief of the National Guard, ousted President Argüello after only twenty-seven days in power, installing another civilian in his place. A year later General Somoza was again elected and remained president until his death.[13]

It should be noted that our indicator applies only to relatively acute manifestations of *personalismo,* which, as in the case of Somoza, have often taken the *condottieri* form. Nevertheless, traces of *personalismo* are practically always apparent, given the prevalence of the personalistic syndrome in Latin American political culture.

In conclusion, it should be pointed out that the personal-interests explanation intersects the organization-problem interpretation presented in the first chapter. In particular, *personalismo* tends to weaken formal organizational structures by rendering difficult the arts of coordination and compromise. This point will be elaborated more fully in a later chapter.

[12] Gillin, "Some Signposts for Policy," p. 31. Emphasis added.
[13] Robert J. Alexander, "The Army in Politics," in *Government and Politics in Latin America,* ed. Harold E. Davis (New York, 1958), pp. 148-149.

U.S. Interference

Another explanation of Latin American *golpes* points to U.S. interference as an important cause of coup activity. Latin American left-wing
intellectuals and journalists are particularly fond of attributing *golpes* to
American political intervention, a tool of economic "imperialism." For
example, a Brazilian leftist, Edmar Morel, contends that the 1964 coup
in that country "began in Washington."[14] Others point to Guatemala
in 1954 and the Dominican Republic in 1965 as blatant cases of U.S.
encouragement of coup activity. Nor are these claims restricted to Latin
American observers. Both Edwin Lieuwen and Irving Horowitz, noted
North American social scientists, have interpreted U.S. military assistance to Latin America as thinly veiled politicking, intended to prevent
the succession to power by left-wing groups which might prove hostile to
the United States' "strategic interests."[15] This type of aid has, in the
words of Lieuwen, "produced some of the most striking examples of
unprincipled and tyrannical rule in the history of Latin America."[16]
Within this frame of reference, the United States is seen placing itself
in solid opposition to realization of the demands for increased participation and sharing that are being brought to bear by traditionally deprived
groups.

In establishing an indicator to gauge the significance of U.S. interference in the context of coup activity, it is necessary to take into consideration the possibility of ideologically motivated accusations which
may have little substance in fact. The presence of American interference
as a factor contributing to the triggering of any given coup is accepted
as substantial only in those instances in which it can be shown that
American personnel, either military or diplomatic, participated in or
encouraged action on the part of the armed forces. For example, Skidmore has documented the involvement of Ambassador Lincoln Gordon
and Colonel Vernon Walters in the events leading up to the overthrow
of João Goulart by the Brazilian armed forces in April, 1964.[17] In short,
U.S. involvement in *golpes* is accepted as a precipitant of the coups only
when our source materials document their accusations with facts that
can be checked against other sources. As for the claims about the alleged
coup effects of U.S. investment and military assistance in Latin America,
statistical analysis (as opposed to qualitative indicators) provides the

[14] Edmar Morel, *O Golpe Começou em Washington* (Rio de Janeiro, 1965).
[15] See Lieuwen, *Arms and Politics,* and Horowitz, *Three Worlds.*
[16] Lieuwen, *Arms and Politics,* pp. 186-187.
[17] Skidmore, *Politics in Brazil,* pp. 322-330.

best test of these hypotheses. The results of such an analysis will be presented later in the text.

Military Corporate Interests

As does any existing organization, the armed forces have a set of private group interests that relate to their maintenance and welfare as an on-going group. These corporate or group interests are often singled out as an important cause of Latin American *golpes*.[18] Coups may be triggered by threats to those interests or by failure to provide for their satisfaction.

In line with this reasoning, we can specify as one useful indicator of the corporate interests argument those cases in which the military perceives a particular political group as posing a direct threat to its continued existence. Military fear of widespread purges, or a weakening of the armed forces' monopolistic control over the means of coercion — as when the government threatens to create a civilian militia — are liable to move the military to action to defend its group interests. The anti-reformist *golpes* in both Peru and Venezuela in 1948 are cases in point.

As noted in Chapter 1, coups conducted in defense of corporate interests are often executed against leftist political groups that are attempting to channel the increasing participatory pressures of relatively deprived sectors. In attempting to reallocate decision-making power and the material benefits produced in the society, military corporate interests may be threatened and coup activity thereby encouraged. As in instances of escalated interclass conflict, coups involving military fear of a political group may either be aimed against threatening governments (e.g., Venezuela in 1948) or preventive in character when designed to block the accession to power by menacing groups (e.g., Peru in 1962).

In some cases, coups resulting from fear of a political group have resulted in the removal of governments that posed a direct threat to the upper classes as well as to the military. The Brazilian coup of April, 1964, is an example.[19] In other instances, as in the case of Peru in 1962, long-lasting mutual distrust between the military and a political group can lead to a *golpe*, even when this fosters the accession to power by other groups which are just as threatening to the upper classes as the

[18] See, for example, Lieuwen, *Generals vs. Presidents*.
[19] Skidmore, *Politics in Brazil*.

group which is checked by the coup.[20] In this latter case, military group interests are different from upper class interests, and the military acts on the basis of its own. In sum, military fear of a political group that it perceives as a threat to its integrity or security can be used as an indicator of the corporate interests explanation of the *golpes*.

There is another possible indicator of the corporate interests argument: the armed forces' desire for adequate levels of material benefits, such as money and equipment. In general terms, a discontented military is one in which military personnel feel that they are not receiving a large enough share of the national budget for purposes of maintaining adequate levels of remuneration and organizational preparedness. If a *golpe* were preceded by the refusal of the government to meet military requests for higher levels of material benefits or by cuts in its share of the national budget, one could infer that military corporate interests played some part in bringing about the coup. In this sense, demands for a "fair" share of material benefits might be employed as an indicator of the corporate interests explanation of the *golpes*. Unfortunately, we were unable to obtain sufficient information for the coups under investigation to permit use of this indicator. Given this limitation, only the fear-of-group indicator can be employed. The material benefits argument, on the other hand, is best investigated by bringing to bear statistical data on the relationship between the size of the military budget and the frequency of coups in any given country. The presentation of this quantitative evidence will be deferred to the appropriate context in Chapter 4.

Low Levels of Military Professionalism

It has frequently been suggested that a low level of military professionalism is an important cause of military intervention in politics.[21] This explanation assumes a clear-cut distinction between the military and political realms, a distinction which is more moral preachment than a description of reality in most Latin American nations. To a certain extent, also, much of the literature on professionalism and the military has been guilty of tautological thinking. On the one hand, it is claimed that the professionalized military establishment has a very low propensity with respect to political intervention. At the same time, profes-

---

[20] See Liisa North, *Civil-Military Relations in Argentina, Chile and Peru* (Berkeley, Calif., 1966).

[21] See, for example, Lieuwen, *Arms and Politics*.

sionalization has often been *defined* in terms of noninvolvement in politics.[22] Another shortcoming prevalent in the literature is that professionalization is all too often construed almost solely in terms of the possession of sophisticated materiel and the degree of technical education of military personnel.[23] It is our feeling that while these factors may constitute a necessary condition for professionalization of the military, they are not a sufficient condition. The essence of military professionalism is better stated in other terms, which are set forth below.

Beyond these remarks of a critical nature, it is still possible to make a solid case for linking the absence of "professionalism" with the relatively high frequency of coups d'état in Latin America. In this context, a professionalized military is one in which advancement within the organization is achieved in accordance with the norms of technical excellence, as demonstrated via performance. (It should be emphasized that demonstrated performance is something distinct from the number of years of technical training.) Moreover, a professionalized military is necessarily characterized by high levels of discipline, cohesion, and morale. When understood in this sense, low levels of professionalism spell a military organization with a variety of internal problems: low levels of morale, poor coordination, and difficulties in maintaining discipline or securing obedience. These internal organizational problems, indicative of low levels of professionalism, are conducive to a divided, conflict-ridden armed forces. At times the internal conflict may escalate to include the government, especially the executive. In this case military factions, unable to resolve their differences in a definitive fashion, will be inclined to broaden the scope of the conflict, thus involving the executive in the dispute. In some cases the president himself may be responsible for sowing the seeds of conflict, if he adopts a policy which extends promotions in accordance with particularistic, nonprofessional norms. In both cases the organizational weaknesses characteristic of low levels of professionalism may lead to escalated conflict and coup d'état, as the stronger military faction grabs executive power for the purpose of insuring its own security. In this sense, low levels of professionalism encourage coup activity.

[22] This is apparent at points in Samuel P. Huntington, *The Soldier and the State: The Theory and Politics of Civil-Military Relations* (Cambridge, Mass., 1957).

[23] See, for example, Arthur P. Whitaker, "Nationalism and Social Change in Latin America," in *Politics of Change in Latin America*, ed. Joseph Maier and Richard W. Weatherhead (New York, 1964), pp. 98-99.

Given this understanding of professionalism in military organizations, we have established three different indicators for low levels of professionalism in the context of the *golpe:* (1) sustained substitution of military personnel in the coup situation, (2) internal conflicts arising from pressures for promotion, and (3) open physical clashes between military factions.

A persistent and high-level rate of turnover or substitution of military personnel (especially at higher echelons) in the armed forces by purges, promotions, or demotions is symptomatic of low levels of professionalism within the military. In situations of this nature favoritism based on family or partisan considerations, as opposed to technical performance criteria, constitutes the basis for change in military status. Status insecurities and occupational frustrations arise as a consequence, and levels of cohesion and morale are also likely to be precariously low. In extreme cases this combination of factors may lead to *golpes* designed to restore some measure of regularity and cohesion to the military organization. Argentina in 1966 experienced a coup which fits this pattern.

Ironically, there is evidence which indicates that coups intended to restore cohesion to the military are capable of yielding just the opposite effect. The politicization that accompanies a coup d'état can undermine military organization. In the words of one Paraguayan army colonel: "If the generals are granted the right to raise themselves up as judges over their hierarchical superior — monarch or president — no reason of obedience will deny this same right to the colonels, so that they in turn criticize the generals, and the commanders, the colonels, and the captains, the commanders; and so on in descending and demolishing fashion until reaching the troops and authorizing the rebellion of the Sargeants."[24] In short, military intervention may undermine discipline and drive levels of cohesion even lower than they were prior to the *golpe,* thus describing a vicious, unintended circle. As a consequence of this vicious circle, the *golpe* may not be able to prevent the carryover of high rates of personnel turnover into the post-coup period. This carryover effect in turn may result in a process of successive coups d'état, as was the case in Ecuador in 1947, when a second coup followed the first within a two-week period.

A second indicator of low levels of professionalism in coup situations refers to those instances in which junior officers find themselves at odds with their superiors as a result of promotional bottlenecks that confine them to a condition of inferior pay and working conditions. In circum-

[24] Colonel Arturo Bray, quoted in Payne, *Conflict in Colombia,* p. 137.

stances of this nature it is usually the case that high-ranking officers have been unwilling or unable to provide for the welfare of the "rank and file." Given the fact that high-level command positions offer increased material benefits, pressures for a coup instigated by unmet desires for promotion are likely to be high in this kind of situation. The Cuban *golpe* of 1933 is the most extreme example of a "promotional" coup in Latin America in this century.

It should be noted that *golpes* with promotional characteristics are somewhat different in a logical sense from those situations in which military corporate interests are responsible for bringing about the illegal seizure of power. In the former case logic suggests that there is no corporate or group interest, as lower echelons confront higher-ups in disagreement respecting what ought to be done to satisfy the demands of the "rank and file" for increased material benefits. When military corporate interests are involved, on the other hand, the military establishment presents a relatively united front in its demands for a larger share of the national budget. In the latter case one can properly speak of a military corporate or group interest, while in the former one cannot. In the case of promotional coups, consensus with respect to group-wide interests has disintegrated. At the same time, the logic of this distinction does not mean that the promotional and corporate interest factors cannot exist in the same real-life situation. Indeed, top officers may invoke the corporate interests argument in an attempt to divert attention from internal military dissatisfactions, as happened in Brazil prior to the 1964 coup.

Our final indicator of low levels of professionalism is designated by those instances in which military factions engage in overt physical clashes in the coup setting, with one faction supporting the *golpe* and the other resisting. The sources of the conflict between factions in this case may involve factors already mentioned in connection with other indicators of low levels of professionalism — status insecurities, occupational frustrations such as those produced by promotional bottlenecks, and lower-echelon discontent with low pay and poor working conditions. In other instances the seeds of the open clash may be found in ideological or class-related divisions, as was the case in Venezuela in 1945 and in Bolivia one year later. In some cases, such as that of the Dominican Republic in 1965, all of these factors may be involved. Whatever the case, physical clashes within the military in coup settings are indicative of problems of morale, cohesion, and discipline that are characteristic of military organizations with low levels of professionalism.

Weakness of Electoral Mechanisms

Some explanations of Latin American *golpes* argue that weaknesses in electoral organization do not lend themselves to peaceful transfers of power from one executive to the next. These weak mechanisms, unable to perform their function, tend to be substituted by armed force. Under such circumstances military intervention, as opposed to electoral processes, may become "institutionalized" as the medium through which the transfer of executive power is accomplished. In this respect Stokes has remarked: "It is my hypothesis . . . that elections in the Anglo-American sense for the determination of executive leadership are resorted to mainly in Latin America when more satisfactory methods have for one reason or another proved inadequate."[25]

Two indicators of weak electoral mechanisms may be established on the basis of a review of available source materials: (1) overthrow of the government in conjunction with electoral outcomes, and (2) coups executed in response to *continuismo*. In the first case the military conducts a *golpe* for the purpose of nullifying a potential or actual electoral result. In other words, coup activity may occur soon before or immediately after the holding of elections. An example of the former was the case of Cuba in 1952, in which a presidential candidate, Fulgencio Batista, fearing electoral defeat, led a coup in conjunction with junior army officers three months prior to the election. Post-election coups, on the other hand, can be triggered by a dispute within the civilian sector over the honesty of the elections (e.g., Peru in 1962) or by an impartial electoral outcome which is unacceptable to the military (e.g., Venezuela in 1952). Whatever the case may be, coups executed in conjunction with electoral outcomes are acute reminders of the absence of legal, regularized mechanisms for the transfer of executive power.

Continuismo, the second indicator of weak electoral mechanisms, describes a number of techniques that the chief executive may resort to in the attempt to remain in power beyond his formal or legal term in office.[26] At times the military perceives that the president will attempt to rig election laws beforehand in an effort to secure his continuation in power, as was the case with the Brazilian dictator Getúlio Vargas during the closing months of his *Estado Nôvo*. More commonly, the president desiring to remain in power will seek abrogation of the usual constitutional prohibition on election for successive terms, presumably allow-

[25] Stokes, "Violence in Latin American Politics," p. 465.

[26] Many of these techniques are treated in detail in Russell H. Fitzgibbon, " 'Continuismo' in Central America and the Caribbean," *Inter-American Quarterly,* July, 1940, pp. 56-74.

ing him to seek reelection successfully. This tactic, for example, was resorted to by President Paz of Bolivia in 1964. In the cases of both Vargas and Paz the military refused to accept the continuistic solution, and both presidents were removed by *golpes* prior to the holding of elections. At other times, as in the case of Venezuela in 1958, elections may actually occur before the military steps in to thwart the ambitions of the president who has attempted to secure his continuation in power by rigging election laws. In all of the instances cited the important fact is the president's attempt to secure his continuation in power by tampering with the laws that govern election and succession of the chief executive, not whether elections are actually held. The vulnerability of election laws that characterizes *continuismo* is indicative, in turn, of the weakness of electoral mechanisms that characterizes many Latin American regimes.

In summary, coups occurring in conjunction with electoral outcomes and attempts at *continuismo* are indicative of the ineffectiveness of peaceful, regularized mechanisms that might allow for the smooth transfer of executive power. In our discussion of one variation of the organization-problem interpretation of the *golpes,* it was pointed out that weak political party organization is an important factor making for political instability around questions of presidential succession. More will be said of this in the next chapter. For now, the important point is that determination of who will be the president often rests with those who hold a monopoly of coercive force — the armed forces — when legal alternatives are not effectively institutionalized.

Governmental Ineffectiveness and Illegitimacy

Low levels of governmental effectiveness and legitimacy are frequently singled out as causes for coups d'état.[27] Governmental ineffectiveness and illegitimacy are phenomena that describe a vicious circle of sorts that prevails in many Latin American countries. On one hand, many Latin American societies exhibit a low level of consensus with respect to the "oughtness" or legitimacy of government. This legitimacy problem makes it very difficult for government to find support for positive action. In such a situation government does well simply to keep itself abreast of the everyday problems with which it is faced. In periods of political change, however, a government with little support is apt to

[27] See, for example, the discussion by Seymour M. Lipset, "Some Social Requisites of Democracy: Economic Development and Political Legitimacy," *American Political Science Review,* 53 (1959), 69-105.

prove itself highly ineffective. Governmental ineffectiveness in turn is likely to lead to ever lower levels of governmental support and legitimacy.[28] An ineffective government, in other words, can do little to justify its continued existence. In this sense, low levels of governmental performance and legitimacy reinforce each other. Impotent government ought not to prevail! Sentiments of this nature, when multiplied sufficiently, create pressures for military intervention which may become irresistible. If the military fails to deliver a merciful *coup de grâce* under these circumstances, it too may become discredited in the eyes of the civilian sectors. Faced with this alternative, the military may well opt for the more popular course of action — a coup d'état.

On the basis of a review of our source materials we have established three indicators of governmental ineffectiveness and illegitimacy in the coup setting. Although others are surely possible, the following three indicators should suffice for present purposes: (1) acute congressional-presidential conflict, (2) high levels of civilian violence or direct action, and (3) overt civilian-military coalition against the government. The presence of one or more of these indicators in the context of coup activity is taken as adequate demonstration of the importance of the governmental effectiveness and legitimacy factors.

Acute congressional-presidential conflict is closely associated with low levels of governmental effectiveness and legitimacy. Confrontations of this nature bring immobility to government. The congress adamantly refuses to endorse government bills, mutual accusations are hurled back and forth, and administrative agencies are likely to adopt a wait-and-see attitude, all of which combine to reduce levels of government performance sharply. Low levels of performance in turn produce unrest in the civilian sectors, and the government steadily loses legitimacy in the process. In the terms employed in our discussion of the organization-problem interpretation, one might say that the failure of president and congress to coordinate their actions produces a weakness of governmental structures, thereby increasing the likelihood of governmental breakdown. If the congressional-presidential deadlock is not resolved within a reasonable period of time, the likelihood of some type of military intervention will rise. In the extreme, a *golpe* may be executed for the purpose of "saving the country" or at least to reactivate the stalled engines of government. The coup, which by definition is an anti-executive act, can be made in coalition with the congress or against both in-

[28] For an explication of this relationship in terms of learning theory, see Richard M. Merelman, "Learning and Legitimacy," *American Political Science Review*, 60 (1966), 548-561.

stitutions. An example of the former case was the Haitian coup of 1950, whereas both the executive and the congress were effectively removed by Manuel Odría's 1948 Peruvian *golpe*.

Another indicator of low government effectiveness and legitimacy involves increased levels of civilian violence and direct action prior to coup activity. Assassinations, strikes, and student demonstrations reflect governmental legitimacy problems and also tend to reduce levels of positive performance, as government must direct attention to questions of self-maintenance, thereby diverting energies from public policy matters. Violence and direct action are types of participation that cannot be easily compromised. They are disruptive. Government organization is badly strained by pressures of this kind. If the government is unable to control the situation, the armed forces finally may step in to prevent the total breakdown of order. Such was the case in Colombia in 1953, for example, when widespread violence was a key factor leading to the coup. At times, a government fearing its imminent collapse may even organize direct action on its own behalf in an effort to forestall its downfall. Brazil in 1945 offers a case in point.

Finally, our review of sources suggested a third indicator of low levels of governmental legitimacy and effectiveness — overt civilian-military coalition against the government. The logic behind this indicator is obvious. With substantial numbers of civilians joining with military personnel in overt opposition to the continued existence of the government, the legitimacy of the regime is manifestly quite low. Under such circumstances government will find it virtually impossible to take effective action. In a manner of speaking, the handwriting is on the wall. Ordinarily, only the day and the hour remain in doubt. In cases of this nature it has not been possible for us to determine the relative frequency of instances in which the civilian as opposed to the military leadership has taken the initiative in making informal contacts toward the formation of the coalition. It seems that in some cases, as in Panama in 1951, the military initiated the move, while in others, such as in Colombia in 1957, the civilian sector was the initiator. Whatever the case, the formation of a sizable, overt coalition of civilian and military types in opposition to the government is nearly always followed by a coup d'état.

Concluding Remarks

Having established indicators for each of these eight explanations that are often employed in the literature to account for Latin American coups, we undertook a review of primary and secondary source materials on the thirty coups studied for the purpose of computing the frequencies with which the respective indicators manifested themselves. Table 1 summarizes the results. In the next chapter a detailed discussion and analysis of the various explanations will be presented. But first, a few remarks should be offered about the nature of our indicators and framework as outlined in Table 1.

The reader should note that with the exception of indicators 1 through 3, the remaining indicators are not mutually exclusive. Indicators 1 and 2 are mutually exclusive because no one coup can be both for and against socioeconomic reforms. Also, indicator 3 is defined by the absence of 1 and 2 in any given coup situation, so the interclass and intraclass indicators are mutually exclusive in the sense that we use them, though as noted, both types of conflict often coexist in the real world. In other words, with the exception of the first three indicators, any single coup can exhibit a variable combination of factors.[29] In fact, such combinations are the rule rather than the exception. The plain fact is that no Latin American coup can be adequately accounted for by any single one of the eight explanations. All *golpes* exhibit a variety of causes.

We have constructed Table 2 in order to show how this combination of factors operates. From the three mutually exclusive indicators, it is possible to establish two basic types of coups: interclass and intraclass *golpes*. The former can be subdivided into two subtypes: anti-leftist and pro-leftist coups. Table 2 indicates the combination of factors present per coup type. As the reader will note, there is some variability in the combination of factors leading to the different types of coups. This permits us to assign different weights to the explanations according to the type of *golpe* in which they are found. For example, U.S. interference does not appear to be an important factor in triggering intraclass coups in Latin America.

There is an important feature about the nature of the explanations, as operationalized by our indicators, which merits discussion. The causes, as defined by the various specific indicators, do not provide a set of conditions sufficient for the occurrence of a coup. That is, we cannot say that the presence of any one indicator is sufficient to produce a *golpe*. As a matter of fact, no single indicator is necessary for the occurrence of a coup. Table 2 suggests that a coup may still occur in the absence of any

[29] One partial exception to this rule is indicator 4 (acute personalism). As we define it, 4 cannot coexist with indicators 1 and 2 (interclass conflict) as it can with the others.

TABLE 2. Triggering Factors per Type of Coup

	Personal Interests of a Leader	U.S. Interference	Military Corporate Interests	Low Levels of Military Professionalism			Weakness of Electoral Mechanisms		Governmental Ineffectiveness and Illegitimacy		
	Acute Personalism	U.S. Personnel Involvement	Fear of Group	Substitution of Personnel	Promotional Bottle-necks	Physical Clashes	Elections	Continuismo	President-Congress Conflict	Civilian Violence and Direct Action	Overt Civilian-Military Coalition
Type I — Interclass Coups											
A. Anti-leftist:											
Percent of subtype A by indicator	0.0	45.5	63.6	36.4	18.2	36.4	18.2	45.5	18.2	72.7	63.6
Percent of subtype A by explanation	0.0	45.5	63.6	54.5			54.5		72.7		63.6
B. Pro-leftist:											
Percent of subtype B by indicator	0.0	0.0	0.0	23.6	71.4	42.9	57.1	28.6	0.0	42.9	57.1
Percent of subtype B by explanation	0.0	0.0	0.0	85.7			57.1		71.4		57.1
Percent of type I (A and B) by explanation	0.0	27.8	38.9	66.7			55.6		72.2		
Type II — Intraclass Coups											
Percent of type II by indicator	16.7	0.0	8.3	3.3	25.0	8.3	25.0	41.7	16.7	50.0	41.7
Percent of type II by explanation	16.7	0.0	8.3	25.0			58.3		58.3		41.7

one of them. In effect, no column adds up to a total of 100 percent.[30] In this context it is useful to distinguish between the "precipitating" and the more fundamental, or "endemic," causes of coup activity. By analogy, a spark is to gunpowder what a precipitant is to an endemic cause. Alternatively, one can speak about differences between "triggering" factors and "predisposing" factors. Differences between these two types of factors can be drawn along the dimensions of duration and abstractness. The predisposing or endemic factors are both more enduring and more abstract than are the triggering or precipitating ones. That is, the predisposing causes are relatively constant ones; they change only over relatively long periods of time. The precipitating causes are far more ephemeral or changeable in contrast. Viewed along a second dimension, the predisposing factors are relatively more abstract than are the precipitants. In other words, the former are more removed from actual events than are the latter. The endemic or predisposing factors are "constructed" by social scientists, while the triggering or precipitating causes are more clearly perceived by the "man in the street." As an example of these distinctions, it should be clear that a particular stage of socioeconomic development is a predisposing or endemic cause of coups, while a spiraling rate of inflation is a triggering or precipitating cause.

These distinctions are of course a matter of degree, as phenomena are more or less enduring and abstract. Therefore, other more refined classification schemes are possible.[31] Yet classificatory schemes should be chosen with an eye to facilitating interpretation of empirical data, and for our purposes the dyadic scheme facilitates understanding of the causes of Latin American *golpes*. As noted, the endemic factor is "waiting for" the precipitant to trigger a coup, in a manner of speaking. Although both types of factors are "required" to produce the *golpe,* the endemic causes are obviously more important, and they must therefore be assigned more weight in our interpretive scheme. While any number of processes can trigger a coup, endemic factors show a lesser measure of substitutability. Employing a notion already established, we can say that predisposing factors collectively constitute a necessary condition for the occurrence of a *golpe*. In other words, coups cannot occur in the absence of endemic causes; the precipitants cannot work in the absence of the predisposing factors. However, a given coup can be triggered by different combinations of precipitating factors.

[30] Of course, given the logic of our definitions, either interclass or intraclass conflict must be present in the coup situation, but this does not imply that either type of conflict will inevitably lead to a coup d'état.

[31] See, for example, the one proposed by Neil J. Smelser, *Theory of Collective Behavior* (New York, 1963).

Returning to the discussion about the nature of the explanations, as operationalized by our indicators, a distinction must be made between the explanations and the indicators themselves. Some explanations — for example, the weakness of electoral mechanisms — obviously refer to structural characteristics of enduring or endemic import[32] and, we might add, can be related to other enduring factors, such as the cultural syndrome of *personalismo*. In this respect, some explanations can be considered to be predisposing factors. Obviously, the weakness of electoral mechanisms is a necessary condition for coups d'état.[33] The indicators employed to operationalize the various explanations are, however, best dealt with as precipitating factors. For example, the indicators of the weakness of electoral mechanisms — the election outcome and the continuistic attempt — refer to specific, temporally bound events and processes that serve to trigger or precipitate the coup. Therefore, the indicators are neither necessary nor sufficient conditions for a coup to occur. A *golpe* can occur, for example, in the absence of an election, and the power of a continuistic dictator can end with his natural death rather than via a coup d'état. Given the facts that our indicators represent triggering factors, and that these factors are characterized by substitutability, Table 2 shows that coups are accompanied by various combinations of indicators.[34] Of course this does not imply that some configurations of triggering factors will not prevail more with certain types of coups than with others. In the following chapter we shall deal with this aspect of coups. The point that must be stressed here is that *golpes* can be triggered by various combinations of precipitants.

To conclude, in this chapter we have presented fourteen indicators corresponding to eight explanations for Latin American *golpes*. The indicators represent factors that have triggered coups in the area in the post–World War II period. Our data show substantial variability in the configuration of precipitants which accompany coups. These variations affect the type of *golpe*. For example, Table 2 shows that certain triggers are more likely to occur in interclass than in intraclass coups. However,

[32] For a discussion of the predisposing factors in Latin American coups, see Chapters 5 and 6.

[33] As discussed in Chapter 1, all *golpes* are illegal. That is, they violate laws of tenure that would not be broken if strong electoral mechanisms were available for the purpose of allowing the peaceful changeover of chief executives.

[34] In this respect we must disagree with Smelser, who sees a unique sequence or ordering of causal elements in the production of political breakdown. See his discussion of the "value-added" concept in *idem*. Our own research indicates that coups are produced by a varying combination of causal factors. No single sequence is predominant. We do, however, adhere to his perspective of breakdown as a cumulative process.

there is one additional factor to keep in mind in this connection: there is substitutability among the precipitating factors within each type of coup. Thus the type of *golpe* itself shows variability. In this sense, there are coup subtypes. In the light of this evidence, the reader may question the ability of our indicators to predict coups. Basically, the indicators suggest critical phenomena that can produce coups, given the presence of certain predisposing structural and cultural characteristics within a society. In this respect, the triggers cannot be considered in isolation. They can, however, provide awareness of processes that are potentially conducive to political breakdown via coup d'état. Finally, our perspective of the coup phenomenon suggests that, *ceteris paribus,* the likelihood of a coup increases as the precipitants accumulate. These basic notions, though developed briefly here, will become clearer as we proceed.

4

DISCUSSION AND ANALYSIS
OF THE EXPLANATIONS

This chapter is organized around a discussion of the eight explanations and the related indicators that were presented in the preceding chapter. Specifically, two different objectives are pursued here. First, the discussion analyzes a number of substantive processes associated with the occurrence of coups in Latin America in connection with our treatment of the various explanations. This qualitative portion of the analysis highlights the processes that have triggered *golpes* in the area. Second, the results of our research of source materials are presented with the intention of adducing quantitative evidence that will enable us to come to some conclusions about the general value of the different explanations that have been offered by specialists to account for the high frequency of coups in Latin Ameria. In so doing, it will become clear that some of the explanations have more utility than others.

Interclass and Intraclass Conflicts

In this section we can best begin by examining a number of concepts and processes that are necessary for understanding some of the similarities and differences between coups that are produced by the two forms of escalated political conflict — interclass and intraclass. Once these matters have been discussed it will be easier to present and account for the results of our data analysis for the two contrasting explanations. Therefore, we shall turn first to the nature of the coups and associated processes. Toward the end of this section the findings of our data analysis will be set forth and discussed.

In the first chapter, the point was made that *golpes* resulting from interclass conflict are common to the so-called period of "transition," while those produced by intraclass conflict usually are attributed to a variety of structural and cultural constants. Scholars employing the former explanation ordinarily treat transition as a historical phenomenon that has become widespread in Latin America since the end of World War II. The high rates of social and economic change that characterize this period have mobilized traditionally deprived groups that are continually demanding a greater voice in deciding how material benefits are distributed in their society. These participatory pressures interact with the fact of limited economic production to produce substantial opposition by the society's established groups. Escalated interclass conflict and the subsequent possibility of coups d'état follow logically from this typical description of the contemporary transitional stage of Latin American development. *Golpes* produced by escalated intraclass conflict, on the other hand, are ordinarily associated with a bygone era of self-seeking *caudillos* and private armies by those who espouse the transitional explanation. In the words of Needler, "this type of [coup] is no longer as common as it once was. [It occurs only] on occasion."[1] As noted in Chapter 1, sources that interpret coups as the product of acute intraclass conflict typically attribute coup activity to a variety of long-established, relatively enduring structural and cultural factors, such as the particularistic character of political parties and the personalistic syndrome present in the political culture. Those who adopt this "nontransitional" perspective believe that little has changed in Latin American societies.

The close association ordinarily established between transitional phenomena and contemporary history, and the subsequent relegation of more traditional patterns of conflict to the historical museum, is unfortunate in at least one respect. It suggests that acute interclass conflict is a continual source of political instability in contemporary Latin America, while implying that the traditional, intraclass sources of instability are no longer very significant. In fact, there is reason to believe that interclass conflict has been neither a continual source of political breakdown nor as important a cause of coups in contemporary Latin America as one might think on the basis of the tight relationship usually established between transition and the present historical era. As indicated by Table 1, 40 percent of the thirty coups sampled for the period 1943-67 were caused by the more traditional intraclass patterns of conflict.

This does not mean that the frequency of coups caused by acute interclass conflict is not greater today than it was at the turn of the century.

---

[1] Needler, *Political Development in Latin America*, p. 50.

A long-run trend in the direction of more coups caused by this type of conflict is to be expected, given the social and economic changes that Latin America has been experiencing during this century. What is objectionable is the one-to-one relationship established between transitional phenomena and the contemporary era. The danger, of course, is that all coups will be explained in terms of the rates of socioeconomic change and the interclass conflict characteristic of transition. The problem with such interpretations lies in their failure to consider, first, the very complex nature of the relationship between rates of socioeconomic change and political behavior and, second, that rates of socioeconomic change are not continually at a critical point during the contemporary era. As for the first point, the literature frequently gives the erroneous impression that the rates of socioeconomic change that are deemed "transitional" (i.e., characteristic of the contemporary era) invariably produce transitional politics (i.e., acute interclass conflict). Second, there is evidence that rates of socioeconomic change are not continuously critical from the point of view of political stability. The point that we wish to stress here is that the relationship between socioeconomic change and political instability is a very complex one that we will investigate in the next chapter. For now, suffice it to note that, for the reasons already mentioned, most explanations of *golpes* in terms of the notion of transition are not as adequate as they might be. In particular, most of these explanations greatly underestimate the continuing importance of intraclass conflict as a source of *golpes* in contemporary Latin America.

Given the tendency toward indiscriminate use of "transition" to account for instability in Latin America since World War II, we must be perfectly clear about our use of the term before proceeding to discuss some of the processes that have led to coups during the period in question. The problems frequently incurred by the literature are best avoided by defining transitional periods in terms of readily observable political behavior. In short, transitional periods are not tied to any single historical period, nor do we define them by reference to rates of socioeconomic change. *Transitional periods* are characterized by observable political pressures for basic social and economic change. Specifically, strong pressures exist for bringing about significant, qualitative changes in power relationships among social classes. As a corollary of this fact, fundamental norms and values tend to be questioned seriously during transitional periods. Interclass conflict manifests itself in the clashing of divergent ideologies. In such an atmosphere, the probability of violence and some kind of political breakdown is high. Coups taking place during

transitional periods assume an ideological dimension — they are conducted either for or against the forces of change — given the interclass
nature of the conflict that characterizes these times.[2] All of these features
are reported in observations of political behavior during these periods.

In contrast to transitional periods, we may describe a politics of "non-
transition," as when conflict centers around issues that are purely political in nature, such as the fact that one group happens to be "in" while
the other is "out" of power. The issue in this type of conflict does not
involve a direct challenge to society's fundamental values or norms, nor
modifications in the relative position of different social classes. On the
contrary, the objective in conflicts of this kind is merely to obtain alteration in the relative power of established groups by changing the identity
of governmental personnel: the "outs" replace the "ins." This squabbling
among members of the politically dominant strata defines conflict that
is intraclass (i.e., strictly political or *political proper*) and nonideological
in character. Historically, nontransitional politics have proven a fertile
source of coups in Latin America.

In sum, transitional politics are defined by the presence of the interclass dimension, while intraclass factors predominate in the nontransitional situation. These ideal-type distinctions are quite useful when it
comes to analyzing differences in the nature of the conflict that produces
the *golpes*. In effect, both interclass and intraclass conflict lead to highly
partisan or *sectarian* behavior in coup situations. In these circumstances,
both types of conflict are accompanied by attempts on the part of the
groups involved to retain or gain power by completely eliminating the
opposition. The stakes of the conflict are defined in terms of total victory or defeat; there is a zero-sum situation. Compromise or the sharing
of power is very difficult to effect under these conditions. Political
compromises produce widespread cynicism and loss of morale in
the polity. To this extent, *golpes* produced by both types of conflict
are similar. At the same time, the sectarian behavior characteristic of
situations involving intraclass conflict is different in important respects
from that produced by interclass conflict; and our definition of the transitional and nontransitional concepts helps to clarify these differences.

Transitional politics involve the extensive questioning of the fundamental norms and values of the social order, and the acute interclass
conflict that produces *golpes* under these circumstances often is accom-

---

[2] The two indicators of interclass conflict described in Chapter 2 were
chosen with this in mind. The reader will recall that our constructs are ideal
types designed to register the type of conflict that predominates in coup situations.

panied by a kind of sectarian behavior that can be called *ideological radicalism*. The ideological radical censures his opponents because they do not embrace those particular norms and values that he believes to be the absolute good or truth. His opponent is a "heretic." During nontransitional periods, on the other hand, fundamental norms and values are not seriously questioned, and the escalated intraclass conflict that produces coups in these instances often is accompanied by a kind of sectarian behavior that we will call *primitive radicalism*. The primitive radical condemns his opponents for violating those norms and values in which they both profess belief. His opponent is a "criminal" or "sinner." These differences can be drawn more sharply once we have considered the nature of the two types of radicalism in greater detail.

The primitive radicalism apparent in coup situations produced by escalated intraclass conflict is an important vehicle for expressing political proper sectarianism in Latin America. This type of radicalism usually manifests itself in prolonged defamatory campaigns, where accusations of criminality and immorality are hurled back and forth between opposing political groups. The participants in such a conflict view their opponents as thoroughly evil, and the political arena is perceived in Manichean nonsecular terms, as a stage where Good and Evil are locked in a furious battle in which no quarter is asked or given. The vitriolic character commonly assumed by primitive radicalism is exemplified by the following commentary written by a former Colombian Conservative president, Laureano Gómez:

> The government of President Olaya Herrera [Liberal, 1930-34], whose provincial agents are *doers of evil,* must understand that Colombian Conservatism is a phenomenon that cannot be intimidated, nor denied importance or existence. In exactly the same way that the *corrupt* labors of this year's congress [1932] ended in failure, so too will end the long and *cruel oppression* gripping those populous provinces that lived in peace prior to the advent of the present regime. An immense pyramid of cadavers . . . constitutes the spoils of this system of Liberal hegemony.[3]

Elsewhere Gómez writes that "the blood of [the sons of the people] continues to drip on the regime and is suffocating it."[4] Besides holding opponents guilty of highly immoral and criminal conduct, primitive radicals never tire of accusations of conspiracy. The forces of Evil are

[3] Laureano Gómez, *Comentarios a un Régimen,* 2nd ed. (Bogotá, 1935), p. 36. Emphasis added.

[4] Laureano Gómez and José de la Vega, *El Crimen de la Magdalena* (Bogotá, 1944), p. 160.

continually mapping their intrigues, alliances, and conspiracies "against the people."[5]

A populistic strain apparent in much of the material exemplifying primitive radicalism is intended to strike a favorable emotional chord. Quite frequently, the moral character of the president is impugned; it is suggested that his actions are designed to injure the people:

> The murders were not a local matter. The execution orders came directly from the [president's] throne. . . . President Olaya Herrera has not lifted a finger to stop those horrible crimes from continuing. In the face of the spectacle of so much innocent blood, the devastation of vast and once fertile lands, the mourning and the stark misery of thousands of his compatriots, President Olaya smiles. His is a cruel, impious soul. He is literally soaked with the honest blood of his brothers. And he smiles.[6]

> The henchmen who sacrificed the life of a [noble] son of the people did so that the president's [honor] might be saved.[7]

Such attacks on the president and his associates interject a decidedly populistic note into the rhetoric of the primitive radical. As a result, one cannot associate this type of radicalism with a completely conservative stance. If anything, primitive radicalism tends to undermine the position of all established authority, without, however, connoting any sort of ideological conflict.

The verbal totalism characteristic of the primitive radical reflects a depth of emotion that far exceeds the standard rhetoric common among North American politicians. At times, the emotional content surpasses all bounds and takes on the air of a dramatic theatrical piece. The important fact is that such words reflect a genuine and deeply felt set of perceptions and sentiments about the nature of one's opponents and the role of the self vis-à-vis such "murderous" men. The frequency of *golpes* touched off by the primitive radicalism associated with acute intraclass conflict is indicative of the fact that the rhetoric of the primitive radical often translates into radical behavior.

Primitive radicalism tends to encourage coups d'état. If the radical

---

[5] *Ibid., passim.* Shils has suggested that radicals on both the "left" and "right" are prone to interpret reality in conspiratorial terms. See Edward A. Shils, "Authoritarianism: 'Right' and 'Left,' " in *Studies in the Scope and Method of 'The Authoritarian Personality': Continuities in Social Research,* ed. Richard Christie and Marie Jahoda (Glencoe, Ill., 1954), pp. 24-29. In effect, Shils is stating that ideological radicals share the conspiratorial perceptions of the primitive radical. Other similarities between the two types of radicals will be treated shortly.

[6] Gómez, *Comentarios a un Régimen,* pp. 14, 199.

[7] Gómez and de la Vega, *Crimen de la Magdalena,* p. 164.

description of the ruling group as "criminals" can be made to stick, the fact that they deserve total displacement from power and punishment becomes both logical and justifiable. The methods employed by the radical against the government tend to escalate from legal to illegal. Primitive radicalism in Latin America is associated with a pattern of events that may be called the *diffusion of illegality*. This syndrome refers to those situations in which illegal or violent measures emanate from the logic of the radicals' accusations, after the fashion of a self-fulfilling prophecy. Illegal actions are viewed as legitimate and necessary steps taken in self-defense for the purpose of correcting the "immoral" or "criminal" behavior of the government. The government in turn tends to resort to illegal or repressive measures to deal with its opponents, justifying its conduct as necessary to defend itself from the illegal or "criminal" conduct of the opposition.

In extreme situations of this kind, the military will find it increasingly difficult to resist forcible intervention in the political process. In effect, in those cases in which the opponents of the government have made a persuasive case, a coup d'état becomes exceedingly likely because if the military fails to take action against the government, it too will be accused of being "immoral" or "criminal." These accusations, when applied to the military, will injure its status in the eyes of the population at large. In such an atmosphere neutrality is virtually impossible. The armed forces will be forced to act in legitimate self-defense in order to preserve their prestige and perhaps their integrity as an on-going organization. The 1968 Panamanian coup provides a case in point.[8]

The forces unchained by primitive radicalism make any reconciliation between the government and its opponents difficult to achieve. When a situation is defined in nonsecular terms as one involving an all-out struggle between Good and Evil, the chances of compromise and bargaining are small. In situations of this kind, conciliatory pacts are difficult to make. The reason for this is relatively simple. If, as sometimes occurs for strategic reasons, a compromise materializes between the accusers and the group charged with criminal behavior, then the former are accused of having "sold out" to Evil, of guilt by virtue of compromise. Compromise of this nature cannot fail to have generally demoralizing effects, to undermine the legitimacy of all parties involved. Actually, primitive radicalism tends to produce a generalized *desprestigio* — loss of prestige or reputation — which erodes the legitimacy of most

---

[8] See *Expreso* (Panama City), May 15, 1968, pp. 1, 13; and *La Calle* (Panama City), March 30, 1968, p. 3.

politicians. In this sense, it "invites" military intervention and underpins the anti-politician bias that typifies many Latin American authoritarian regimes.

In order to understand more fully why compromise is difficult to come by in situations where primitive radicalism is involved, a few additional comments are in order. Common sense suggests the difficulties involved in making a pact with someone who has publicly called you a "common criminal" and "immoral murderer." Remarks of this nature are in an important sense uncompromisable, and their effects can be irreparable. This is particularly true in view of the great emphasis placed on personal dignity and self-respect throughout most of Latin America.[9] In light of this fact, primitive radicalism deals a severe blow to the ego. Naturally, the authors of the accusations which lead to *desprestigio* become the objects of intense hatred on the part of those suffering the brunt of the attacks. In election campaigns characterized by primitive radicalism, those in power, threatened by the serious nature of the attacks upon their morality, may resort to electoral illegality in order to avoid displacement. The high cost of their possible defeat is not only based on fear of physical persecution or the frequent alternative punishment — political exile. The fact is that under conditions of primitive radicalism, election losses are extremely costly on a symbolic or personal identity level. Defeat in these terms results in an enormous blow to personal integrity and self-respect. In a sense, defeat confirms the widespread suspicion regarding the evil nature of the ruling group and its leaders.

In short, primitive radicalism in Latin America encourages illegal measures designed to save face while effectively minimizing the possibilities of compromise. It leads to the treatment of opponents as criminals and to the diffusion of illegality. Illegalities and uncompromisable differences provide highly fertile ground for *golpes de estado* designed to solve what are in fact the crises of morale and morality that are produced by primitive radicalism.

The ideological radicalism that occurs in Latin America during transitional periods of acute interclass conflict is a complex phenomenon. There are what one might call different "grades" of this second variety of radicalism. In its most sophisticated form, it gives some theoretical consideration to a philosophy of history, with all the teleological implications common to such philosophies. An example of a relatively sophisticated type of radicalism can be found in some of the writings of the Peruvian APRA leader, Víctor Raul Haya de la Torre:

[9] See Gillin, "Some Signposts for Policy."

Aprista *theory* recognizes that imperialism, the *first stage of capitalism* in our countries, brings with it industrialization . . . and it represents *a period* of evolution of the economy and of civilization superior to that of colonial feudalism. . . . imperialism as an economic phenomenon, as the first stage of capitalism in Indio-America — as a stage of *ineluctable,* progressive industrialization — is both dangerous and *necessary.* With it, we run the risk of subjection, but without it, there would be inevitable stagnation and retrogression.[10]

It should be noted, however, that most Latin American ideological radicalism is not marked by a sustained preoccupation with the internal logic or rigorous systematization of ideas. The common grade of ideological radicalism in the area is generally typified by a search for ideology, the dilettantish manipulation of symbols, and perceptions that countergroups represent diametrically opposed idea-values. Take, for example, the low-grade ideology expressed in the following speech given by the Colombian Conservative Laureano Gómez, who had developed into an ideological radical by the time he assumed the presidency in 1950:

When [the Liberals] eradicated *the name of God* from the preamble of the Constitution, when they adulterated the wise principles which reigned over the concordance of the spiritual and civil powers, when the youth in the University and secondary schools were submitted to unmasked instruction in *naturalism* and *atheism,* there emerged a process of disfiguration of our national soul and destruction of our noble *Christian* and free country, giving us instead a structure which forced the people to bypass the *Red* [Marxist] paths of revolution.[11]

The statements of many Latin American politicians of leftist persuasion are similarly weak in systematic ideological content. The focus is on emotional symbols and attacks against the opposition, as opposed to the systematic explanation of ideas and refutation of alternative philosophies. The low-grade character of ideological radicalism in Latin America is further attested to by the infrequency of indoctrination campaigns and the generally low theoretical level of political conflict in the area.[12] This situation contrasts with those European situations in which ideological groups integrated around relatively pure, highly systematic sets of ideas

[10] Víctor Haya de la Torre, "Thirty Years of 'Aprismo,' " in *The Ideologies of Developing Nations,* ed. Paul E. Sigmund (New York, 1963), pp. 292-293.

[11] *El Siglo* (Bogotá), August 8, 1950, p. 1. Emphasis added. Comparison of the primitive and ideological types, and the possible evolution of the former into the latter, will be taken up shortly.

[12] As noted in Chapter 2, the authoritarian dictatorships prevalent in Latin America do not engage in systematic ideological indoctrination.

have emerged.[13] The main example of groups of the latter kind to be found in Latin America today are the relatively small, old-line Communist parties. Aside from these groups, and other occasional exceptions, ideological radicalism in Latin America is far more concerned with emotional reaction than it is with a systematic refutation of philosophies. The tendency is to search for a suitable set of emotional symbols which can be used as weapons against one's opponents in situations of inter-class conflict. For example, in situations involving a high degree of polarization between traditional upper-class and lower strata, as in Brazil in 1964, highly charged rhetoric of this variety is likely to be in evidence. In circumstances of this kind, self-fulfilling prophecies tend to materialize. The upper classes, fearing total displacement by "Communist" or "Marxist" groups, pledge strong action in defense of "God and the traditions of the *Patria*." Groups on the periphery, meanwhile, are radicalized by the perceived lack of flexibility on the part of the upper strata, and they will likely pledge to take all measures necessary to de-fend the "rights of the Workers against exploitation by insensitive Capital and Wealth." This quasi-ideological verbal totalism reinforces initial differences, and polarization is increased. Political breakdown in the form of a coup d'état may be only a step away.

Having discussed the two types of radicalism in some detail, it should be emphasized that the ideological and primitive radicals share much in common, a fact which is hardly surprising in view of the nonsecular political culture that predominates throughout much of Latin America. In both types of radicalism, opponents are viewed as "immoral crim-inals" who are continually "conspiring against the people." In this sense, all ideological radicals are primitive radicals too, but the reverse is not true. To extend the metaphor employed earlier, we might say that the opponents of the ideological radical are both "sinners" and "heretics," while those of the primitive radical are "sinners" only. The crucial dif-ference here is that ideological radicalism appears during transitional periods, when fundamental norms and values are extensively questioned. One's opponents are not only guilty of evil-doing (i.e., they are sinners), but they reject one's basic philosophy as well (i.e., they are heretics). On the other hand, primitive radicalism is present during nontran-sitional periods, when basic norms and values are not being extensively questioned. Under these circumstances, one's opponents are sinners, but they cannot be heretics because all parties are in basic agreement that

[13] For a description of these groups, see Vladimir C. Nahirny, "Some Ob-servations on Ideological Groups," *American Journal of Sociology,* 67 (1962), 397-405.

the fundamental principles that legitimize the social order are desirable. As a result of these differences, political conflict tends to be more severe during transitional periods. This point was suggested by our discussion of the equilibrium framework outlined in Chapter 2 and will be documented later in this chapter.

Viewing this distinction between the primitive and ideological positions from a slightly different perspective, ideological radicalism is distinguished by a lack of consensus over fundamental sociopolitical philosophies, while the primitive variety involves a lack of consensus over the facts and implications of political behavior. The 1952 Cuban coup that brought Batista to power offers an excellent example of the destabilizing nonconsensus that accompanies primitive radicalism.[14] In this case, both Batista and the Prío government that he removed formally espoused the same moral codes and the same democratic philosophy. Consensus was lacking only with respect to (1) what actions had the government taken? (i.e., did it expropriate public funds for private use?); (2) what did the alleged actions mean? (i.e., did they exemplify "illegality," "corruption"?); and (3) what actions did the government plan? (i.e., did it plan electoral fraud?). The Prío government denied the parenthetical accusations while Batista affirmed them. In accordance with the logic of the diffusion of illegality syndrome, the coup was justified in terms of self-defense vis-à-vis a corrupt government that was perceived as acting illegally. In other words, the *golpe* was justified by Batista as necessary to restore honesty and legality to government and to avoid electoral fraud. In the situation where ideological radicalism is prevalent, on the other hand, disagreement over the facts and import of political behavior are also present, but this nonconsensus merely serves to escalate further the conflict between groups that are not in agreement about the fundamental values and norms that underpin the social order. In the Cuban case just discussed, the conflict could have been escalated in this manner if either Batista or Prío had formally advocated an anti-democratic ideology.[15]

Finally, in the context of distinguishing the two types of radicalism, it should be made clear that the primitive radical may evolve into an

---

[14] Solaún, "Democracia en Cuba."

[15] Of course, one might argue that Prío was a democrat in his actions while Batista was not, rhetoric notwithstanding. Still, the character of verbal statements is an important variable affecting the intensity of political conflict, and it is significant that Batista justified his coup in terms of the illegality of the Prío regime rather than attacking the legal principles on which the status quo was founded. Quite simply, primitive radicalism leads to the diffusion of illegality syndrome without involving ideological conflict.

ideological type over time. Examples can be found in the careers of Cuba's Fidel Castro and Colombia's militant Conservative, Laureano Gómez. The possibility of this kind of evolution still does not negate the distinction between the two types of radicalism. It merely indicates that intraclass conflict at times may be transformed into the interclass variety, thus reflecting the changing patterns in the society. Needless to say, our ideal types will seldom appear in reality in the full-blown, nearly mutually exclusive form that they assume in our presentation. Often, as in the case of Colombia in the mid-1940s, both types of conflict will be found together in varying proportions. To the extent that this is the case, the determination as to which type of conflict predominates in the society at any given time is a relative matter subject to empirical inquiry.

We have suggested that the primitive radical accuses the government of violating values and norms in which both profess belief, and that intraclass coups can be precipitated by the crises of morale and morality produced by this type of radicalism.[16] There are additional processes accompanying primitive radicalism that are important in triggering coups. Primitive attacks against governments typically occur under democratic regimes.[17] As previously noted, the logic of radicalization tends to transform the regime into a dictatorship because of the measures that the government feels it must take in order to maintain its moral position. This is one way in which primitive radicalism tends to weaken a democratic regime. Democracy is also undermined when the primitive radical succeeds in gaining support for his position. In effect, if the population is made to perceive that government is staffed by "criminals," then persons will question the effectiveness of a system that permitted these government officials to be elected. In either case, the democratic regime enters into crises, and the military tends to consider the need for a *golpe* that will bring about an authoritarian regime that will cure the "pathology of democracy."

[16] In the terms employed in Chapter 2, primitive radicalism describes a less acute form of overparticipation which tends to trigger intraclass *golpes.* Needless to say, primitive radicalism does not always lead to coups in reality. Like the other factors discussed in this chapter, it is a precipitating factor which is neither a necessary nor sufficient condition for coup d'état. We should also note that there are a few exceptions to the association between primitive radicalism and intraclass *golpes,* such as in Peru in 1968, when a reformist coup followed primitive attacks. Such exceptions seem to follow in part from the fact that our discussion has not accorded sufficient importance to military ideologies as a variable that has some independence from activities in the civilian sector.

[17] Obviously, the restrictions placed on freedoms of speech and assembly by authoritarian dictatorships make it unlikely that the sentiments of the primitive radical will be expressed openly, even though they are present in latent form.

We have already noted that primitive radicalism may evolve into ideological radicalism over time. However, military intervention as a result of primitive radicalism does not necessarily require the emergence of ideological radicalism. Actually, some authoritarian regimes aimed at "curing the pathology of democracy" do not adopt an anti-democratic ideology. Frequently, they tend to justify their rule only as a provisional departure from democracy that will enable a fuller institutionalization of democracy in the future.

Regardless of the process that triggers the *golpes,* the white-hot rhetoric of both types of radicalism often succeeds in bringing about structural fusion, whereby formal governmental structures are "melted down" and fused into less differentiated units. Radicals maintain that the ruling group has "captured" the government. Accusations along this line imply that public office is being treated as the private and exclusive domain of the ruling group or class at others' expense. In effect, the opposition believes that governmental organizations have been given a sectarian reconstitution, that they have lost their autonomy from their "incumbents." As a consequence of this process, and in a self-fulfilling manner, governmental organization "melts down," i.e., the constitutional structure or the regime is defined as being inoperative. Formally institutionalized procedures for obtaining political change become ineffective. In the face of this structural crisis, and given the military's monopoly over violence, the armed forces also experience a process of structural fusion. This is exactly what happens in every *golpe.* As discussed in Chapter 1, in the coup situation the military loses some of its functional specificity as it assumes determination of the executive, even if only provisionally. This *de facto* redefinition of roles produced by the coup results in an amplification of the military role: the executive function is fused with the traditional military one of national defense. More will be said of this later. For now, suffice it to point out that the structural fusion that defines the coup process is a distinctive product of a highly sectarian politics which leaves little room for neutrality or compromise.

Greater appreciation of the destabilizing effects of the two kinds of radicalism in Latin America can be gained by offering a few comparisons with stable, Western democracies such as the United States. First, the rhetoric of successful politicians at the national level in the United States is singularly devoid of the primitive radicalism so apparent in the speech of their Latin American counterparts. Even at the local level, the perennial campaign to "throw the rascals out of city hall" is typically low in primitive radicalism. Opponents are "rascals," not "murderers," as a general rule. As a result of these characteristics, consensus politics tends to develop in the United States during nontransitional periods. Chances for democratic equilibrium are maximized by the fact that differences among key political groups tend to be restricted to political questions surrounding the selection of the "team" which will staff the offices of government. This type of situation stands in sharp contrast to conditions which surround personnel questions in much of Latin America, where primitive radicalism escalates political conflict and heightens the probability of a coup d'état.

The verbal totalism of the ideological radical — the vituperative condemnation of opposing philosophies, the accusations of immoral and criminal behavior, the messianic perceptions of redemption in a future Heaven on Earth — is not entirely foreign to American ears. During transitional periods — for example, during the process of labor union incorporation in the New Deal period, or the current attempt of blacks and students to gain access to society's decision-making processes — the United States has had experience with ideological radicalism. The U.S. Communist party, though never a serious contender for power, had its heyday during the Depression era. In recent years the Black Panther movement has proclaimed its "solidarity with all brothers and sisters throughout the world who are being oppressed by the racist policies of United States imperialism." Flags of anarchy, Communist banners, and Viet Cong battle pennants have been paraded recently by students across many American university campuses. Despite the vigor of these movements, the factor of overriding significance from the point of view of system stability is that they are confined to small, peripheral groups in the society. The vast majority of organized labor, blacks, and students do not engage in ideological radicalism. Moreover, the level of ideological rhetoric in the United States during transitional periods still remains below that characteristic of Latin American societies that are experiencing transition. These points will be discussed at greater length in Chapter 6. We are only raising them briefly now for the purpose of showing that although our two types of radicalism are not unknown in stable democracies, such as the United States, their appearance is more confined and less virulent there than in Latin America. For this reason, stable democracies are able to maintain a rather high level of consensus, and political breakdown is largely avoided as a result. In Latin America, on the other hand, the virulence of primitive and ideological radicalism has devastating effects on political stability.

The remarks presented up to this point about the nature of the processes associated with our two types of political conflict can be summarized briefly. Escalated interclass conflict in Latin America is observed during transitional periods and is often accompanied by an ideological radicalism that leads to the increasing polarization of social and political groups, thereby encouraging some form of political breakdown. Acute intraclass conflict, on the other hand, is characteristic of non-transitional periods during which purely political matters form the center of controversy. Intraclass conflict is still an important cause of coups in the area, and it often assumes the form of a primitive radicalism that has highly disintegrative effects.

Having set forth the qualitative processes associated with the two forms of conflict, we are now ready to consider the quantitative evidence that is presented in Table 1. Sixty percent of the thirty *golpes* analyzed were produced by interclass conflict, while the remaining 40 percent were the product of escalated intraclass conflict. In view of the already noted tendency to interpret contemporary Latin American history as a transitional period characterized by the prevalence of sustained interclass struggle, one would expect far fewer instances of coups being triggered by the intraclass conflict factor. In fact, two *golpes* out of every five were produced by the intraclass variety during the 1943-67 time period that we studied, thereby suggesting that traditional patterns of conflict are still an important cause of coups throughout the area.

The question remains — particularly in view of the transitional bias present in much of the current social science literature on Latin America — why has escalated interclass conflict not been more widespread in the area during the post–World War II era? We can acknowledge that the socioeconomic changes under way in Latin America have made the transitional causes of *golpes* more important in recent years than they were during the first thirty years of this century and still pose this question meaningfully. If the pressures characteristic of transitional periods are growing throughout most of the area, there are a number of factors that mitigate these pressures.

In attempting to achieve an understanding of why interclass conflict is not more widespread in Latin America today than it is, one has to look for factors which work against the polarization or radicalization of social classes. The fact is that although the lower classes always have suffered a great deal of relative deprivation vis-à-vis the upper classes in Latin America, this condition has not posed a constant political problem. It still does not today, even with the high rates of socioeconomic change that are sweeping the area. There are a number of factors that help to account for this fact. First, and despite the extreme poverty of the lower classes, demographic pressures in most of Latin America do not seem to have led so far to problems of widespread land-grabbing and starvation.[18] Second, the traditional norms of fatalism and passivism in the face of deprivation are still strong among the lower classes in many parts of the area, particularly in the rural regions. These norms do not make for awareness of condition, let alone activism, on the part of the lower classes. Moreover, as until recently with American blacks, the coercion practiced on the deprived sectors by those in positions of power has in all probability increased the tendency of the lower strata to accept their condition as one which indeed might be worse than it is. Coercion on the part of the *patrones* discourages future demands on the part of affected parties, thus reinforcing prior dispositions to resignation and hopelessness existing in the lower classes. All of these factors would tend to reduce the availability of the lower classes for interclass violence.[19]

These comments about the state of the Latin American lower classes also suggest the high dependency of these sectors on the middle classes. Efforts at vindication on the part of the lower strata would in all likelihood have to depend excessively on the middle classes for leadership. Indeed, they often have. Both Fidel Castro and Che Guevara came from the ranks of the middle classes. Still, such factors as the relatively small size of the middle sectors, low levels of industrialization, and the resistance of cultural values to change have caused segments of the Latin American middle classes to be rather highly dependent on upper class values and styles and to display a high degree of status consciousness and aristocratic orientation.[20] It is quite probable that these factors tend to split and reduce the capacity of the middle class for sustained radicalization. In fact, placing the discussion in historical perspective, according to Luis Ratinoff, in most Latin American countries middle class ideology has gone through cycles of radicalization-deradicalization in which there was an initial attack on the prerogatives that had been concentrated in the upper classes, followed by an increased conserva-

[18] See David Simpson, "Dimensions of World Poverty," *Scientific American,* 219 (1968), 22, 27-35.

[19] For some exceptions to this, see Henry A. Landsberger, "The Role of Peasant Movements and Revolts in Development," in *Latin American Peasant Movements,* ed. Henry A. Landsberger (Ithaca, N.Y., 1969), pp. 1-61.

[20] In this sense see François Bourricaud, "Structure and Function of the Peruvian Oligarchy," *Studies in Comparative International Development,* vol. 2, no. 2 (St. Louis, 1966) ; Fernando Guillén Martínez, "Los Estados Unidos y América Latina," *Aportes,* Jan., 1968, pp. 4-28; and Hélio Jaguaribe, "The Dynamics of Brazilian Nationalism," in *Obstacles to Change in Latin America,* ed. Claudio Véliz (London, 1965), pp. 162-187.

tism as the middle sectors' economic status improved.[21] The middle sector–working class alliance that marked the period of radicalization (i.e., the 1930s and 1940s in most countries) began to disintegrate with the process of deradicalization. Once certain concessions or gains have been registered, the tendency has been toward middle class conservatism, thus leading many authors to suggest that middle class leaders are interested only in personal gains rather than in basic social change.[22] Given our prior remarks on the *condottieri* or gangster-type behavior of some Latin American political leaders, it is not hard to find a measure of merit in such opinions. Indeed, socioeconomic deprivation vis-à-vis the upper classes need not necessarily lead to demands for social revolution; at times it also can lead to "gangsterism."[23]

Another explanation that helps to account for this trend of deradicalization relates to the changing character of the majority of Latin America's middle class political parties. Several of these parties that were ardent reformers during the 1930s and 1940s have turned toward the center of the political spectrum after having been sobered by a *golpe* designed to prevent them from implementing policies deemed too radical by the armed forces. Venezuela's *Acción Democrática*, Peru's APRA, and Cuba's old *Partido Revolucionario Cubano* fit this pattern. In all of these cases, the deradicalization of the parties was accomplished by a process of "socialization and compromise through violence." Ultimately, this quite simply means that the parties "learned" more moderate ways after having been chastised by the armed forces.[24] This process is an important phenomenon, for it tells one something of the basic character of Latin America's middle sectors.

During the early years of their existence, the reformist zeal of the

[21] Luis A. Ratinoff, "Las Clases Medias en América Latina," *Revista Paraguaya de Sociología,* Sept.-Dec., 1965, pp. 5-31. Nun, "Middle-Class Military Coup," has also made a case for middle-class conservatism.

[22] In this context some leaders have been called "opportunistic," "madly ambitious," and "selfish," all epithets suggesting egotistic motives. See, for example, Payne, *Conflict in Colombia*, pp. 157, 253, 300; and John D. Martz, *Colombia: A Contemporary Political Survey* (Chapel Hill, N.C., 1962), pp. 19, 42, 261, 296, 327, 329.

[23] See Robert K. Merton, *Social Theory and Social Structure,* rev. and enl. ed. (Glencoe, Ill., 1957), pp. 192-194.

[24] In this sense see Mauricio Solaún and Manuel S. Alguero, "Socialización y Compromiso por Medio de la Violencia," *Razón y Fábula*, 10 (1968), 61-76. In the terms employed in Chapter 2, this process of compromise through violence describes a situation in which higher levels of political development are eventually achieved in the wake of a period of acute disequilibrium (coups) and erratic overshooting of the 45° line.

middle class parties that we are referring to resulted in their propagation of programs of basic socioeconomic change. The controversial nature of these programs — often proposed by intellectuals — alienated some support in the middle sectors, which felt threatened by the programs' possible adverse effects on their own economic interests.[25] Withdrawal of a significant portion of middle class support brought with it a loss of confidence in the leadership of these groups and subsequent *golpes* designed to veto the policies that threatened existing economic interests. In the final analysis, the bulk of the middle class reformist parties have become more moderate with the passage of time as a result of the lessons "learned" when they were checked by military intervention. (Of course, this is not meant to imply that leftist parties are the only ones that make concessions; establishment groups also make them.)

Castro's revolution provides the most dramatic example of the unwillingness of the middle classes to sustain a radical position over long periods of time. While programs of social change receive initial backing from the middle sectors, this support may be withdrawn, particularly if change proceeds too rapidly. In general, the lower the productivity of the society in question, and the more rapidly that changes are advanced, the costlier will the redistributive policies be for the middle sectors. Ultimately, the middle class will withdraw its support under these circumstances, as witnessed by the predominantly middle class character of refugees from Castro's Cuba.

In sum, these limits on middle class radicalism combine with other factors making for lower class quiescence to block widespread and sustained polarization of social classes in Latin America. Although, as witnessed by recent developments, interclass conflict is recurrent because of the inability to solve basic social problems, it is still not as pervasive as it might be throughout most of the area. As suggested by the findings in Table 1, escalated intraclass conflict continued to rival acute interclass conflict as a cause of *golpes* during the postwar period.

Before moving on to consider another explanation of the coups, some comments must be entered with regard to the interclass conflict explanation. According to our data in Table 1, the eighteen coups where interclass conflict was present were divided into "reactionary" and "progressive" *golpes*. Some 36.7 percent of the coups were executed against egalitarian or leftist groups, while 23.3 percent involved reformist motivations. (See columns 1 and 2 respectively.) This finding does not

[25] For the critical role of intellectuals in radical politics, see, for instance, Huntington, *Political Order,* p. 8.

support the conservative stereotype of Latin American military establishments. The simple fact of the matter is that during the period under investigation, military recruits were not being drawn primarily from the established, upper classes. Increasingly, Latin American military establishments are recruiting from the ranks of the middle and even the upper lower classes.[26] Given this recruitment pattern, the military has become far less conservative than heretofore, and this fact is clearly recorded in our finding that 23.3 percent of the coups were executed in the interests of reform.

At the same time, anti-reformist *golpes* were still somewhat more numerous, registering 36.7 percent of our sample. There are a number of factors which help to account for this fact. First, there is reason to suspect that professional military training, with its emphasis on hierarchy and obedience, tends to make recruits conservative.[27] Against this fact, one easily can understand the military preference for "order" vis-à-vis the frequently agitational tactics of reformist groups. In addition, Table 1 suggests that those groups most likely to sponsor reforms are the same left-wing groups that are most often anti-military in orientation. In all but one of the eight coups executed by the military for the purpose of protecting its corporate interests (indicator 6), the repression of left-wing groups (indicator 1) was also involved.[28] Actually, as indicated by Table 2, in over 60 percent of the anti-leftist *golpes* the military perceived threats against its corporate interests. In short, all of these factors would tend to incline the military in an anti-reformist direction in situations of acute interclass conflict. Overall, however, the armed forces can no longer be considered a basically conservative force. Our data indicate that in cases of escalated interclass conflict the military was only slightly more likely to side with the conservative or reactionary groups than with the reformers.

To conclude this section, we anticipate our remarks in Chapter 5 by making a few comments on the relationship between levels of socioeconomic development and types of coups in Latin America. The gen-

[26] McAlister, "Role of the Military in Latin America."

[27] In this sense see Morris Janowitz, *The Professional Soldier: A Social and Political Portrait* (Glencoe, Ill., 1960), pp. 239-241.

[28] The Peruvian coup of 1962 is the one exception. In this case the military acted in defense of its corporate interests, but interclass conflict was not a factor because the civilian groups both favored and repressed by the coup (*Acción Popular* and APRA respectively) were virtually indistinguishable in terms of their policies — both were reformist in character. As a matter of fact, AP was a spinoff of the older APRA, which had become much more moderate by the 1960s than it was during the 1930s and 1940s.

eral literature has often categorized societies as traditional, transitional, and modern.[29] Within this schema, coups are often considered characteristic of transitional societies. However, our data indicate that in Latin America *golpes* have occurred at all three levels of socioeconomic development.[30] Furthermore, both intra- and interclass coups have occurred at the three levels of development. The hypothesis that interclass coups are more frequent at higher levels of socioeconomic development is not confirmed by our data. Finally, our data indicate that the hypothesis that conservative coups tend to be more frequent than reformist coups as levels of development increase is not strongly supported.[31] Actually, most Latin American societies have experienced cycles in which intraclass and interclass conflict alternate. This phenomenon manifests itself in variations in the type of *golpe* experienced by a particular country over short periods of time. For example, in a four-year period Colombia experienced both an intraclass (1953) and an interclass coup (1957). Coup types also vary over somewhat longer periods of time. For instance, since 1948 Peru has had anti-leftist (1948), intraclass (1962), and pro-leftist (1968) *golpes*. Given all this variation, the relationship between levels of socioeconomic development and type of coup is clearly a most complex one.

Personal Interests of a Leader

As indicated by Table 1, the personal-interests-of-a-leader explanation was found to be the least useful of all when it came to accounting for the causes of *golpes* in Latin America between 1943 and 1967. Evidence of acute *personalismo,* our indicator for the personal interests explanation, was present in only two of the thirty coups surveyed. This amounts to a mere 6.7 percent of the sampled coups. Nicaragua in 1947 offers a typical instance of a coup where the personal interests of a single leader predominated. In this case General Anastasio Somoza, who had completely dominated the country since the withdrawal of the U.S. Marines in the early 1930s, executed a coup against one of his puppet executives who was beginning to manifest a degree of independence.

The fact that acute *personalismo* was found in just two of the sampled

[29] See, for instance, Fred W. Riggs, *Administration in Developing Countries: The Theory of Prismatic Society* (Boston, 1964), especially chap. 1.

[30] See Table 4, Chapter 5. Actually, during the period of our investigation, the less developed Latin American societies experienced more coups than did the more developed ones.

[31] For this hypothesis defined in terms of the size of the middle class, see Huntington, *Political Order,* pp. 220-221.

coups is indicative of the changing character of the military in many Latin American countries. The professionalization of the armed forces, while still just beginning and not having effectively depoliticized military personnel in most countries throughout the area, has nonetheless altered the character of their political intervention. Unlike earlier periods, coups during the second half of this century have become less personalistic in character, being executed more often in response to group or corporate interests rather than to the interests of the dashing *caudillo*.

Professionalization, even in small and imperfect degrees, is the bane of the highly personalistic leader. There is much evidence which indicates that group interests and organizational strength tend to increase as the armed forces undertake their professionalization; and an inverse relationship exists between organizational strength and *personalismo*.[32] For example, the highly personalistic policies of the late Dominican dictator, Rafael Leónidas Trujillo, eventually resulted in the disintegration of the military organization in 1965.[33]

To conclude, the reader is reminded that our indicator applies only to relatively acute manifestations of *personalismo*. While traces of the phenomenon are still evident, given the resilience of the personalistic orientation in Latin American political culture, acute manifestations tend to be present principally in societies with relatively low levels of socioeconomic development. As developing societies become increasingly differentiated and bureaucratized, the incidence of "personality" coups decreases. Nevertheless, this relationship between levels of socioeconomic development and "personality" coups should not be construed to mean that societies in which this type of *golpe* occurs have not experienced periods of escalated interclass conflict. For example, Panama's personalistic coup of 1949 was followed by an anti-leftist *golpe* in 1951.

U.S. Interference

Compared to most of our other indicators, the frequency of cases in which interference by U.S. personnel encouraged coup activity is relatively small. According to Table 1, U.S. interference was a factor in only 16.7 percent of the *golpes*. However, by examining Table 2 we find

[32] In this sense see Ferenc Merei, "Group Leadership and Institutionalization," in *Readings in Social Psychology*, 3rd ed., ed. Eleanor E. Maccoby, Theodore M. Newcomb, and Eugene L. Hartly (New York, 1958), pp. 522-532.
[33] For remarks on Trujillo's personalistic leadership style, see Crassweller, *Trujillo*.

that overt American pressures were present in 45.5 percent of the anti-leftist coups. These findings reveal that while the overall direct American involvement in Latin American coups was relatively low, it was nevertheless a visible factor in cases in which U.S. interests were threatened. In this respect, a case can be made that the general American involvement was low because U.S. interests were not frequently threatened.

American foreign policy toward Latin America in the post–World War II era has been predominantly anti-leftist in character. Prior to the war, U.S. intervention in the domestic affairs of Latin American countries in this century had obeyed other premises. On one hand, the Roosevelt Corollary to the Monroe Doctrine prescribed overt interdiction of those governments unable to "defend" themselves against the possibility of intervention by European powers. American direction of the Dominican and Haitian governments during the first three decades of this century are cases in point.[34] In other instances — such as Cuba (1898-1934) and Nicaragua (1912-33) — U.S. intervention responded primarily to the needs of commercial interests, thereby incurring the label "dollar diplomacy." In all of these instances, American intervention was highly blatant in character. Neither Theodore Roosevelt's "big stick" nor "gunboat diplomacy" were subtle techniques. The smaller countries of the Caribbean and Central America, given their impotence and their proximity to Uncle Sam, suffered most from these tactics.

Only since World War II has U.S. policy toward Latin America emphasized the need to protect against the threat of subversion by left-wing forces, whose policies are alleged to pose a direct threat to her "strategic interests" in the area.[35] U.S. interference has usually been characterized by subtle pressures brought to bear on the military by American personnel. Such was the case, for example, in April, 1964, when the Brazilian armed forces overthrew the leftist government of President João Goulart. State Department officials had been preoccupied for some months prior to the *golpe* with "leftist infiltration of the Goulart regime,"[36] and the American ambassador and top military attaché were in contact with the *golpistas* for some time prior to the coup. In contrast

[34] See John E. Fagg, *Cuba, Haiti, & the Dominican Republic* (Englewood Cliffs, N.J., 1965).

[35] Actually, according to Powell, in 1962 American policy toward Latin America shifted from concern with hemispheric military defense against external aggression to an emphasis on internal security and counterinsurgency capability. See John Duncan Powell, "Military Assistance and Militarism in Latin America," *Western Political Quarterly*, 18 (1965), 382-392. As suggested in Chapter 1, this shift in emphasis can contribute to the politicization of the military.

[36] Skidmore, *Politics in Brazil*, p. 324.

to the relatively subtle character of U.S. involvement in this case, the commitment of the marines by President Johnson during the anti-leftist Dominican coup of 1965 appeared as a throwback to the tactics employed in the Caribbean during the first decades of the century. On the whole, however, American interference in recent years has been far more subtle in nature. The promise of speedy diplomatic recognition and the extension of some sort of foreign aid or threats to suspend credit are the more usual forms of U.S. encouragement of coup activity.

To a degree, it might be argued that fear for the security of American investments is at the base of the United States' anti-leftist foreign policy toward Latin America. From this perspective, U.S. interests in Venezuelan oil and Bolivian tin can be seen as providing the stimulus for encouragement of the anti-leftist *golpes* that occurred in those countries in 1948 and 1951 respectively. In both cases, American investments were directly threatened by reformist policies prior to the coups. Still, it would be inaccurate to say that the United States' encouragement of *golpes* during the post-war period has resulted only from its apprehensiveness concerning the security of American business interests. The fear of left-wing groups was also prefaced by a more general concern for the "security" of the entire Western hemisphere against the presence of subversive forces. Moreover, there is some evidence of a quantitative character that advises against the easy attribution of *golpes* to the presence of U.S. investments. Midlarsky and Tanter have found no relationship between the density of American investments and coup activity in Latin America's more democratic countries.[37]

Finally, there is some evidence which suggests that U.S. military aid has not figured importantly in military intervention in the political arena. A study by Charles Wolf, Jr., on the relationship between military aid and the political characteristics of Latin American countries concludes that there is no statistically significant relationship between the amount of military assistance given to a Latin American country and a tendency for "democracy to erode." In the words of Wolf: "Dictatorships, military or otherwise, are a frequent and disturbing phenomenon in Latin America. But their occurrence and recurrence are not properly attributable to simple causes like military aid. . . . Indeed, [this

[37] Manus Midlarsky and Raymond Tanter, "Toward a Theory of Political Instability in Latin America," *Journal of Peace Research*, 3 (1967), 209-227. As indicated by the ITT papers published by the Allende government, the 1970 coup attempt in Chile in which the ITT was a leading instigator failed in part due to a lack of support from the U.S. Department of State. See Secretaría General de Gobierno, *Documentos Secretos de la ITT* (Santiago, 1972).

factor does] not appear to play a significant role in the process at all."[38]
As a matter of fact, a case can be made that American military aid actually decreases pressures for coups by reducing civilian-military competition for scarce resources.[39] In effect, if we divide Latin American
countries into three categories according to the number of coups experienced during the 1950-62 period, we discover an inverse relationship
between the cumulative U.S. military aid per member of the armed
forces of the host country and coup frequency.[40] Of course, it is possible
to question the extent to which published figures accurately represent
the amount of U.S. financial involvement in Latin American military
organizations.

In summary, available data suggest that when considering both intra-
and interclass coups, the actual involvement of U.S. personnel was not
a very important trigger of Latin American *golpes*. Indeed, there are
examples, such as Peru in 1962 and the Dominican Republic in 1963,
in which coups have taken place in the face of strong and explicit
American opposition.[41] The fact remains, however, that Table 2 points
to overt American personnel involvement in a substantial number of
coups in the anti-leftist category. For this reason, we cannot discard
American interference as irrelevant to coup processes. At the same time,
the amount of American interference in the total coup sample is too
small for it to be considered as a fundamental precipitant of coups in
the area. Here is an example of a case in which it seems safer to relate
the high frequency of *golpes* in Latin America to the character of certain predisposing factors, such as indigenous cultural patterns and socioeconomic and political institutions, than to interference from abroad.
Some might argue that the United States has played an important role
in shaping the "indigenous" patterns and institutions that are the fre-

[38] Wolf, "Military Programs," p. 890.
[39] See the comments of Kenneth Southwood, "Riot and Revolt: Sociological
Theories of Political Violence," *Peace Research Reviews*, no. 3, 1967, p. 33.
[40] The three categories were formed by countries without coups, those that
had one or two *golpes*, and those that experienced more than two coups during
the 1950-62 period. The average aid for each group of countries was $1,204.50,
$648.30, and $602.50 per armed forces member, respectively. Coup frequency
is based on our Appendix C. Data for American military aid were taken from
Powell, "Military Assistance," p. 385.
[41] See the comments of the former U.S. ambassador to the Dominican Republic, John B. Martin, *Overtaken by Events: The Dominican Crisis from the
Fall of Trujillo to the Civil War* (New York, 1966), pp. 120-122. It should be
noted that after the Batista post-coup regime resulted in the Castro revolution,
the United States unsuccessfully attempted to discourage *golpes* as well as
"leftist" and "rightist" dictatorships, as a formula to justify the Cuban embargo
and prevent future Marxist-Leninist victories.

quent source of *golpes* in the area. In other words, U.S. "cultural imperialism" may be seen as a factor contributing to the "pathology of democracy" syndrome. In this sense American responsibility would not be detected by our indicator of U.S. interference. There may be some truth in this argument, but it can be dealt with better in the context of a subsequent chapter, where the character of these patterns and institutions will be explored in depth. For now, suffice it to note that the actual encouragement of *golpes* by American personnel is manifest in only five of the thirty coups that we examined. On the basis of this evidence, it would be easy to exaggerate the role of American imperialism in Latin American *golpes*.

Military Corporate Interests

Analysis of Table 1 points to military corporate interests, measured by the fear-of-group indicator, as a moderately important source of coups d'état in Latin America. Corporate interests were involved in 26.7 percent of the coups studied. In these cases, civilian groups are perceived by the military as offering some type of threat to its group interests. For example, the civilian group may threaten to purge the armed forces (e.g., Peru in 1948) or to create an armed militia not subject to formal military control (e.g., Venezuela in 1948). The threat to organizational survival or integrity that is posed in such cases may spur the military to action in its own self-defense. The diffusion of illegality syndrome discussed earlier is very apparent in these cases. The military questions the legality of purges of the armed forces and the establishment of a civilian militia; and in order to prevent their occurrence, the coup, another illegal act, is executed in self-defense. The eight *golpes* that fit this pattern have as a direct effect the repression of those groups which presented the threat to the military's corporate interests — in this case, its viability as an on-going organization.

It is interesting to note that all but one of the coups studied involving military fear of a civilian group were also cases in which the *golpes* were executed against egalitarian or left-wing groups. In this respect, there appears to be a definite relationship between anti-militarism and liberal-leftist positions. Table 2 shows that the fear-of-group category was present in 63.6 percent of the anti-leftist coups. This is partly due, of course, to the tendency of these groups to view the military as a force diametrically opposed to their programs. These groups generally have in their ranks a large number of intellectuals, who are most likely to adopt the ideological radicalism that was discussed in the first section of this chapter. Given their left-wing position, the radicals will be inclined to condemn the armed forces as "an evil bastion of Reaction and Conservatism." The military is blamed for all of the country's ills. The bombast of the ideological radical is frequently accompanied by the profession of "total" or "revolutionary" solutions. In other words, their approach to the institutions and problems of the society is messianic rather than gradualist in character.[42] If they were to achieve power, the military might be apprehensive with very good reason, especially in view of the scarcity of alternative sources of employment that frequently characterizes Latin American countries. For example, during the early years of Haya de la Torre's Peruvian APRA, the destruction of the armed forces was linked to the party's political victory. In this light, it is hardly surprising that the 1948 *golpe* in that country was designed to block the *Aprista* accession to power. In situations of this kind, the military will be inclined to view the radicals as "irresponsible" and "illegitimate" contenders for political power. As the radicals attempt to make the military into scapegoats, so the military will attempt to do the same thing. Antagonisms escalate as these "anti" attitudes feed on each other. In extreme situations, a military self-defense coup becomes highly probable. This is especially true if the radicals back up their messianic rhetoric with actual violence, as happened in five of the eight *golpe* situations where military corporate interests were involved.

This relationship between anti-militarism, totalistic rhetoric, and the resort to violence is not uncommon in areas outside Latin America; nor is the military reaction to them. Witness the character of the anti-war militants in the United States. Groups engaged in direct action are involved in physical encounters with police and military forces, who are defined as enemies. In the heat of the confrontation, the forces of "law and order" are degraded by being labeled "murderers," "fascist pigs," etc. Accusations of "brutality" and "immorality" fly back and forth. In these circumstances, the reaction of the defenders of public order is predictable. Total rhetoric and violence are met in kind. (After all, the police and military forces are the ones who must endure the physical and verbal abuse dished out by the militants.) The vituperation of the militants tends to politicize the very same forces of law and order whose job is to repress those already radicalized. Police involvement in campaigns against civilian review boards in various large cities and in the 1969 reelection of Cleveland's black mayor, Carl Stokes, even in the

---

[42] For a description of this messianic trait and some of its implications in Latin America, see Albert O. Hirschman, "Out of Phase," *Encounter*, 25 (1965), 21-23.

face of explicit prohibitions against politicking by police, attest to the strong feelings which underlie the politicization of the supposedly "neutral" defenders of public law and order.

This tendency toward politicization is important. What it entails is the breakdown of the functional specificity of the defenders of law and order. The "proper" function of the military or the police — defense of country or the impartial upholding of law and order — is supplemented by a political one. In extreme cases, and here Latin America provides us with numerous examples, the specific and differentiated character of the military and police will be replaced by a situation of structural fusion in which the holders of the means of coercion enlarge the scope of their activity by assuming an overtly political role, which ultimately may escalate to include determination of the country's governmental institutions. As previously noted, this is exactly what happens in every coup situation. The point that should be emphasized here is that the ideological radicalism of left-wing intellectuals can be a powerful stimulus to military politicization and the structural fusion epitomized by the *golpe*. The events leading up to the Venezuelan coup of 1948 provide a clear case in point.

Up to now, we have been considering primarily those cases in which the military has acted to prevent the accession to power of left-wing groups inimical to its corporate interests. At the same time, situations arise in which the military carries out a self-defense coup against an incumbent left-wing government, particularly if the government endeavors to create lower class, "grass roots" organizations for its own purposes. In this case, the government initiates a state of structural fusion, the result being a situation in which there is little differentiation between the government and particularistic class interests. In undertaking the mobilization of the lower classes, the government damages its ability to act as an integrating or "aggregating" institution. This simply means that it finds it increasingly difficult to perform the very important function of mediating conflict between opposing private pressure groups. By cultivating its own grass roots organizations, the government is perceived by the establishment to be a highly partisan rather than a mediating force. In this sense, and as opposed to those instances in which the mobilization of marginal groups has a relatively autonomous character, the government cannot justify its policies as "reactions" needed to integrate the society. In situations of this kind, both the military and civilian establishment groups are likely to grow increasingly restive, as the government is now viewed as conducting itself in a highly partisan nonaggregative manner.

The reasons for the restiveness of these established groups can best be understood by referring briefly to the nature of the processes triggered by an environment that favors the fusion of left-wing governments and lower class organizations. The economic underdevelopment of much of Latin America is a factor that discourages the formation of autonomous working-class organizations.[43] The traditional attitudes of fatalism and quietism prevalent in the culture also undermine autonomy, especially among the lower classes. A left-wing government seeking support for policies of social change among the working classes therefore must undertake to create working-class organizations, which thereafter are considered to "belong to" the government. The important point for understanding why established interests both inside and outside the military become restive with this process, however, relates to the nature of the techniques used by the government to organize working-class support. In organizing the masses, the government sows excessive expectations among the nascent organizations. The tendency for leftists to resort to ideological radicalism and the already mentioned messianic character of their rhetoric lead invariably to extreme pronouncements that excite the workers. This in turn frightens away the support of some upper and middle class sectors, as was previously discussed. Distrust and suspicion of the government multiply in the salons of the society's established interests.[44] Many of these interests will begin to pressure the military to remove the threatening leftist government.[45] The interclass dimensions of the developing conflict become increasingly apparent. Worried by the possibility of a coup, the government will be induced to arm its lower class organizations or to purge the military, which in turn poses a clear and present danger to military corporate interests. In the process of attempting to provide for its security, the government solidifies military opposition, which up to that time was probably divided as to whether the policies of the government constituted a threat to its group interests. In the last resort, a vicious circle of defensive moves may trigger the anti-leftist coup. The government,

[43] For the direct relationship between the economic weakness of labor and its politicization, see Robert J. Alexander, *Latin-American Politics and Government* (New York, 1965), pp. 101-102.

[44] For a description of the high levels of distrust in Latin American culture and some of the implications, see Robert E. Scott, "Mexico: The Established Revolution," in *Political Culture and Political Development,* ed. Lucian W. Pye and Sidney Verba (Princeton, N.J., 1965), pp. 330-395.

[45] As indicated by Table 2, in 63.6 percent of the anti-leftist coups there was an overt coalition between military and civilian groups in opposition to the government. Furthermore, in contrast to the two other coup types, a civil-military coalition was present most often in anti-leftist *golpes.*

attempting to defend itself, takes an action which causes the military to respond with a self-defense coup designed to protect its threatened corporate interests. This pattern was clearly exemplified in the 1948 anti-leftist *golpe* in Venezuela.[46]

In summary, the military's fear for the protection of its corporate interests usually coincides with the repression of left-wing groups, be they incumbent governments or contenders for power.

Yet not all coups executed for the purpose of protecting corporate interests are anti-leftist in character. As was already mentioned, the 1962 Peruvian *golpe* cannot be considered anti-leftist. Another coup involving corporate interests without the anti-leftist dimension took place in Panama in 1968. These cases suggest the presence of more general factors working in the direction of corporate interests coups, independent of any ideological bias.

The 1962 Peruvian *golpe* demonstrates the significance of traditional group antagonisms in producing a coup that involves military fear of a political group. As noted in a previous context, Peru's APRA had become a relatively moderate party by the early 1960's, partly as a result of the sanctions that had been imposed on it by the military in earlier years, especially at the time of the 1948 coup. Despite this moderation, thirty years of military *Aprista* conflict served to traditionalize hatreds between the two forces, so that in 1962 the military still feared APRA's intentions and therefore acted to prevent its accession to power. This case points up the importance of "hereditary hatreds" that at times may produce high levels of civilian-military conflict and subsequent fear-of-group *golpes,* independent of the ideological persuasion of the civilian group in question.[47]

A second factor which is independent of ideological considerations and that makes for coups designed to safeguard corporate interests

[46] See Bernstein, *Venezuela and Colombia,* p. 61. We might note here that while the structural fusion between government and lower-class organizations tends to produce coups during transitional periods, the fusion can lead to inter-class "peace" when "moderate" governments control labor groups, thus transforming them into captive organizations. Also, and as suggested by post-Perón Argentina, a highly autonomous and politicized labor movement can sometimes produce political instability and a high frequency of coups. According to Payne, autonomous labor groups may use the threat of a coup as a means to obtain pro-labor concessions in bargaining with government. See James L. Payne, *Labor and Politics: The System of Political Bargaining* (New Haven, Conn., 1965).

[47] The term is taken from Robert H. Dix, *Colombia: The Political Dimensions of Change* (New Haven, Conn., 1967), pp. 211, 370, 372. This traditional sort of confrontation devoid of ostensible ideological content can also polarize civilian groups and lead to coups that seek to pacify the country. This was the case of Colombia in the months prior to the 1953 coup.

refers to the role of the military as agents of force in the society. The military occupation carries with it the almost complete monopoly over the instruments of violence. As the escalated conflict and radicalism characteristic of Latin American politics do not allow for neutrality, the military is often forced to take sides in the competition for power. In so doing, it is likely to alienate losing civilian groups. These nonvictorious groups come to view the military as the dominant or "repressive" force in society, an attitude that fosters the development of a climate of eventual revenge on the part of these "out" groups. These anti-military sentiments are likely in turn to lead to strong anti-civilian attitudes on the part of the military. Pride of profession and *esprit de corps* feed the fires of anti-civilian feeling. In this situation, a vicious circle develops in which anti-civilian and anti-military attitudes continue to accumulate over time. If the "out" groups should ever attain power, as occurred in Panama in 1968, the military will feel threatened by these groups and may therefore conduct a *golpe* designed to protect its corporate interests.[48] The important point about this process is that it originates in society's division of labor — the military monopolizes the instruments of coercion. When the armed forces act for the purpose of safeguarding this role, they manifest an occupational partisanship in its purest form; and this sort of partisanship can operate independently of the ideological persuasion or social class basis of the civilian groups involved.

In summary, we have seen that *golpes* executed out of fear of a civilian group (indicator 6) frequently coincide with anti-leftist motivations (indicator 1). Still, anti-militarism and left-wing philosophy are not coterminous. Factors such as traditional group hatreds and military occupational sectarianism also can lead at times to coups designed to protect against threatening civilian groups.

Having presented our findings with respect to the fear-of-group indicator, we can conclude that the corporate interests explanation of coup activity was particularly important in the context of anti-leftist coups, but it was only moderately important when considering all coup types. However, we have not been able to provide a thoroughly satisfactory test for the corporate interests hypothesis. In particular, one important part of this hypothesis has been overlooked up to this point because we do not have sufficient information to warrant establishing an indicator to test for its presence in the coups studied. Specifically, it is possible that *golpes* may be caused at times by the military establishment's unmet

[48] See *The New York Times,* Oct. 2, 1968, p. 22; and *Visión,* 35, no. 10 (1968), 15-16.

desires for greater material benefits, such as higher salaries and better equipment. Payne calls this the "organizational benefits" explanation of coups.[49] If a coup occurred in the wake of either a refusal of the government to provide increased benefits or a cut in the military budget, one might reasonably adduce the corporate interests explanation to help account for the *golpe*. Unfortunately, the information available for the sampled coups is not sufficient to warrant establishing an indicator of this sort. Matters of military expenditure are often shrouded in secrecy.

There is, however, some quantitative evidence that can be brought to bear on the organizational benefits thesis, based on the hypothesis that if true, the thesis should mean that a relatively high level of military expenditures is found in those countries that have experienced a relatively high frequency of *golpes* over a prolonged period of time. This logic suggests that the military's share of the national budget increases as a result of its "greedy" perpetration of coup activity. Our own computations, however, indicate that there is little support for this hypothesis. Taking as variables the number of coups and average percentage of the national budget going to the military for the period 1938-65, there is only a very weak positive correlation (0.18) between these variables.[50] To set the question in a still broader context, some stable Western democracies, even those with few international commitments, such as Canada and Sweden, spend a far greater share of their national income on defense expenditures than do the Latin American countries.[51] At the same time, these countries are free of coups while Latin America, needless to say, is not. In terms of this quantitative evidence, therefore, the organizational benefits explanation does not appear very useful. Still, this type of evidence is not fully satisfactory. As noted, budgetary

[49] Payne, *Conflict in Colombia*, pp. 152-155.

[50] For the sources of our data on these two variables, see, respectively, the works used to compile Table 3 in this study (see Appendix C) and Joseph E. Loftus, *Latin American Defense Expenditures, 1938-1965* (Santa Monica, Calif., 1968), p. 37. Loftus does not present sufficient data for four of the countries — Cuba, Nicaragua, Panama, and Uruguay. For this reason our computations are based on data from the remaining sixteen countries. However, for the 1956-65 period Putnam found a .55 correlation between "military intervention" and defense expenditures as a percentage of gross national product. Robert D. Putnam, "Toward Explaining Military Intervention in Latin American Politics," *World Politics*, 20 (1967), 83-110.

[51] Loftus, *Latin American Defense Expenditures*. According to Einaudi, Latin America "spends less on defense than any other area of the world." See Luigi R. Einaudi, *Peruvian Military Relations with the United States* (Santa Monica, Calif., 1970), p. 3. In addition, the size of the armed forces relative to civilian population appears unrelated to military intervention. In this sense see Stepan, *Military in Politics*, chap. 2.

figures could not be obtained from four of the countries. Some might even question the veracity of the figures that are available. Finally, the obtained correlation is based on averaged data which, it can be argued, does not get at the more important relationship between the incidence of coups and year-by-year changes in the military share of the budget.

But even if the organizational benefits thesis is tested against annual military budget changes, our results are still inconclusive. If the organizational benefits thesis is correct, one would expect to find that reductions in the military share of the budget are followed the next year by a *golpe* and that military expenditures rise subsequent to the overthrow. But the data yield an erratic pattern. In fact, only about one-half of the cases for which annual military budget figures are available fit this expectation, while the other half present just the opposite pattern — increases in budget prior to the *golpe,* with reductions following.[52]

To summarize, available evidence that can be brought to bear on the organizational benefits thesis is inconclusive for the reasons presented. The best that can be said is that it appears to be applicable in some cases. For example, in Cuba in 1952 the *golpistas* decreed increases in the military budget the very same day that the coup took place.[53] Conversely, as suggested by Payne, on other occasions, such as in Colombia in 1953, governments threatened by low levels of legitimacy may increase military budgets in an unsuccessful attempt to prevent a coup by "buying off" the military.[54] Given such evidence, we cannot rule out the possibility that at times unsatisfied military demands for material benefits may contribute to the triggering of a particular coup. On the basis of our data, however, it would be inaccurate to say that the benefits thesis provides consistent support for the military corporate interests explanation of the *golpes.* Most of the support for the corporate interests interpretation must rest on our fear-of-group indicator. On this basis, and until better evidence can be brought to bear on the organizational benefits hypothesis, we can tentatively conclude that the corporate in-

[52] See Loftus, *Latin American Defense Expenditures,* p. 36. The exact results of our analysis are as follows: (1) for the thirty-nine cases in which data for two years prior to the coup are available, 54 percent fit the benefits thesis (budgetary cuts); 41 percent contradict it (budgetary increases); 5 percent are neutral (no budgetary change); (2) for the thirty-six cases in which data for the year after the coup are available, 50 percent fit the thesis (budgetary increases), while 50 percent refute it (cuts in the budget). These results do not differ markedly even when the type of conflict that produced the coup — interclass *vs.* intraclass — is controlled for.

[53] See Solaún, "Democracia en Cuba."

[54] Payne, *Conflict in Colombia.* Allende has attempted to bolster his Chilean government by following a similar strategy.

terests explanation is particularly important in anti-leftist coups and moderately important in Latin American coups in general.

Low Levels of Military Professionalism

Table 1 shows that one-half of the sampled coups involved low levels of military professionalism as a factor leading to the *golpe*. As noted in the previous chapter, high levels of morale, cohesion, and discipline are essential for a highly professionalized military establishment. We therefore selected high turnover of military personnel, unmet desires for promotion, and overt clashes between military factions in the coup situation as indicators of a weakly professionalized armed forces. In this section of this chapter some of the processes underlying the organizational weakness of the military are described. In most cases our remarks will be somewhat anecdotal in character, reflecting the fact that very little research has been done on the politics of military cohesion in Latin America. When feasible, the research of organizational variables, personnel policies in particular, recommends itself as an important matter for future investigation. From the point of view of the policy-maker, the professionalization of the military is of crucial concern. As is often recognized by Latin American military leaders, a professional armed forces reduces the frequency of coups d'état by diminishing the incidence of military organizational problems that provide fertile ground for coups.

Sustained substitution of military personnel was present in the coup situation in 23.3 percent of the cases analyzed. This high-level turnover is encouraged by personnel policies governed by nonprofessional, particularistic criteria. First of all, military occupational monopoly of the instruments of violence induces the executive to maintain strict control over the armed forces. This is all the more necessary in societies characterized by frequent and acute political conflict, in which there are strong pressures at work that tend to politicize the military. Given the well-established tradition of forceful removal of the executive that prevails in most Latin American countries, the president must be especially careful to maintain his control over the armed forces.[55] To this end, the government often will resort to particularistic personnel policies in order to insure the loyalty of high-ranking military officers. The tendency is to seek military loyalty by reshuffling personnel along partisan lines, at the

[55] Coleman states that once a particular pattern of conflict resolution (e.g., coup d'état) develops in a society, it tends to repeat itself. See James S. Coleman, *Community Conflict* (Glencoe, Ill., 1957).

expense of certain cliques within the military establishment. While this practice may be functional to the maintenance of regimes over the short run, the turnover of top personnel divides the military over time and in so doing tends to reduce military cohesion, discipline, and morale. Under these circumstances, if the external political situation worsens, thereby reducing support for the government, military discontent may erupt into a coup situation, as restive groups of officers take advantage of changed external conditions in an effort to reduce the insecurities and frustrations associated with the high rates of turnover by removing the executive responsible for this highly divisive personnel policy. At any rate, the presence of high rates of turnover in the context of a *golpe* is indicative of the low levels of cohesion and morale that typify the weakly professionalized armed forces.[56] The Ecuadorian coup of September, 1947, is a prime example of this pattern.

Particularistic personnel policies also may lead to coups that manifest promotional characteristics. Coups of this kind, representing one-third of our sample, usually indicate that personnel policies are considered unfair by certain well-defined groups in the armed forces. *Golpes* involving promotional motivations are most common in those instances in which there are pressures from left-wing groups for social change. As indicated by Table 2, 71.4 percent of the reform coups also involved the promotional factor.

The reasons for this coincidence between the pro-reform and promotional factors can be accounted for as follows. Authoritarian regimes typically have little respect for legal regulations, and their political support is precarious. As a result, these regimes are likely to define promotional practices in terms of political expediency, as opposed to professional performance. In addition to this fact, the scarcity of alternative employment in the relatively underdeveloped countries where these regimes tend to prevail means that older personnel are not forced into retirement as they would be in, let us say, the U.S. military. All of these factors make for a situation in which systematic retirements and promotions are not followed. Most important, a very real promotional bottleneck exists for many officers under these circumstances. Eventually this bottleneck may create pressures for a coup by lower-grade officers seeking redress of this state of affairs. If civilian opposition to the regime

---

[56] We might note here that when a military organization is divided into professionalized and politicized personnel, the former group may lead a coup partly to increase the professionalization of the armed forces. We are indebted to Colonel Luther F. Long, former U.S. military attaché in the Dominican Republic, for this interpretation of the Dominican 1965 *golpe*.

increases, and this is most likely during transitional periods of interclass conflict, the groups of younger officers who have suffered most from the particularistic promotional policies of the regime are likely to seize the occasion as a perfect opportunity for eliminating the promotional bottleneck. What results, in effect, is a coalition of younger military officers and their left-wing civilian counterparts, who come together to carry through a pro-reform *golpe* that results in an abrupt generational change in both military and civilian leadership. In these instances, the interests of the civilian and military *golpistas* coincide, though they are not necessarily identical. Ordinarily, pressures for social reform and promotional grievances tend to seek out one another, in a manner of speaking. Coups in Guatemala (October, 1944) and Venezuela (1945) provide examples of this pattern.

Low pay and bad working conditions are other factors which, when added to the promotional bottleneck situation, tend to create pressures for a coup with promotional characteristics. The bad pay and conditions suffered by low-grade officers in most Latin American countries have a rather obvious effect in reducing morale and discipline in the armed forces. When combined with the bottleneck factors, as in Venezuela in 1945, the pressures for a promotional coup are high.

If more stable countries such as the United States and Great Britain are any indication, the formation and maintenance of a highly professionalized armed forces is a very expensive proposition. Making high expenditures on the top cadre alone is not sufficient. In all probability, the high levels of morale and discipline that professionalization brings cannot be achieved without providing generous material benefits to all levels within the military establishment.

One final note on the pressures that make for promotional coups is necessary at this time. The noncohesiveness of the military establishment that is fostered by promotional bottlenecks, poor pay for junior officers, etc., may lead senior officers to see the handwriting on the wall, particularly if left-wing civilian groups are attempting to politicize the lower echelons. At times this awareness may lead senior officers to conduct a "preventive" coup for the purpose of maintaining their position in the face of increasing discontent among the junior officers or sergeants. This seems to have been the case in Peru in 1948 and again in Brazil in 1964, when the president himself had encouraged insubordination among the lower echelons. Logically enough, these preventive coups are generally anti-reform in character, given the fact that they are designed to prevent a promotional *golpe* that frequently coincides with pressures for social reform.

In summary, pressures for promotions can lead at times to preventive coups directed by higher echelon personnel. In this context it is interesting to note that such *golpes* tend to be rationalized by creating a scapegoat in the civilian sector. In effect, the higher-level officers leading the coup are trying to restore unity to the military by appealing to dangers outside the military establishment. In a sense this scapegoating represents an overreaction vis-à-vis the civilian sector, but it is functional from the point of view of restoring and maintaining military cohesion. Seen in this light, the apparent harshness of some military regimes, such as the post-Goulart Brazilian ones, can be better understood as at least in part a response to internal problems in the military establishment. Also, it may not be pure coincidence that one of the most cohesive military organizations in Latin America — the Peruvian — engages in yearly anti-*Aprista* rituals.[57] By focusing on external dangers, problems arising from internal difficulties are assuaged.

Overt physical clashes within the military in the coup situation, our third indicator of low levels of professionalism, are often nothing more than the reflection of those processes already described in connection with high levels of personnel turnover and promotional problems. In the absence of effective steps taken to stem the development of these processes, levels of morale, cohesion, and discipline within the armed forces will decline sharply, and open conflict between military factions will become increasingly likely. As indicated by Table 2, in most instances physical clashes are the result of divergent stands on ideological issues or class conflict. In other cases, such as in the Dominican Republic in 1965, divisions as to whether constitutional provisions should be respected may also provide a rationale for open conflict. Whatever the particular case, overt physical clashes between military factions represent perilously low levels of morale, cohesion, and discipline within the armed forces, features diametrically opposite to those found in a highly professionalized military establishment.

On the whole, the military throughout much of Latin America exhibits low levels of professionalism. Problems of morale and discipline are often severe. The organizational weaknesses that mark this situation — high rates of personnel substitution, promotional bottlenecks, and clashes between various military factions — are a highly significant source of coup activity in the area, particularly during transitional periods of escalated interclass conflict.

[57] In this sense see North, *Civil-Military Relations,* and Einaudi, *Peruvian Military Relations.*

In concluding this section, we might return for a moment to a point raised in the preceding chapter: technical training and the possession of sophisticated equipment are not sufficient in and of themselves for professionalization of the armed forces in Latin America. Argentina is the perfect example of this assertion. The Argentine military exhibits relatively high levels of training and materiel sophistication, yet it not only has engaged in much coup activity, but has also shown high levels of internal divisiveness, particularly during the post-Perón period.[58] One important reason for this state of affairs is best given in terms of the total institutional and cultural framework within which the military moves. Specifically, factors such as the increasing levels of civilian conflict and subsequent attempts by civilian politicians to co-opt military personnel for political conflict, radicalism, and nonprofessional personnel policies originating in the executive — all factors that transcend the military establishment — make it very difficult for the armed forces to remain aloof from the political arena, where their involvement all too often leads to coups d'état. This is not to say that coups are not encouraged by factors internal to the military. Internal feuding and desires for material aggrandizement also play a part at times in producing the organizational weaknesses that have been discussed in this section. The point that should be made here is that these organizational problems and, ultimately, the professionalization of the military must be framed in a picture that places the armed forces in proper societal perspective. In the words of Germani and Silvert: "Military intromission in the political power structure always indicates, of course, at least a relative inability of other social institutions to marshal their power effectively, and at most an advanced state of institutional decomposition. This is to say, if the armed forces are viewed as having a limited and specialized set of functions having only to do with internal order and external defense, then a widening of castrensic activities into other social domains implies a generally weakened and sick social system. . . ."[59]

In this connection, there is some question as to the effectiveness of the current social science orientation of some of the Latin American military academies in terms of the ultimate goal of increased professionalization. Theoretically, this socially oriented training, as with any type of training, should increase professionalization, which in turn reduces the probability of coups through increased internal cohesion and

---

[58] For an analysis of the sources of these internal problems, see José Luis de Imaz, *Los que Mandan* (Buenos Aires, 1964).

[59] Germani and Silvert, "Military Intervention," p. 62.

discipline. It may be hypothesized, however, that this new approach actually increases the propensity toward coups. That is, as the military develops a greater awareness of social problems it will become increasingly conscious of the failures of civilian institutions. Rather than cohesion, this attitude can lead to internal factionalism. There is substantial evidence that a politicized military provides fertile ground for the development of a factionalized military,[60] which is anathema to any professionally sound military establishment. On the whole, factors transcending the military are every bit as important as internal ones when it comes to accounting for the low levels of professionalism that characterize most of Latin America's military establishments.

Weakness of Electoral Mechanisms

Indicators 10 and 11 in Table 1 gauge the significance of weak electoral mechanisms as a factor that triggered Latin American coups during the period 1943-67. Disputed electoral processes (elections) and tampering with electoral laws by the president for the purpose of maintaining himself in power (*continuismo*) were precipitants of *golpes* in more than one-half of the coups studied. In this section we shall present some of the reasons for this high incidence of weak electoral mechanisms and the implications of this state of affairs for military intervention in the political arena. Beginning with a discussion of those coups which occurred in conjunction with election outcomes, and then shifting the focus of analysis to *continuismo,* the contribution of organizational, cultural, and economic factors to the anemic character of electoral mechanisms will be examined. But before we proceed, the reader must be reminded about the nature of this explanation and its two indicators. As discussed at the end of Chapter 3, the weakness of electoral mechanisms is a predisposing or necessary condition for coups d'état. In effect, the very nature of coups implies the absence of institutionalized legal procedures to change the executive, i.e., of effective electoral organization. This is an axiomatic proposition that need not be tested. We have constructed the two indicators, however, as a means of testing the extent to which *golpes* were precipitated by actual disputes over electoral processes and by tampering with electoral laws prior to the coup. In this respect, our indicators are triggering factors that are neither necessary nor sufficient conditions for the occurrence of *golpes*.

[60] See, for instance, Huntington, *Political Order,* p. 194, and Stepan, *Military in Politics, passim*.

A substantial minority of the coups, 30 percent according to Table 1, have occurred in connection with election outcomes. This points to what has been a fundamental problem in most Latin American countries — the inability to establish effective formal-legal structures that insure a predictable and peaceful means for the transfer of governmental power. Under such conditions, it is extremely difficult to institutionalize representative democracy, for stable democracy relies on electoral mechanisms unlike any other form of government.

It is interesting to note that this difficulty exists even in the absence of anti-democratic ideologies of any notable strength. As discussed earlier, most authoritarian dictatorships in the Latin American context have not formally rejected the desirability of democracy. More frequently than not, authoritarian regimes in Latin America have either upheld the pretense of democracy or have attempted to justify their rule as a temporary departure from democracy necessary to correct its "pathologies." Batista's Cuba and Trujillo's Dominican Republic are examples of the former, while the current Argentine and Brazilian regimes are cases of the latter. In short, there is hardly any support for arguments that attempt to attribute the absence of effective electoral mechanisms and subsequent political instability in Latin America to the presence of ideologies that negate the ultimate desirability of democracy. We must look elsewhere in order to understand why elections are so often accompanied by violence and military intervention.

First, the occurrence of *golpes* in conjunction with elections is an indication of the weakness of the rule of law and formal government organizations. Specifically, it is an indication of the fact that the will of a small number of men substitutes for formal law and that the state becomes the personal property of the men who are no longer its incumbents, in the strict sense of the term. In effect, the political group of the office holders tends to merge with the formal structures of government. In other words, in most Latin American countries there is little differentiation between the political sphere (i.e., the ruling group) and the realm of government (i.e., the state). This fusion between the partisan political and the governmental structures takes place to an extent seldom witnessed in stable Western democracies, and it provides fertile ground for the occurrence of coups in the context of electoral campaigns. In an environment where the concept of formal office is poorly developed in practice, and where government incumbents tend to become proprietors of the state in accordance with the regal philosophy — *"L'état c'est moi"* — the impersonal character of government is lost and the institutions of government undergo a debilitating and highly partisan or sectarian transformation. There is a tendency, in other words, for groups in power to perceive the formal structures of the state as personal property, designed for their own exclusive use. This attitude in turn fosters attempts to remain in power by means of electoral fraud and whatever other extra-constitutional instruments happen to be available. As a result, under these conditions the opposition is likely to perceive the government in highly partisan terms and to vigorously contest election outcomes, while at times resorting to coercive methods to achieve control over the government apparatus. In Latin America the contesting of electoral outcomes at times involves the use of violence or direct action techniques, thereby encouraging military intervention for the purpose of restoring order. The coup that took place in Peru in 1962 fits this pattern.

In addition to encouraging violence and direct action, the partisan transformation of formal government also fosters acute conflict and the subsequent possibility of *golpes* because government tends to lose its universal and integrating character under the conditions of extreme partisanship.[61] Partisans have difficulty claiming that they are impartial mediators of divergent interests. The president cannot hope to step outside of his partisan identity. He cannot claim to be acting in the interests of the whole people on a nonpartisan basis and hope to be believed. In effect, he loses flexibility and support by being locked into a partisan role. Moreover, all of the laws passed by his government will be perceived as biased in a partisan direction. Under these circumstances, it is little wonder that the opposition frequently resorts to extralegal measures in the attempt to wrest control of government from the incumbents.

The partisan definition of the formal offices of government can take on various forms. It can be highly personalistic, as in the case of Trujillo. It can have a wider group basis, such as in the case of the "dictatorial" party which has characterized much of Colombia's political history. It can be militaristic, as is largely the case with the current Brazilian regime.[62] In accordance with Marxist doctrine, government is viewed as a mere appendage of the ruling class. A slightly different instance of this phenomenon is to be found in the history of the United States, when the institutions of government are perceived as "belonging

---

[61] For a similar interpretation of the need for political "autonomy" in order to obtain political institutionalization, see Huntington, *Political Order*, pp. 20-22.

[62] The coup propensities of these regimes will be discussed in later chapters.

to" whites to the exclusion of blacks. Whatever form the partisan definition assumes, however, the important thing is that this kind of definition of formal government tends to encourage acute conflict, thereby providing fertile ground for coups d'état, especially during high-tension election campaigns.

A number of cultural factors also contribute to the high incidence of coups in conjunction with elections. It has already been suggested that political conflict in Latin America tends to be viewed in a quasi-religious, nonsecular fashion; both primitive and ideological radicalism view political conflict as a struggle between all-good and all-evil forces. Electoral outcomes tend to be viewed in apocalyptic terms. Elections can create expectations of a new dawn, the arrival of the millennium. Under these conditions, defeat is an unacceptable outcome. As noted, defeat reinforces popular beliefs as to the "criminality" or "immorality" of the government, and tends to be tied to its total displacement from power, i.e., exile and other forms of persecution. As a result, there is a tendency to resort to illegal techniques in the attempt to reverse the outcome of the voting. In this context, it should be noted that election fraud has not been uncommon in Latin America, and this fact gives more substance to the opposition's claims of foul play. Furthermore, the high levels of distrust characteristic of the culture lead to self-fulfilling prophecies in which groups actually engage in fraud because they suspect their opponents of doing the same. The distrust leads to the already mentioned "diffusion of illegality." Conflict is intense in situations of this kind, and the tendency to define all groups as Good or Evil forces the military to take sides. In executing the coup, the military "pacifies" the country by repressing the political hyperactivity of the radical groups. In this context the *golpistas* often legitimize their actions by proclaiming the need for a "temporary" departure from democracy to cure its "pathology."

As a final factor contributing to *golpes* that occur in conjunction with elections, mention should be made of the relative poverty of most Latin American countries. If there is little material wealth to spread about, and the government tends to be treated as a private estate by the party in power, it follows that electoral defeat may be highly threatening. For some groups, particularly those which comprise the middle and lower levels of leadership, exclusion from the security of government "welfare" or patronage may jeopardize their livelihood. They may have no other source of support to fall back on in the case of defeat. For this reason, the political conflict for scarce resources is exceedingly bitter, and the incentive to resort to illegal means to insure victory will be all the stronger. We will have more to say on this matter in Chapter 6.

Continuismo, our second indicator of weak electoral mechanisms, was present in 40 percent of the *golpes* analyzed. This factor can also be understood in terms of some of the foregoing explanations. The scarcity of material resources may encourage governmental incumbents to attempt to perpetuate their tenure in office. Also, the nonsecular character of political conflict is apparent in cases of *continuismo;* in these instances, the incumbents will attempt to pass themselves off as "saviors," while their propaganda will depict opposition groups as "gangsters."[63] The opposition, of course, will try to make the reverse symbolism stick. Again, as with our first indicator of weak electoral mechanisms, *continuismo* often provokes acute conflict and increases the probability of violence. As indicated by Table 1, 75 percent of the coups executed in response to *continuismo* also took place in an atmosphere of increased civilian violence and direct action. The reason for this is not difficult to understand. The incumbents, wishing to extend their tenure, block or "fix" the channels available for regular and pacific change — elections. This practically forces opposing groups to resort to violent tactics if they hope to have a chance to attain governmental power. In effect, *continuismo* reduces the ability of the political system to achieve change in the absence of violence. If violence does break out, the likelihood that the military will remove the executive for the purpose of restoring order increases significantly. The Bolivian coup of 1964, which removed Víctor Paz Estenssoro from office, fits this pattern.

Of particular relevance for coup activity is the characteristic organizational weakness of "continuistic" authoritarian regimes. As discussed in Chapter 2, an important peculiarity pointing to their organizational weakness is their lack of institutionalized mechanisms of succession and institutional maintenance. Most involve personal dictatorial forms accompanied by weak party organizations. Without viable party structures, there is no organizational basis for a successful democratic experiment. When coups occur in response to *continuismo,* the bane of democracy is plainly evident. Direct action by the military counters the nondemocratic practices of the incumbents. But, normally, neither *continuismo* nor its "cure" institutionalize means for the peaceful, democratic transfer of power. In other words, while the military justifies an anti-continuistic *golpe* as necessary to correct for the "pathology of democracy," the tenure in power of the armed forces does not usually result in the

---

[63] See, for example, Batista, *Respuesta.*

formation of strong party organizations. In effect, military rule tends to be highly anti-party in character. In the cases where the military has attempted to forge parties, such as in post-Goulart Brazil, its efforts have left much to be desired. Actually, the military preference for order and hierarchy stifles the participation necessary for the cultivation of strong political parties. More will be said on this point in the following chapter. At any rate, when the military finally permits the restoration of democratic rules, the probability of a successful experiment under these rules is low, because the requisite strong party system is absent.[64] The military may again have to step in and freeze the situation. The end result is the cyclical alternation of authoritarian and democratic regimes that characterizes many Latin American countries.[65]

On the whole, Latin America provides support for the existence of a rather clear inverse relationship between strong party organization and *continuismo*. In countries that have experienced continuistic attempts, party organization has been weak. In addition, *continuismo* tends to weaken party organization seriously. In this context we must be careful to distinguish the *continuismo* of *el jefe* (i.e., a single person) from those instances in which a political party is able to continue or maintain its control over the governmental apparatus for long periods of time. Parties such as Mexico's PRI are quite strong, and on the whole they are far less prone to coups than are personalistic regimes. A parallel case can be made for Colombia's Conservative and Liberal parties during the first half of this century. Under such strong and continuistic party regimes, pressures for *golpes* are reduced in part because the regimes have managed to institutionalize mechanisms for periodic executive turnover within the ruling party. In addition, these regimes usually allow for limited democratic freedoms, such as a relatively free press. In both of these respects, the regimes' greater flexibility permits the maintenance of relatively high levels of political morale, and the pressures for coups are lessened as a result. More will be said on these points later.

Before closing this section, mention should be made of the relationship between our two indicators and the type of *golpe*. Table 2 shows that electoral weaknesses were almost equally important in triggering interclass and intraclass *golpes*, thus suggesting the general import of weak electoral organization for breakdown regardless of the type of conflict that predominates in the coup situation. In addition, it is inter-

---

[64] In this sense see Seymour M. Lipset, *Political Man: The Social Bases of Politics* (Garden City, N.Y., 1963).

[65] Needler, *Political Development in Latin America,* chap. 2.

esting to note that anti-leftist coups were relatively more frequent in situations characterized by *continuismo* when contrasted with the pro-leftist variety, which were relatively more common at times of elections. While there is no conclusive evidence to account for this pattern, we might nevertheless offer the following remarks by way of speculation. In the pro-leftist coup situation the government perceives itself as being in a very weak position. Most importantly, Table 2 shows that the incumbent cannot count on the severely divided military to support any desires he might have to continue in office. Under these circumstances pressure for an electoral solution is great, even though it is not realized in the final analysis without military intervention. In the anti-leftist coup situation, on the other hand, military disunity, although still present, is not as severe. Moreover, the president may miscalculate that the military will back him personally in a showdown with left-wing groups, which Table 2 shows to be engaging in frequent violence and direct action in this type of situation. These factors may give the incumbent a false sense of strength that encourages him to attempt his own continuation in power. Though admittedly speculative in character, these differences might help to account for the fact that pro-leftist *golpes* tend to occur in conjunction with elections while anti-leftist ones tend to be accompanied by attempts at *continuismo*.

In summarizing the comments made in this section, we have seen that weak electoral mechanisms have been an important trigger of coups d'état in Latin America between 1943 and 1967. Various factors — such as the low levels of differentiation between the political and governmental spheres, the weakness of party organization, the nonsecular character of political conflict, and the scarcity of economic resources — are responsible for the existence of these anemic electoral mechanisms. Electoral fraud, *continuismo*, and coups d'état are mere symptoms of the basic dilemma — the inability to institutionalize regular, legal channels for the peaceful turnover of executive power.

Governmental Ineffectiveness and Illegitimacy

A brief inspection of Table 1 shows that low levels of legitimacy and effectiveness on the part of government constituted the largest single precipitant of coups d'état in Latin America between 1943 and 1967. One or more of our three indicators of this explanation were found to be present in two-thirds of the *golpes* examined. This is not surprising because in a sense explanations relying on governmental ineffectiveness and illegitimacy serve as an umbrella for a number of those processes already discussed in connection with some of the preceding explanations. This will become apparent as we proceed because a number of factors previously treated in other contexts must be raised again in our analysis of governmental ineffectiveness and illegitimacy.

First of all, acute conflict between the president and congress, present in some 13 percent of the coups investigated, is an indication of low levels of governmental effectiveness and legitimacy. As previously noted, governmental immobility is produced by conflict of this kind. Policy is not made or implemented, as the institutions of formal government are locked in battle, each attempting to protect its integrity from threats made by the other. As governmental performance declines, so too does its legitimacy in the eyes of the population at large. A government less and less able to perform its functions in situations of this kind tends to become less and less a government and ceases to command the respect of its people. If the deadlock between the two institutions is not some-how broken, the replacement of the executive and even the congress by the military becomes increasingly probable. In effect, the coup is a response to a growing sentiment that prefers any form of government to no government at all.

Acute conflict between the executive and congress assumes different forms. At times it can be the product of intense interclass sectarianism, as was the case in Peru in 1948, when the two institutions took the sides of groups with different social class composition. In other instances, the conflict that surrounds the congressional-presidential deadlock is pre-dominantly intraclass in character. The Haitian *golpe* of 1950 provides a case in point. Finally, either of these forms of congressional-presi-dential conflict may betray the presence of a type of institutional sec-tarianism, when the corporate or group interests of the two institutions are defined in mutually exclusive terms. In this case, each side views the demands of the other as highly prejudicial to its own institutional inter-ests. For example, executive demands for congressional approval of a grant of power not allowed by the constitution would be against the congress' own group interests, for such a move would dilute its power vis-à-vis the executive. The coups in Haiti in 1950 and in Panama one year later are examples of this sort of case. In both instances the con-gressional-presidential confrontation that helped bring on the coup arose when congress refused to alter the constitutional clause barring pres-idential *continuismo*.

A number of other factors can be adduced to account for the inci-dence of acute conflict between the executive and the legislature in Latin America. First of all, the high levels of distrust present in the culture and the tendency to negate the instrumental-task dimension of formal roles do not facilitate the compromise and bargaining that are necessary for the maintenance of a viable working relationship between the executive and congress in a presidential system.[66] The nonsecular character of political conflict and its tendency to escalate under the impact of the rhetoric of primitive and ideological radicals also makes it difficult to compromise initial positions taken in the course of the policy-making process. When these factors are added to the fact that the president and the members of congress are responsive to the demands of different constituencies, it is surprising that the coups analyzed do not offer a larger number of cases in which escalated executive-congressional conflict was present. In fact, only four of the thirty coups involved conflict of this kind.

There are two facts that help to account for this finding. First, the executive ordinarily is a good deal more powerful than congress in most Latin American countries, and this fact may discourage the legislative body from challenging the president.[67] Second, the relatively high occurrence of authoritarian rule in the area also tends to reduce the incidence of acute presidential-congressional conflict because independent legislative bodies do not exist under such regimes. Whatever the case, escalated executive-legislative conflict, given its tendency to reduce governmental effectiveness and legitimacy, is a potential triggering factor of coups in Latin America.

Our final two indicators of low levels of governmental effectiveness and legitimacy are increased levels of civilian violence and direct action and overt coalition between military and civilian groups in the coup setting. As indicated by Table 1, the former was a factor in 56.7 percent of the coups examined, the latter in 53.3 percent of them. In effect, both of these indicators suggest the high frequency of escalated rather than limited conflict in Latin America.

In societies that have had more than their share of authoritarian regimes, open conflict is not legitimized. That is to say, conflict in authoritarian systems is not accepted as a necessary means for the reconciliation of divergent interests. Authoritarian regimes tend to block effective participation; participation is either controlled by "the state" or it is considered to be revolutionary and therefore illegitimate. In this

[66] The weakness of the instrumental-task dimension is discussed in Payne, *Conflict in Colombia.*

[67] For a general discussion of Latin American legislative bodies, see Robert E. Scott, "Legislatures and Legislation," in *Government and Politics in Latin America,* ed. Harold E. Davis (New York, 1958), pp. 290-332.

setting, it is difficult to obtain limited or regulated conflict. Opponents of the regime must wage a relatively clandestine struggle which tends to escalate into violent confrontation as the movement gains strength. The recent upswing of urban terrorism and guerrilla warfare throughout much of Latin America illustrates this pattern.

We should mention that this is the opposite of the situation which prevails in stable democratic systems where open disagreement is legitimized and where there are appropriate formal mechanisms for the expression of views and the turnover of governmental personnel. In contrast, many Latin American countries do not have formal-legal structures of sufficient strength to keep conflict within the boundaries of the political system. Electoral mechanisms are characteristically weak, and the already noted tendency toward the partisan transformation of formal governmental roles — the fusion of partisan political and formal governmental roles — attests to the weakness of formal-legal structures. Under these conditions, the tendency is not only toward escalated conflict but also to its being accompanied by apocalyptic visions that conflict and strife will produce a total collapse of the social fabric. Political and social conflicts augment phenomenally in a self-fulfilling manner, and the probability of military coups increases as the situation worsens. In cases of this kind, the military produces an abrupt change in the formal political organization in order to prevent unfavorable alternative collapses. In addition, the coup can also perform a latent function from the point of view of the society at large. It provides a catharsis after a period of rising tensions. This helps to explain why many Latin American coups are followed by an outflow of exceedingly optimistic predictions in a carnival-like atmosphere. The reduction of tension produced by the coup gives way to relieved expressions of renewed hope and, not uncommonly, much festiveness.[68]

At the same time, the coups seldom result in much more than changes of a purely political nature. As indicated in Table 1, only about one coup in four involved reformist motivations, and the extent to which subsequent reform measures actually produced significant socioeconomic change is debatable. Instead of meaningful social change, most coups are marked by a "constitutional fetishism" in which the old constitution

---

[68] The greater the level of conflict prior to the *golpe,* the more generalized the tension-release effect after the coup. Colombia's 1953 coup is an excellent example of a far-reaching catharsis. See Vernon L. Fluharty, *Dance of the Millions: Military Rule and the Social Revolution in Colombia, 1930-1956* (Pittsburgh, 1957). In other instances, the tension release is confined to the society's military elites. For example, see *Alerta* (Havana), March 11, 1952, pp. 1, 10, for reports of the 1952 Cuban *golpe.*

is replaced by a new document. This fetishism again reflects the messianic expectations that frequently accompany political conflict in Latin America. There is a tendency to expect that only "total" changes in governmental formal-legal organization can "solve" the country's problems.

These remarks also suggest the difficulty that most Latin American countries experience in attempting to provide for gradual change. In an environment characterized by escalated political conflict, violence and repression, messianic perceptions of reality, and weak formal structures, gradual change has little chance. The fact that *golpes* occur with such frequency throughout most of the area illustrates this difficulty; only infrequently do they result in a serious commitment to something other than purely political modifications.[69]

In contrast to this picture, stable Western democracies, when faced with sharp conflict and pressures for change, tend to limit and institutionalize the conflict, to reintegrate the society and obtain gradual changes, by making slight modifications in the constitutional or formal-legal organization of the society. Generally, only those norms of the regime which relate directly to the contested issue are changed. For example, the incorporation of labor into the political system of these stable democracies was accomplished by institutionalizing the right to strike and by extending the franchise. Minor constitutional changes served to blunt interclass conflict, to institutionalize it after a fashion, without destroying other institutions. This does not imply that change has not been accompanied by violence in these currently stable democracies. For example, U.S. labor history has often been marked by bloodshed. Still, this should not detract from the crucial point: over the years, these stable democracies have managed to evolve a set of resilient, highly differentiated formal institutions that have allowed for the gradual incorporation of peripheral groups, for the realization of gradual socioeconomic change.

On the other hand, the generally weak formal-legal structures found in most Latin American countries cannot stand up under escalated pressures for social change. The formal governmental institutions tend to lose their differentiated character and to encompass extra-legal partisan roles that effectively undermine their ability to mediate conflict and aggregate divergent interests. In this setting, governmental effectiveness and legitimacy fall off seriously. Escalated conflict marked by civilian

[69] This is probably why many scholars have observed that Latin American politics seldom produce marked changes in socioeconomic structures, despite high levels of violence and repression throughout the area. In this sense see Anderson, *Latin America*.

violence and direct action — general strikes, popular demonstrations, boycotts — tends to increase. In the end, the military intervenes for the purpose of restoring order. The weakness and low legitimacy of the government are attested to by the relatively high incidence of coups which involve an overt coalition of civilian and military groups in opposition to the executive — slightly more than one-half of the thirty coups studied.

In short, a set of highly differentiated formal-legal institutions is essential to the regulation or limitation of conflict and the provision for gradual social change. By institutionalizing and limiting conflict, these institutions play an important part in reducing the frequency of coup activity. In their absence, the high incidence of violence and coup activity characteristic of many Latin American countries provides the alternative. Using the terms employed in Chapter 2, we can say that although some Latin American societies have registered gains in political development, much more energy has been expended in the coup-studded pattern of disequilibrium that typifies situations of political stagnation or even decay.

In this section we have seen how a number of the factors already mentioned in connection with other coup explanations are summarized in the low levels of governmental effectiveness and legitimacy. The fusion of governmental and partisan roles, weak electoral mechanisms, the messianic perceptions of reality, the inflamed rhetoric of radicalism, and the high levels of distrust in the nonsecular culture all tend to produce a situation in which unregulated conflict and violence encourage coups d'état and the so-called "pathology of democracy." From this perspective, as evidenced by the high incidence of categories 13 and 14, the military can hardly be "blamed" entirely for the high frequency of *golpes* in Latin America. Factors in the larger environment create pressures that often "compel" the armed forces to action.

Finally, brief mention should be made of one additional point that will be explored in the following chapters: the low levels of socioeconomic development prevalent throughout most of Latin America make it very difficult for government to establish an effective set of institutions that might serve to integrate the society. The social mobilization and subsequent pressures for change that accompany transitional periods are becoming more frequent throughout the area. As indicated by Table 2, escalated interclass conflict has been particularly associated with substantial drops in governmental effectiveness and legitimacy in the area. The picture is an ironic one. Demands for increased material benefits and a more egalitarian distribution of wealth are being made before most countries are sufficiently affluent to cope with them. Political instability and military intervention are a probable outcome of this difficult situation.

Concluding Remarks

In this chapter we have analyzed a number of processes that have triggered Latin American coups d'état. By calculating the frequency of these processes in coup situations during the 1943-67 period, we are able to evaluate the relative significance of the eight explanations set forth in Chapter 3. As indicated by Table 1, some explanations of coup activity were a good deal more significant than others in the overall Latin American picture in accounting for the precipitants of the thirty *golpes* analyzed. For example, the personal interests explanation had the least significance, although it was critical in particular cases. Against this, processes couched in terms of governmental ineffectiveness and illegitimacy were a good deal more significant.

Our data also bear upon some of the hypotheses concerning political breakdown that were deduced from the equilibrium framework presented in Chapter 2. The reader will recall that we interpreted *golpes* as the product of relatively severe imbalances between levels of participation and organization in the political system. In general terms, the logic of the equilibrium framework suggested that interclass coups involve a greater degree of imbalance than do those of the intraclass variety. Table 2 lends a measure of support to this hypothesis. In effect, the higher incidence of civilian violence, direct action, and overt coalition-making with the military that characterize the interclass coup situation in contrast to the intraclass context are indicative of the greater intensity of civilian participation in the former. Furthermore, the indicators of military professionalism in Table 2 indicate that organizational problems in government were relatively more severe in the interclass coup context than they were in instances of intraclass *golpes*. The equilibrium framework also suggested that anti-leftist (conservative) coups tend to take place in the context of civilian political hyperactivity (over-participation) and, conversely, that pro-leftist (reformist) coups tend to occur in situations of relative underparticipation (i.e., where government is excessively "centralized"). Some support for these relationships can be found in Table 2. In effect, all the indicators of governmental ineffectiveness and illegitimacy, military corporate interests, and U.S. interference suggest a greater volume of disruptive participation in the anti-leftist context when compared to the pro-leftist situation. In addition to the lower incidence of civilian violence in the pro-leftist case, the greater degree of underparticipation in government that characterizes this type of *golpe* in contrast with the anti-leftist variety is suggested by the fact that military promotional bottlenecks were much more severe in the pro-leftist situation. These remarks bring a measure of empirical support to the analytical formulations advanced in Chapter 2, and they also suggest that the type of *golpe* that occurs in any given instance is a function of the overall situational context in which the polity finds itself.

Table 2 also shows how the factors that trigger coups combine in different situations to produce distinctive types of *golpes*. In the Latin American context between 1943 and 1967 anti-leftist *golpes* were particularly likely to occur as a result of civilian strife in which conservative groups urged the military to take action. In most instances the probability of a coup was heightened by the military's perception of a substantial threat to its corporate interests. In nearly half of the anti-leftist coups a president suffering from acute crises of legitimacy and from his inability to control civilian unrest made an unsuccessful attempt to continue in office through illegal means. In addition to these factors, the intrigues of U.S. personnel played a role in the events which led up to the conservative *golpe* in a substantial number of cases. In contrast to this picture, pro-leftist coups were triggered most often in instances in which promotional dissatisfactions on the part of junior officers provided fertile ground on which reformist politicians could encourage a *golpe* allegedly designed to redistribute the benefits of political participation. In most of these cases civilian reformers and their junior officer allies judged that elections would not be sufficient to overcome resistance and produce the desired changes. As suggested by the frequency of open physical conflict between military factions in these pro-leftist coup situations, there was actual resistance to the implementation of reformist goals.

In contrast to these interclass coup types, intraclass *golpes* manifested lesser degrees of imbalance between the participation and organization variables. Still, the intraclass coups involved substantial problems of governmental ineffectiveness and illegitimacy. Civilian unrest, often triggered by *continuismo,* precipitated coups in societies in which electoral mechanisms were not effectively institutionalized even for the transfer of power among elite groups. These low levels of political development were attested to by the presence of "personality" coups, in which the personal interests of a *caudillo* led to *golpes* devoid of implications for social change.

As noted in Chapter 2, no single precipitant can be considered a necessary or sufficient condition for a coup d'état. Coup processes are cumulative in character. Nonetheless, the factors discussed in this chapter provide an awareness of the processes that are potentially conducive to *golpes*, and by employing the indicators as we have done, it is possible to get some sense of the overall relative utility of the various processes in producing coups in the Latin American context. By showing the ways in which the various indicators have combined, we have also been able to produce a rough, preliminary categorization of Latin American coup types for the 1943-67 period. More refined, alternative typologies are surely possible and desirable. Yet we feel that we have made a beginning for future research along these lines by setting forth the contrasting constellations of coup-triggering factors as far as our data permit.

Our analysis in terms of the triggering factors has several limitations related to the application of empirical methods to the exceedingly complex character of the coup processes. For example, our equilibrium framework adopts a macrosociological perspective that emphasizes the reactive role of the military vis-à-vis the civilian sectors and institutions of government. We overcome this difficulty in part by inserting the military-organization dimension. But the problem still remains to some extent for our analysis here pays little attention to military ideologies or role perceptions, an important conditioner of probabilities for the types of military intervention in the political process.[70]

In addition, our analysis in this chapter makes use of rather crude, restrictive indicators that are poor measures of the intensity of the conflict that leads to coups d'état. For one thing, it would be very difficult to quantify some of the properties referred to by our explanations (e.g., acute *personalismo*). Also, our sources, particularly the newspapers and periodicals, are not usually detailed enough to allow for such precision. Despite this weakness, however, our indicators are useful as guides to those processes that may trigger military intervention. Moreover, and as suggested by recent events in Chile, these processes are central to the equation that governs propensities toward breakdown. In Chile the ongoing political crisis has been assuaged somewhat by pacts designed to safeguard electoral processes and to maintain the neutrality of the armed forces, thereby seeking to avoid Marxist *continuismo* in the future and

[70] Military role perceptions are an important factor in the works by Einaudi, *Peruvian Military Relations,* and Stepan, *Military in Politics.* Quite simply, particularly in countries with low levels of political institutionalization, coup forms are somewhat erratic because of the relative autonomy of military behavior in the coup situation. A more sophisticated treatment of coup phenomena requires a detailed consideration of the relative weight that must be given to internal military variables in the overall situational context that produce the different coup types.

to insure that the military's discipline and cohesion will not be eroded nor its corporate interests unduly threatened.

Finally, our analysis in this chapter does not account for the variability of sociopolitical structures that is apparent throughout Latin America. Without considering this structural factor, our indicators might give a false impression of the actual probabilities toward breakdown in specific cases. For example, the nearly equal levels of support for the ruling party and the opposition that characterized Colombia during much of this century created a structural condition in the political system which was not very conducive to military mediation via coup d'état. Partly for this reason, Colombia required a lengthy period of unprecedented interparty warfare (*la violencia*) and a continuistic attempt to produce in 1953 the country's first coup since 1901. The point of this case and others like it is that it is not enough to consider in isolation the triggering factors that are capable of precipitating military intervention. One must also consider the broader structural context in order to enhance the accuracy with which probabilities toward breakdown can be established. Some of the main structural factors that affect coup probabilities are analyzed and, finally, related to our discussion of the triggering factors in the succeeding two chapters.

5

SOCIOECONOMIC DIMENSIONS
AND POLITICAL STRUCTURE

In this chapter we shall begin by investigating the extent to which Latin American coups can be understood in terms of socioeconomic factors, and this investigation will lead us to consider the effects of political structure on stability. As for the socioeconomic dimensions, we should note that attempts to relate socioeconomic variables to political stability are by no means new. The relevance of these variables for the political stability dimension was recognized by the earliest political philosophers of the Western world. For our purposes, two contrasting socioeconomic approaches to the interpretation of *golpes* may be discerned — one static, the other dynamic.

Static approaches link political behavior generally, and political stability in particular, to achieved levels of socioeconomic development. The underlying assumption here is that there are certain enduring socioeconomic factors that have an influence on political behavior. While it is acknowledged that all societies are in a state of flux, they in fact possess certain socioeconomic structural characteristics that are relatively fixed. For example, the basic socioeconomic characteristics that generally differentiate an industrial from an agricultural society — a large middle class, a high proportion of literate, urban dwellers, and a set of highly differentiated financial institutions, for example — change rather slowly and over relatively long periods of time. Those who engage in static analysis feel that much of value about political behavior in a particular society can be learned from exploring the nature of the relationships between these relatively constant socioeconomic characteristics and the political process. They also feel that cross-national comparisons of political behavior can be advanced by investigating possible differences in these basic socioeconomic structures, as, for example, the fact that one country is relatively "advanced" or "developed" (i.e., industrial) while another is comparatively "underdeveloped" (i.e., agricultural).

The notion of different "levels" or "stages" of development emerges from this type of orientation. Within the static frame of analysis, "levels" or "stages" of development are the key explanatory concepts. The basic socioeconomic structures characteristic of a given level of development are alleged to affect political institutions either directly or indirectly via the influence they exercise on the culture of the society in question. As an example of the former, Merle Kling argues that economic under-development in Latin America — typically characterized by foreign economic control that minimizes opportunities for most natives — leads directly to excessive competition in the political sector, which remains a relatively open arena for personal mobility in the society. This excessive competition weakens political organizations, thereby increasing the pressures for a coup d'état.[1] John Johnson, on the other hand, offers an example of static analysis that links levels of development to political behavior via the indirect route of culture. Specifically, Johnson suggests that the early stages of industrialization have brought a secular element to Latin American culture. As we shall see in more detail later on, this increased secularism strengthens political organizations, thereby reducing the pressures for *golpes*.[2]

In short, static analysis focuses on the relationship between political behavior and levels of socioeconomic development at a fixed point in time. In general terms, high levels of achieved development are linked with political stability and vice versa.

Dynamic analyses of the relationship between socioeconomic and political variables, on the other hand, are concerned with investigating the impact of various kinds of socioeconomic change on political behavior generally and political stability in particular. In this context, an effort is made to interpret political stability, or the lack of it, in terms of socioeconomic change. In contrast with the static approaches, which are content to deal with fixed levels of development, dynamic interpretations are interested in the impact of socioeconomic change on political stability. In the useful terms employed by Huntington, static analysis is concerned with the impact of "modernity" on politics, while dynamic analysis deals with the political implications of "modernization."[3]

With their focus on the implications of change, all dynamic interpre-

[1] See Kling, "Political Instability."

[2] See John J. Johnson, "The Political Role of the Latin-American Middle Sectors," *Annals of the American Academy of Political and Social Science,* 334 (1961), 20-29.

[3] Huntington, *Political Order,* p. 41.

tations are similar. In another sense, however, they exhibit differences by focusing on the effects of change over varying periods of time. Some studies emphasize the unsettling effects of short-run economic changes, such as sudden fluctuations in production or price levels. Political instability and *golpes* are often interpreted as a response to short-run changes of this sort.[4] Other advocates of dynamic analysis focus on the political impact of socioeconomic changes over somewhat longer periods of time. For example, middle-term analysis of this kind may select a process such as urbanization during the post–World War II period as a suitable object for study. In this context, it is often argued by Latin American specialists that the high rates of urbanization characteristic of this period increase the probability of political breakdown because of the traumatic changes in norms and values that necessarily accompany the transition from rural to urban areas.[5] Whatever the particular case, dynamic analyses are unified in proclaiming the relevance of socioeconomic change for problems of political equilibrium or stability.

Although the static and dynamic approaches might appear to be at odds, they are similar to the participation-problem and organization-problem interpretations discussed in Chapter 1 in that they can usefully be viewed as complementary. In effect, static analysis suggests the importance of relatively enduring socioeconomic characteristics that serve as parameters for the dynamic processes of socioeconomic change. The failure to consider this interrelationship can result in serious problems. Take, for example, the relationship between political stability and high rates of industrial growth. These high rates of growth would have a variable political impact, depending on the level of socioeconomic development already achieved by the country in question. High rates of industrial growth in a relatively underdeveloped country will necessitate changes in fundamental values and norms. A nascent labor movement must violate age-old norms governing the conduct of the masses in order to obtain a bargaining position in the society. In this situation, transitional conflict of the interclass variety and the possibility of political breakdown are likely to be present. In relatively more developed societies, on the other hand, high rates of industrial growth may not threaten breakdown. In these modern societies there already exists an institutional framework capable of absorbing high rates of change with-

[4] See, for example, the first section of Martin C. Needler, "Political Development and Military Intervention in Latin America," *American Political Science Review*, 60 (1966), 616–626.

[5] See, for instance, Torcuato S. Di Tella, *El Sistema Político Argentino y la Clase Obrera* (Buenos Aires, 1964). The reader will recall that the participation-problem interpretation of coups manifests this dynamic perspective.

out suffering serious disruption. In this context, labor unions and their position in society are likely to be well established. Subsequent union organization can therefore take place without incurring high levels of conflict. Only minor adjustments will be needed, as unions are already accepted as legitimate in most modern industrial societies. In short, both static and dynamic analyses are necessary complements to understanding the relationship between political stability and socioeconomic variables. In the example just given, assessment of the impact of rates of change depends critically on knowledge of achieved levels of socioeconomic development — whether the society in question is relatively more or less modern.

In connection with remarks presented above, we should mention that some scholars have addressed themselves to the question of prerequisites for successful "modernization," which may be defined as the process by which strong institutions capable of withstanding subsequent change without breakdown are established.[6] This approach has an evolutionary perspective, which includes both the static and dynamic dimensions. A central theme of this evolutionary interpretation is that beyond a certain point in the process of socioeconomic change a critical point in the development process is reached. Having achieved this hypothetical, fixed level of socioeconomic development, usually after a long period of time, the political system presumably acquires a sufficient degree of cultural secularization and structural differentiation which will enable it to cope successfully with most challenges to its continuity. In this context, Eisenstadt, for example, suggests that once this critical level is reached, the political system is likely to be strong and flexible enough to persist through transitional periods, with their accompanying pressures for change.

This discussion suggests an important point that must be reiterated here. High rates of socioeconomic change will not always produce political breakdown. This is why in the previous chapter we defined transitional periods in terms of observable political phenomena, as opposed to rates of socioeconomic change, as is most often done. As discussed in this chapter, the impact of socioeconomic change on political stability appears to depend in part on the level of socioeconomic development that the society in question has achieved. In other words, we shall see that both the dynamic and static approaches are necessary to an understanding of the way in which socioeconomic factors affect political stability in Latin America.

[6] See, for instance, Eisenstadt, *Modernization*.

Static Analysis

In order to investigate the extent to which socioeconomic factors can be used to account for political instability in Latin America, we began by using a static approach. For this purpose, the total frequency of coups during the 1943-67 period under study was determined (see Appendix C) and related to fixed levels of socioeconomic development near the midpoint of this period. The twenty Latin American countries were divided into two equal groups — the relatively developed and the relatively underdeveloped — on the basis of six developmental criteria employed by Germani and Silvert.[7] On the basis of this procedure, it was found that the ten least developed countries experienced twice as many coups as the ten most developed ones. Table 3 summarizes the findings.

In general terms, it appears that higher levels of socioeconomic development, while not a sufficient condition to avoid *golpes,* were accompanied by a lower frequency of coups. As noted, coups in the more underdeveloped group of countries were twice as frequent as those in the group of relatively more developed countries. All of the less developed countries have had coups, and as a group they were twice as likely to experience breakdown as were the more developed ones. Also, the three countries that did not experience *golpes* during the period under study — Uruguay, Chile, and Mexico — were located in the more developed group, in the second, third, and sixth places respectively. In this sense, relatively high levels of socioeconomic development were a necessary condition to avoid coups during the period under study.

The reader should note that if we divide the countries into three categories of achieved socioeconomic development — low, medium, and high — the inverse relationship between level of socioeconomic development and coup frequency does not change.[8] In this respect, considering the 1943-67 period as a whole, a case cannot be made that in Latin America there is a group of highly "traditional," socioeconom-

---

[7] Germani and Silvert, "Military Intervention." Criteria directly related to level of socioeconomic development are (a) percent middle and upper strata, (b) percent in cities of 20,000 or more inhabitants, (c) percent middle and upper urban strata, (d) percent literates, and (e) university students per 1,000 inhabitants. Percent in primary activities is inversely related to level of socioeconomic development. Our ranking of countries agrees with Germani and Silvert's in all cases except for that of Cuba, which should be ranked fourth according to their own data, instead of seventh, where they place it for undetermined reasons.

[8] Taking the seven countries with relatively low levels of development followed by the next seven countries with higher levels, and the remaining six countries with the highest levels of development, as forming the three categories, we find that their coup frequency was 29, 24, and 10 respectively.

TABLE 3. Level of Socioeconomic Development and
Number of Coups d'État per Country, 1943-67

Countries with Higher Level of Development	Number of Coups	Countries with Lower Level of Development	Number of Coups
Argentina	7	Paraguay	5
Uruguay	0	Peru	2
Chile	0	Ecuador	6
Cuba[a]	2	El Salvador	6
Costa Rica	1	Bolivia[a]	4
Mexico	0	Guatemala[c]	5
Brazil[b]	3	Nicaragua[c]	1
Venezuela[c]	4	Dominican Republic[c]	3
Colombia	2	Honduras	3
Panama[c]	2	Haiti	7
Totals	21		42

[a] There was also a revolution.
[b] There was also a presidential suicide.
[c] There was also a presidential assassination.

ically underdeveloped nations whose isolation from the "currents of modernization" results in political stability.[9] Indeed, given the cultural dependency of most Latin American countries on the more developed Western societies, the converse is often the case. That is, the effort to impose "imported" modern forms in a relatively underdeveloped context often increases the pressures for breakdown.

These remarks, of course, do not explain why low levels of socioeconomic development are associated with coups. On the basis of the data presented in Table 3, one can say only that low levels of development and relatively high coup frequencies tend to occur together, for whatever reason. At the same time, the underlying assumption, already alluded to earlier, is that levels of socioeconomic development have an effect on the frequency of coups by way of intervening cultural and organizational variables. It is assumed that rising levels of socioeconomic development have a "healthy" impact on the political culture and on both civilian and military organizations, which in turn reduces the frequency of *golpes*. At present, suffice it to say that when we speak of low levels of socioeconomic development "producing" or "leading to" coup situations, the intervening mechanisms are being assumed. In the next

[9] Table 3 shows that Nicaragua, with just one coup, was the only country close to being an exception during the entire 1943-67 period under study.

chapter, some of these intervening links will be explored when the over-all impact of culture and political organization on military intervention is considered.

Although Table 3 indicates that the level of socioeconomic develop-ment is an important factor to consider in assessing the incidence of coups in Latin America, it is by no means the only one. The relation-ship between levels of development and coup frequency is not a linear one. Argentina, the most developed country in terms of a composite socioeconomic dimension, is tied with the least developed country for the top position in terms of the total number of coups during the period of time under study. In this sense, Argentina is to Latin America what France has been to Western Europe — a case that has not matched the levels of political stability achieved by other countries with similar levels of socioeconomic development. In comparative perspective, ranking ac-cording to levels of socioeconomic development would lead one to expect fewer coups in Argentina than in Nicaragua, another exceptional case that has a far lower level of socioeconomic development. Yet this is not the case. Argentina suffered seven coups between 1943 and 1967, while Nicaragua had only one. This suggests that there are political variables, not wholly determined by levels of socioeconomic develop-ment, which affect the tendency for coups to occur.

The relative independence of political institutions from levels of socio-economic development must be explored in order to interpret the pro-pensity of societies toward *golpes*. But before we discuss this important topic, we must briefly consider the extent to which levels of socio-economic development affect the types of coups experienced by Latin American societies. Table 4 has been constructed to aid us in this analysis.[10] Although our sample size is admittedly small and our group-ing of countries necessarily involves a rather arbitrary decision with respect to establishment of cut-off points for the three groups, we never-theless feel that there is some utility in our tentative interpretations.

An inspection of Table 4 suggests that both interclass and intraclass coups occurred at all three levels of socioeconomic development. A con-trast of countries with low and medium levels of development indicates that they experienced approximately the same proportion of interclass coups. However, the incidence of reformist interclass *golpes* was slightly

[10] The determination of the three groups of countries according to their levels of socioeconomic development — low, medium, and high — is based on the criterion set in footnote 8. The classification of coups is based on Table 1. The number of sampled *golpes* per development group was as follows: low, 13; medium, 15; and high, 2.

TABLE 4. Socioeconomic Development and Type of Coup, 1943-67
(in percentages)

	Interclass Coups			Intraclass Coups	Total
	Oppose Left	Make Reforms	Subtotal		
High Development	50.0	None	50.0	50.0	100.0
Medium Development	40.0	20.0	60.0	40.0	100.0
Low Development	30.8	30.8	61.6	38.4	100.0

higher in countries with lower levels of development. In this respect, the direction of the relationship provides modest support for the hypothesis that the military adopts a conservative role as levels of socioeconomic development increase.[11] This is particularly evident in the case of post-Perón Argentina, Latin America's most socioeconomically developed country. Since 1955, most Argentine golpes have been anti-leftist (i.e., anti-Peronist) in character. As the type of coup is conditioned by the situational context and socioeconomically developed countries tend to be characterized by high levels of political participation, military intervention in these societies often tends to adopt a conservative stance in order to dampen the intensity of activity in the polity. At the same time, and as suggested by the 1971 Argentine coup, one cannot find a consistent conservative bias in Latin American golpes, even at the highest levels of socioeconomic development.[12] Finally, with the aid of Table 1, we can establish that the group of most developed countries experienced no "personality" intraclass golpes, i.e., coups that were precipitated by acute personalismo, whereas both the medium and low groups of countries by socioeconomic criteria did.

In summary, the 1943-67 experience suggests that although high levels

[11] This might partly account for Needler's finding to the effect that contemporary Latin American coups have become increasingly conservative in character. See Needler, *Political Development in Latin America*, pp. 64-65.

[12] By the early 1970s, the Argentine situation appeared to have reached a point of stalemate between the military and the Peronists. In accordance with the logic of the already mentioned process of "socialization and compromise through violence," the key political actors have modified their original positions and have sought a measure of accommodation with their adversaries.

of socioeconomic development were a sufficient condition for the absence of "personality" coups, the type of *golpe* was not entirely determined by socioeconomic development. In effect, "traditional" intraclass coups were present in societies with various levels of development. Furthermore, particularly when considering countries with medium and low levels of development, it is apparent that the ideological position of the military was not strongly linked to levels of socioeconomic development, as these countries experienced both conservative and reformist coups.

In Chapter 2 we briefly discussed the relationship between political development and the propensity of regimes toward coups d'état. Theoretical considerations suggested that the politically less developed authoritarian ideal type was highly susceptible to *golpes,* while the relatively developed democratic ideal type was deemed highly capable of absorbing pressures for change without breakdown. Table 3 offers a measure of support for the hypothesized direct relationship between political development and the avoidance of breakdown in Latin America. In effect, the only three countries that were able to avoid coups during the 1943-67 period — Chile, Mexico, and Uruguay — were among the relatively more democratic and politically developed Latin American countries.[13] In fact, these three democratic regimes have lasted longer than any of Latin America's numerous authoritarian regimes. Table 3 also shows that these three countries were among the socioeconomically more developed countries, thereby suggesting a possible direct relationship between both political and socioeconomic development and the avoidance of coups in the Latin American context. While there is some evidence for this generalization,[14] the situation is in fact a good deal more complex.

On the basis of our data it appears that socioeconomic development is a necessary, but not a sufficient, condition for both the complete avoidance of *golpes* and democratic institutionalization over relatively long periods of time. However, the level of political institutionalization or stability is not wholly determined by the achieved level of socioeconomic development. That is, political structure manifests a degree of

[13] As suggested in Chapter 2, these countries may be considered relatively democratic in the Latin American context by virtue of their constitutional continuity, civilian rule, periodic changes of the chief executive by way of scheduled elections, and the fact that they show a measure of respect for individual freedoms during all but the most serious periods of crisis.

[14] According to Needler, there is a positive statistical relationship between political development, as measured by both the observance of constitutional norms and popular participation in politics, and economic development in Latin America. See Needler, "Case of Latin America," p. 895.

independence from the socioeconomic dimension. These generalizations are exemplified by the experiences of Argentina and Nicaragua during the 1943-67 period. Argentina, the most socioeconomically developed Latin American country according to Table 3, was also one of the least stable politically. Conversely, underdeveloped Nicaragua suffered only one coup during the post-war era. These exceptional cases suggest the need to transcend socioeconomic development and political development as isolated concepts if we are to arrive at a fuller comprehension of political institutionalization or stability in Latin America since World War II.

The concept of balanced sociopolitical development, briefly introduced in Chapter 2, can be used to transcend the limitations alluded to above. Political stability in Latin America is best understood as a product of the congruity or "fit" between political and socioeconomic structures. Thus the low frequency of *golpes* in Nicaragua during the 1943-67 time period can be understood as the product of a relatively high level of synchronization between its politically underdeveloped, authoritarian regime and its low level of socioeconomic development. That is, political equilibrium in Nicaragua has been approximated by virtue of the rather harmonious imposition of a patrimonial, quasi-monarchical regime on a highly personalistic and familistic political culture that is typical of Latin American countries with a relatively low level of socioeconomic development. By way of contrast, the attempt to impose highly complex democratic forms in a socioeconomically underdeveloped context produces a high degree of incongruity or imbalance which results in the pathology of democracy syndrome — the frequent, coup-studded alternation of weak democratic and authoritarian regimes. In light of the equilibrium framework presented in Chapter 2, one can say that the attempt to impose democratic forms in a context of relative socioeconomic underdevelopment results in disruptive increases in participation that are not consolidated effectively by corresponding adjustments in political organization. Thus gains in political development are not consolidated, and political breakdown is likely to become a recurrent phenomenon. In effect, and as suggested by cases like Nicaragua under the Somozas, relatively long-lasting regimes in the socioeconomically less developed Latin American countries have been likely to assume a relatively underdeveloped, patrimonial-authoritarian complexion.

One can also gain an insight into the perplexing instability of post-Perón Argentina by reference to the notion of balanced sociopolitical development. Argentina since Perón has suffered from a conspicuous political "lag" of sorts; that is, increases in political participation spawned by a relatively high level of socioeconomic development have not been accompanied by adjustments in political organization that would allow for effective coordination of the increases in activity, and frequent coups have occurred as a result. From a slightly different perspective, one might view the high coup frequency of post-Perón Argentina as a product of authoritarian attempts to demobilize political actors in a society with the high levels of social mobilization and labor activism that typify societies with a relatively high level of socioeconomic development. More will be said about the Argentine case later in the chapter.

In summary, neither political development nor socioeconomic development standing in isolation is sufficient to a full understanding of political institutionalization or stability in the Latin American context. In particular, while the data in Table 3 suggest that a high level of socioeconomic development is a necessary condition for the institutionalization of democratic regimes and political stability over long periods of time, it is not a sufficient condition. Quite simply, political structures exhibit a measure of autonomy from the socioeconomic dimension. This matter is taken up in the following section.

Political Structure and Coup d'État

Strong, flexible civilian political structures are an important factor making for political stability. In this respect, the emergence of a strong party system is a very important factor in reducing the propensity for coups to occur in the long run. In support of this generalization, we should note that Chile, Mexico, and Uruguay — the only three Latin American countries that were able to avoid coups completely during the post-war period — have had strong party systems. In addition, when compared with all other regimes in the Latin American setting, these regimes that have had strong party systems have lasted for the longest periods of time without suffering breakdown.

As noted in Chapter 2, the presence of strong parties is characteristic of relatively high levels of political development and is inversely related to the frequency of coups. We argued then that a developed party system was required to achieve high levels of political participation because a prime function of political parties is to mobilize the civilian population for the purpose of determining and/or supporting governments. Also, from the organizational standpoint, a party system is relatively developed in that it is characterized by greater organizational complexity than, for example, interest groups. That is, in contrast to the latter, party systems aggregate or coordinate numerous interests in order to form and support governments. Therefore, there are two reasons why a strong party system inhibits coups d'état. First, as one of the parties' specialized functions is to choose the chief executive, the military will not be called upon to fulfill this function. Second, strong parties will rally sufficient popular support so that governments will not be faced with frequent crises of legitimacy. As suggested earlier, military intervention under conditions of high civilian participation in the party system is discouraged because of the perceived likelihood that intervention under these conditions would be ineffective and that it might even lead to civil war. In other words, under conditions of high civilian participation and acute polarization in the party system military intervention tends to alienate just as much support as it could possibly hope to gain. In addition, under conditions of high civilian participation in the party system majoritarian forces are likely to seek power through elections. These factors appear, for example, to be discouraging military intervention in the current Chilean situation. They also discouraged intervention in Colombia under crisis conditions for many years until the combination of high levels of civilian violence and a continuistic attempt finally triggered the 1953 *golpe*.

Although it can be argued that a minimum level of socioeconomic development is necessary for the emergence of a strong party system, particularly in a nontotalitarian context, the relationship that exists between the strength of party systems and levels of socioeconomic development is quite complex. While those Latin American countries that currently possess relatively strong party systems are to be found in the group of relatively developed countries in Table 3, there are other countries like Argentina in this group in which the party system is very weak. This fact suggests that there are factors affecting party strength that are not wholly determined by levels of socioeconomic development. Thus, contrary to the implications of the static socioeconomic approach to the study of coups, high levels of socioeconomic development are not a sufficient condition for the existence of a strong party system. One must also consider other factors which are not strictly "tied" to achieved levels of socioeconomic development. In this section we will analyze some general characteristics of a strong party system as a prelude to consideration of some of the "untied" factors in the following section. In so doing we will be specifying some requirements for political party system effectiveness in the Latin American context.

First, a strong party system is characterized by the predominance of a relatively small number of mass-based parties that represent groups from various social strata. This requirement is logical enough, as only a small number of mass-based parties can be effectively accommodated by a single population. In the absence of a small number of these parties, government finds it very difficult to aggregate narrow interests effectively, and escalated political conflict, low levels of legitimacy, and instability tend to prevail. General support for these comments can be drawn from Banks and Textor's *Cross-Polity Survey,* which reports a strong positive relationship between political stability and the existence of few party structures.[15] The Latin American experience during the 1943-67 period suggests that the absence of coups is not determined so much by the number of parties per se but by the presence of a small number of mass-based parties enjoying significant civilian participation. In effect, the three countries that did not experience *golpes* during the time period in question — Mexico, Uruguay, and Chile — had mass-based one-party, two-party, and multi-party systems, respectively. By way of contrast, as previously discussed, authoritarian regimes which were highly prone toward *golpes* were generally characterized by an absence of mass-based party support. As a rule these regimes either banned political party activity or did not concentrate their efforts on the development of official mass-based parties.

Another characteristic of strong party systems in Latin America is their ability to enforce scheduled changes in the country's chief executive. As Latin American countries with strong party systems tend to manifest the prevalence of a relatively democratic ethos, it is hardly surprising that they are able to prevent *continuismo.* However, in this context it is necessary to distinguish the "*continuismo*" of the ruling party from that of the individual leader because there are instances in which presidents have been changed by way of intraparty, rather than interparty, elections. In short, Latin America's strong party systems are effective in preventing the *continuismo* of the individual leader but not necessarily that of the party. (Of course, the exception to our comments is the recent and unique case of totalitarian Cuba. For an analysis of the coup propensity in totalitarian regimes see Chapter 2.)

These brief preliminary comments describe some of the more important characteristics of effective party systems in the Latin American context. The importance of a strong party system from the viewpoint of achieving political stability can be exemplified by contrasting party systems in four Latin American countries — Argentina, Colombia, Cuba

[15] Arthur S. Banks and Robert B. Textor, *A Cross-Polity Survey* (Cambridge, Mass., 1963).

(before Castro), and Mexico. In selecting these countries for discussion we attempted to locate some examples whose coup frequency deviates from what one would expect if stability were a simple function of achieved levels of socioeconomic development. In so doing, the importance of strong party structures for stability as a factor not wholly tied to achieved levels of socioeconomic development should become clear.

First of all, both Argentina and pre-Castro Cuba are cases of political "lag." That is, their political institutions functioned less effectively than one would have expected on the basis of their relatively favorable socioeconomic ranking. Although Argentina is the most socioeconomically developed country in Latin America, Table 3 shows that in terms of coups it has experienced as much political instability as has the least developed country, Haiti. Cuba, too, has had relatively more political instability than have the other countries toward the top of the listing of the more developed countries. The political lag of both countries is understandable, however, in view of the fact that neither was able to institutionalize a strong party system capable of aggregating mass support and preventing *continuismo*.

The nonaggregative character of Argentine parties became all too apparent during the 1930s. During this period the mobilization of the rural population and its migration into urban centers was high. The predominantly rural and lower class background of the migrants contributed to their alienation from the existing political parties, which were largely urban and whose support did not extend substantially into the ranks of the lower classes. These parties were unable to gain the loyalty of the migrants, whose alienation from the parties facilitated Juan Perón's rise to power in the mid-1940s. As suggested by Di Tella, the recently arrived and still unincorporated urban masses were fertile material for Perón's demagogic talents.[16] Yet Perón failed to convert the mass support of his *descamisados* into an effective political party organization. Rather, his regime largely corresponds to the authoritarian type discussed in Chapter 2. Perón's regime reflected the corporate state pattern common to Europe's quasi-fascist experiments, especially those of Spain's Primo de Rivera and Francisco Franco.[17] Typical

[16] Di Tella, *Sistema Político Argentino*.

[17] Perón was greatly influenced by the example of these regimes. See Arthur P. Whitaker, *Argentina* (Englewood Cliffs, N.J., 1964), especially chap. 6. For an interesting discussion of the corporate pattern in Latin America, see Kalman H. Silvert, ed., *Expectant Peoples: Nationalism and Development* (New York, 1963), pp. 359-361. For a discussion of Brazilian corporatism, see Schmitter, *Interest Conflict, passim*.

of corporate regimes is the reliance on personal charisma and interest group support, rather than political party organization. In Perón's case, labor, the military, the Catholic Church,[18] and emergent industrial interests provided the main bases of support. The important point here is that this corporatist pattern is inimical to the strength of political parties. When such a pattern was combined with his charismatic, authoritarian style — his preference for continuistic rule — there can be little wonder that Perón failed to forge a strong party organization. With his departure from the scene in 1955, the weakness of Argentine parties manifested itself in the continuing alienation of labor and fragmentation of parties. Not only was labor isolated from the party system. The excessive plurality of parties did not permit the existence of governments with solid party support.[19] Argentina's high coup frequency during the post-war period was in part a consequence of this situation.

Although the Cuban situation prior to Castro differs from that prevailing in Argentina in certain respects, especially in their differing levels of social mobilization, they are similar in that in both cases weak parties encouraged armed intervention in the political process. Prior to Castro, the political history of twentieth-century Cuba was characterized by the cyclical alternation of weak civilian "party rule" with authoritarian regimes. Both types of regimes were characterized by a tendency toward *continuismo*. Typically, the parties lacked sustained support among the various sectors of the population. The situation was characterized by the appearance of what Cubans call *partidos de bolsillo,* or "pocket" parties, which were organized in an ad hoc fashion by individual leaders with a view to upcoming elections. Having served their purpose as electoral vehicles, the *partidos de bolsillo* would often disintegrate for all intents and purposes when the elections were over.[20] The Cuban party system was weakened by the absence of traditionalized, enduring parties. Twice in recent history (in 1933 and 1959) all pre-existing political parties virtually collapsed with the intervention of

[18] Although the Church and its advocates are at great pains to distinguish Catholic corporate theory from that espoused by some European dictators prior to World War II, there are some similarities between Catholic and quasi-fascist corporatism. In this respect, there are grounds for tracing Latin American corporatism to Catholic thought. For the origins of corporatist thinking in the social philosophy of the Catholic Church, see Edward J. Williams, *Latin American Christian Democratic Parties* (Knoxville, Tenn., 1967), pp. 118-122, 232-237.

[19] According to Snow, over fifty parties participated in national elections during the post-Perón period. See Peter G. Snow, "Parties and Politics in Argentina: The Elections of 1962 and 1963," *Midwest Journal of Political Science,* 9 (1965), 1-36.

[20] See Calixto Masó Vázquez, *Historia de Cuba* (Caracas, 1963-67).

armed force. In both instances, government fell into the hands of groups staffed by men in their twenties, who had not been socialized into the existing parties. In sum, in Cuba as in Argentina, parties lacking in broad support and unable to prevent the *continuismo* of strong leaders have been conducive to political instability and breakdown.

In contrast to the Argentine and pre-Castro Cuban cases, both Mexico and Colombia have been characterized by strong party systems. If anything, their ranking in Table 3, when compared with their records of political stability, suggests that their political institutions were somewhat more effective than one might expect if stability were a simple function of achieved levels of socioeconomic development. As shown by Table 3, Mexico was considerably less developed socioeconomically than were the only other two countries that did not have coups during the period investigated, Uruguay and Chile. Also, Mexico was the only country among those in the second half of the more developed grouping that was able to avoid breakdown. While Colombia experienced a coup frequency only slightly lower than the average for its grouping during the 1943-67 period, the comparative strength of its civilian political institutions becomes more evident if we broaden our historical perspective a bit. In fact, since 1901 Colombia has had only two *golpes,* a record comparable only to those of Uruguay and Chile, the most socioeconomically advanced and politically stable countries in the area. The two *golpes* suffered by Colombia in the 1950s represent a partial weakening of the country's party system as a result of the social changes that are currently being felt in the society. Still, Colombia's twentieth-century history on the whole presents a case of virtually uninterrupted civilian rule.

In Mexico, a modified one-party system emerged from the Revolution of 1910, after almost two decades of disorder and violence. For all intents and purposes, the *Partido Revolucionario Institucional* (PRI) is Mexico's "official" party.[21] The party has been quite successful in aggregating the diverse interests of many sectors in the population. The formal affiliation of agricultural, labor, and various other interest groups with the PRI offers evidence of the party's success in institutionalizing the aggregative function. Moreover, as beneficiary of the symbols of the Revolution, the PRI has enjoyed the traditional support of the majority of politically aware Mexicans. Finally, the party has institutionalized a stable mechanism for the transfer of the presidency from one individual to another on a noncontinuistic basis. As already suggested, given the prevalence of a formal democratic ideology among most of Latin

[21] For a good general discussion of the PRI, see Scott, *Mexican Government.*

America's ruling parties, strong parties and *continuismo* of the leader are inversely related in the area. While it is true that in Mexico there is little differentiation between the PRI and the formal structures of the state — the state and the official party are fused by and large — no president is allowed to remain in office beyond the six-year term specified in the constitution.[22] In other words, the Mexican political system is characterized by the "*continuismo*" of the party as opposed to that of the individual leader. Still, Mexico qualifies as a relatively democratic country in the Latin American context: some opposition is allowed; a measure of intraparty competition is present; and the individual freedoms of the citizenry are at least partially respected. In sum, the perfect record of political stability achieved by the Mexican PRI as indicated by the absence of *golpes* makes it exemplary of the stabilizing influence of a strong party system.

Colombia also is characterized by a relatively strong party system, although it has begun to show some signs of weakening over the last two decades. The overall strength of Colombia's parties is reflected in the country's record of civilian rule and infrequency of coups during this century. Since 1901, this record was broken only between 1953 and 1957, by the military dictatorship of Rojas Pinilla. The country's well-established two-party system has endured since the early post-independence period. Both the Conservative and Liberal parties have been fairly adept at aggregating mass support, as is evidenced by the fact that both parties have encompassed large numbers of people from all social classes, including the rural masses.[23] Moreover, both have enjoyed the support provided by the existence of strong traditional identifications on the part of their respective followings. In contrast to what happened in Cuba after Batista's 1933 coup and Castro's 1959 revolution, Colombia's traditional parties were able to ride out armed intervention and return to power. In fact, given the high levels of violence during the five years prior to the *golpe* of 1953, it is amazing that Colombian parties did not utterly collapse when Rojas took over.[24] Finally, the strength and flexibility of the Colombian party system is

[22] Viable one-party states are an exception to the general comments presented in the previous chapter, where the fusion of political and formal governmental spheres was related to political breakdown. While a good general rule for Latin America, viable one-party states, whether communist or (like Mexico) noncommunist, constitute an important exception. More will be said on this point in Chapter 6.

[23] See Orlando Fals-Borda, *Peasant Society in the Colombian Andes: A Sociological Study of Saucío* (Gainesville, Fla., 1955).

[24] For a comprehensive study of Colombia's infamous time of *violencia*, see Germán Guzmán Campos, Orlando Fals-Borda, and Eduardo Umaña Luna, *La*

exemplified by the infrequency of *continuismo* among party leadership and by the frequent willingness of the two parties to form coalition governments when necessary to prevent breakdowns. Similar to the case of Mexico, *continuismo* has been avoided in Colombia largely through intraparty competition for the presidency. Prior to the formation of the *Frente Nacional* in 1958, there were only two instances in which the party controlling the presidency changed — 1930 and 1946 — creating a partially democratic situation in which there was virtual one-party control during lengthy periods. Unlike the Mexican case, however, the opposition party has frequently participated in coalitions with the ruling party because both Colombian parties always had substantial support. The ruling party has often had to share government positions with the opposition in order to prevent the outbreak of violence. Such "wisdom" could not have been effected if the party organization had not been strong and adaptable.

In summary, a strong party system is an important factor inhibiting political breakdown. As shown by Table 3, the two countries suffering from a political lag, Argentina and pre-Castro Cuba, experienced more instability during the 1943-67 period than did the two countries with relatively effective political parties, Mexico and Colombia. During this span of time, the four countries can be ranked for political stability as follows:

1. Mexico — perfect record
2. Colombia — two coups
3. Cuba — two coups; one revolution
4. Argentina — seven coups

If political instability were strictly tied to fixed levels of socioeconomic development, as suggested by static analysis, one would expect a very different ranking:

1. Argentina
2. Cuba
3. Mexico
4. Colombia

This nearly complete inversion of the true picture can only mean that political instability is not completely tied to levels of socioeconomic de-

Violencia en Colombia: Estudio de un Proceso Social (Bogotá, 1964). Actually, the intensity of *la violencia* was in part a consequence of the ability of Colombia's two parties to mobilize the rural lower classes. As we shall see in the next section, strong party identifications may exhibit some destabilizing characteristics under certain conditions.

velopment. Political variables enjoy a certain independence of levels of development. This helps account for the fact that the two more socio-economically developed countries, Argentina and Cuba, have had greater political instability than less developed Mexico and Colombia. As we have seen, the more socioeconomically developed countries are the ones suffering from a destabilizing political lag.

In line with this discussion, the strength of the party system is not completely determined by levels of socioeconomic development. There are a number of factors bearing upon the emergence and maintenance of strong parties which are not tied to socioeconomic variables in a rigorous fashion. Some of these factors are discussed in the following section.

Factors Affecting the Strength of Party Systems

In exploring the nature of effective Latin American party systems we have attempted to specify a number of factors conducive to the emergence and maintenance of strong parties throughout the area. This amounts to a search for answers to the general question of why some countries have a strong party system while others do not. While much more comparative work on Latin American party systems is needed, we find three variables that might enable one to offer some tentative answers to this question. Specifically, the following three factors appear useful in accounting for the existence of strong party systems:

1. The type of violence employed to effect socioeconomic change during transitional periods
2. The nature of popular identification with the parties
3. The socioeconomic background of party elites

In the following discussion of these factors it will become clear that they are not strictly determined by levels of socioeconomic development. In this sense, our remarks depart from and qualify the main implication of static socioeconomic analysis: that political instability and coups d'état can be understood solely in terms of attained levels of socioeconomic development.

Violence employed to bring about socioeconomic change during transitional periods in Latin America normally assumes one of two different forms: (1) revolutions, and (2) *golpes* that manifest reformist tendencies. The latter type has, of course, been a good deal more frequent than the former, as there have been only three social revolutions in Latin America during this century: Mexico (1910), Bolivia (1952), and Cuba (1959). Although our findings are not conclusive, it appears that revolutions have produced stronger political parties than have the "progressive" coups. In this sense, the character of the violence employed in the process of producing socioeconomic change appears to be a variable governing the probability that a strong party system will emerge.

Coups that result in a measure of reform may produce relatively democratic regimes generally favorable to party activity, or they may yield populistic authoritarian regimes that discourage party activity. Guatemala in 1944 and Venezuela in 1945 had "progressive" coups which fit the former pattern, while Vargas' *Estado Nôvo* and Perón's Argentine regime are examples of the populistic authoritarian type of regime.[25] In neither case, however, did effective parties emerge. Reformist democratic regimes were usually produced by coups in which a recently established party formed a coalition with junior army officers against a right-wing authoritarian regime. These reformist regimes, typically left-wing in character, were prone to removal by subsequent *golpes* executed by their former military allies; and these *golpes* were usually not long in coming. The length of time between the progressive coup and the second one, which was normally reactionary in character, has varied from a minimum of less than one year (Cuba, 1933), to a maximum of ten years (Guatemala, 1944-54).[26] Whatever the exact timing, the relatively short duration of these regimes indicates that the coups were not conducive to the establishment of strong, effective political parties capable of remaining in power for more than a short period.

While the populistic authoritarian regimes remained in power for longer periods than the coup-emergent democratic reformers, such regimes were not markedly more successful in creating strong parties. As authoritarian leaders, Vargas and Perón practiced *continuismo*, and they did not devote much energy to the establishment of political parties.[27] Both preferred to rely on the corporate state pattern, in which

[25] This area of terminology is full of semantic difficulties because the regimes of Perón and Vargas manifested certain corporatist and fascist dimensions. Nonetheless, they also had a prominent leftist dimension: they organized the urban working classes while promoting their welfare. For this reason, the term populistic or "leftist" authoritarian clarifies their nature, in our opinion. The more recent term, Nasserist, could also be applied to them.

[26] The exception among our sampled coups is the progressive Venezuelan *golpe* of January, 1958. Of all the reformist *golpes* listed in Table 1, only this one was not followed by another coup.

[27] Vargas' attention to cultivation of his *Partido Trabalhista Brasileiro* began during his "democratic" era, after the demise of the *Estado Nôvo*. Perón always relied primarily on his labor union support.

support is based largely upon personal charisma and interest groups, such as labor and the military. Coups ended the authoritarian regimes of both men, and *golpes* have recurred subsequently in both Brazil and Argentina. In retrospect, the dictators Vargas and Perón appear to have had ideal opportunities for establishing strong parties. Both appear to have had substantial backing at one time or another from most key groups in their countries. Furthermore, the fact that they mobilized new groups into the polity could have resulted in the establishment of strong party identity. Their failure to form such parties, on the other hand, has contributed to the institutional weakness and fragmentation that continues to characterize both Brazil and Argentina down to the present.

Revolutions, unlike the reform regimes installed by coups, have had greater potential for producing strong political parties. As already described, the Mexican Revolution resulted in the establishment of the PRI, one of the strongest parties in all of Latin America. While it is still too soon to assess properly Castro's *Partido Comunista de Cuba* (PCC), which was only established in 1965, its birth seems to indicate a growing tendency toward institutionalization of the Revolution by way of establishing a strong party structure. The intensive ideological indoctrination characteristic of totalitarian regimes should help to strengthen the party, while if the cases of Lenin and Mao are any indication, the *continuismo* of a strong personality need not be highly dysfunctional to party strength in communist systems, as it would be in nontotalitarian ones. Quite simply, dictatorship is legitimized by communist ideology. Also, if the Committees for Defense of the Revolution, which are presently outside the party, are incorporated into the PCC, its strength and durability would be greatly increased. It appears, then, that the Cuban Revolution may result in the production of a strong party organization. Finally, only in the case of Bolivia did social revolution fail to produce a party strong enough to resist the subsequent recurrence of coups d'état. The country's revolutionary party, the *Movimiento Nacionalista Revolucionario* (MNR), was banished in the wake of the 1964 *golpe* that took place in response to a continuistic attempt by President Víctor Paz Estenssoro.[28] However, if we take into consideration that the MNR experiment took place in a society with very low levels of socioeconomic development, the unprecedented

[28] For the emergence and development of the MNR, see Robert J. Alexander, *The Bolivian National Revolution* (New Brunswick, N.J., 1958). For an excellent discussion on the failure of the Bolivian revolution, see Huntington, *Political Order*, pp. 325-334. As noted, the ability to prevent *continuismo* of the leader is a hallmark of party strength in nontotalitarian Latin American societies.

twelve years of civilian party rule for Bolivia does indicate a measure of party strength. In any case, this twelve-year period was longer than the time which generally has been allowed to democratic reformist regimes produced by *golpes*.

In sum, revolutions seem a more fruitful potential source of strong party organizations than do reformist coups, but we must still ask why this is so. First of all, revolutions, unlike reform *golpes,* produce extensive readjustments of the pre-existing socioeconomic and political orders. In the process, violence directed at the traditional centers of power is ordinarily prolonged and intense. Potential and actual opposition to the forces of the revolution can, in other words, be minimized by the simple expedient of physical elimination. If such "clearing of the air" proceeds far enough, the possibilities governing the emergence of a strong, integrating political party will be enhanced. In this context, the destruction of the military that accompanies the revolutionary process favors the growth of a strong party by removing the single most important potential source of opposition.[29] Actually, as revolutions seek the decimation of the armed forces and mobilize and politicize the civilian population, they are likely to form strong parties.

Looked at from a slightly different perspective, the interclass conflict characteristic of transitional politics is maximized in the revolutionary situation. The high levels of tension and apocalyptic expectations that materialize in this situation can be employed to forge the beginnings of a strong political party. In effect, the association of the momentous events of a revolution with a particular party organization results in that structure becoming the beneficiary of powerful, quasi-religious identifications. In following years, the revolutionary party may rely heavily on its position as keeper of the revolutionary myths. By manipulating these sacred symbols, the party finds it easier to obtain substantial support. It is a strong party in part by virtue of the traditionalization of this symbolism, which does not appear to accrue with equal intensity to reform parties that have achieved power through coup d'état. In fact, the most powerful or functional of myths is forged only in the crucible of social revolution. Symbols surrounding coups are less powerful for having been shaped in less traumatic circumstances.

There are other reasons why coups seldom produce strong parties. As mentioned in Chapter 4, coup-emergent regimes led by reformist parties find it exceedingly difficult to implement an aggregative policy

[29] The armed forces were completely destroyed in both the Mexican and Cuban revolutions; they were seriously crippled in the immediate aftermath of the Bolivian revolution, though they recovered in later years. See Lieuwen, *Arms and Politics,* p. 80.

capable of neutralizing anti-establishment forces while protecting military corporate interests at the same time. In addition, the coup-emergent authoritarian regime which is led by military men or is dependent on them for its prime base of support will find it exceedingly difficult to institutionalize a strong party system by virtue of the character of its military leadership and/or support. First, military training fosters authoritarian orientations which create negative attitudes toward political bargaining. The military often views political deals as corrupt. Consequently, it often tends to bypass the professional politician in favor of a technocratic approach toward problem-solving, as happened in Brazil immediately after the 1964 *golpe*. If we add to this factor the fact that the military often intervenes in the political process in response to the alleged corruption of civilian institutions, it becomes clear that military prejudices are reinforced. Second, Latin American coup-emergent military regimes often rationalize their rule as a necessary, albeit transitory, remedy for the weakness of civilian political institutions — the pathology of democracy syndrome. Under these "exceptional" circumstances governments are not likely to establish long-lasting institutions. The tendency for coup-emergent authoritarian regimes to rely heavily on the military for support creates a tendency to downplay the importance of civilian support. At the same time, these regimes face a basic dilemma regarding their support within the armed forces. If they formally extend to the military the legal right to select the president — a course of action that is hardly likely in view of the philosophical resistance to legitimizing the principle of naked force — then the principle of military subordination to the executive tends to be eroded. Given the difficulties inherent in this option, coup-emergent authoritarian regimes often adopt a continuistic orientation, but this "solution" is also fraught with destabilizing consequences because the military must often step in to dismantle such regimes in the absence of regularized legal procedures allowing for executive succession! Finally, if the coup-emergent regime were to attempt to form a political party, there is always the danger that the boundaries between the military and political organizations might break down, thereby increasing the probability of eroding military discipline and cohesion. As noted in Chapter 4, coup-emergent regimes have often found it difficult to resist this politicization of the military with all of its destabilizing consequences.[30]

In conclusion, while there are several factors that tend to strengthen revolutionary parties, there are also certain characteristics of regimes

[30] In this sense see Stepan, *Military in Politics.*

produced by *golpes* that tend to weaken party structure. On the whole, revolution as a mechanism for inducing socioeconomic change during transitional periods tends to foster the growth of effective political parties more so than the reformist *golpe*. Moreover, it should be mentioned that the mechanism employed to effect socioeconomic change is not strictly determined by pre-existing levels of socioeconomic development, as the static socioeconomic perspective would have us believe. This is particularly evident if one compares, for example, the widely different levels of development in Cuba and Bolivia at the time of their respective revolutions. As a variable positively related to the subsequent strength of political parties, the occurrence of revolutions is not closely bound to given levels of socioeconomic development. As strong parties discourage coups, one can say by extension that the frequency of coups is not strictly bound by development levels either.

There are two other factors which contribute to party strength and which manifest a measure of independence from levels of socioeconomic development. First, one must consider the nature of party identifications among the population. In general terms, traditional party identifications, handed down from one generation to succeeding ones, provide parties with a relatively strong and durable base of support. By its very nature, then, traditional or inherited identification tends to strengthen parties. In terms of its scope or frequency among the population, parties suffering from low levels of traditional identification tend to be weak, by virtue of the lack of commitment implied by the low levels of inherited identification. On the other hand, if traditional party identifications are so extensive that uncommitted groups are insignificant, then the tendencies toward extreme partisanship, political instability, and the subsequent weakness of the party system will be encouraged in the long run because the parties will have little incentive to follow a middle-of-the-road course in order to obtain the support of the uncommitted.[31] It is only when inherited identifications are moderately high that the

[31] The logic of this process is well explained in Anthony Downs, *An Economic Theory of Democracy* (New York, 1957). These comments, of course, are restricted to systems where some semblance of political competition exists. By way of example, it is interesting to note that Colombia at times has had to cope with the problem of excessive party identification. Indeed, this was one of the factors that encouraged *la violencia* in the 1940s and early 1950s and eventually helped to trigger the 1953 coup that weakened the party system somewhat. Still, the effects of party identification in Colombia have had a stabilizing influence, as the country has suffered only two coups since 1901. In effect, the relatively high resilience of the Colombian party system was again demonstrated in 1958 with the creation of the interparty coalition that has ruled to the present day. For a detailed discussion, see Mauricio Solaún, "Political Violence in Colombia," unpub. diss., University of Chicago, 1971.

ideal of long-run equilibrium is approximated. Under these circumstances, the parties enjoy substantial traditional support, while the existence of still uncommitted groups encourages them to follow moderate policies for the purpose of gaining still more support.

Moderately high levels of inherited party identification favor the presence of a strong party system. Moreover, the level of traditional identification is not strictly determined by levels of socioeconomic development, as can be verified by a brief comparison of France and the United States. Both have relatively high levels of development, while the former does not enjoy the moderately high levels of inherited party identification found in the latter. In France, low levels of traditional party identification have tended to weaken the parties while encouraging political instability.[32]

As far as Latin America is concerned, several secondary sources have implied the weakness of traditional party identifications in many countries.[33] This is certainly plausible in view of the high party mortality rate prevalent throughout much of the area. In some instances, such as in Cuba in 1933 and 1959, the perishability of Latin American parties has been linked to generational change. This implies that there are problems in transmitting party identifications from one generation to the next. Weak socialization processes reduce the likelihood of establishing inherited party identifications. Conversely, the attainment of moderately high levels of traditional party identification tends to strengthen the party system, thereby reducing the tendency toward political instability and coups d'état. In this sense, there are clearly some traditional factors that serve to stabilize "modern" societies.[34] In Latin America, however, traditional party identifications appear generally weak, a fact that would help to account for its relatively high levels of political instability and coups d'état.

There is a third and final factor affecting the strength of party systems which is not wholly determined by levels of socioeconomic development: the socioeconomic background of party elites. The proposition here is that a sharp separation of socioeconomic and party elites weakens the

---

[32] See Philip E. Converse and Georges Dupeux, "Politicization of the Electorate in France and the United States," in *Elections and the Political Order,* ed. Angus Campbell *et al.* (New York, 1966), pp. 269-291.

[33] See, for instance, Russell H. Fitzgibbon, "Party Potpourri in Latin America," *Western Political Quarterly,* 10 (1957), 3-22.

[34] All too often the ideal-type dichotomy established between "tradition" and "modernity" is overdone. For a general discussion, see Joseph R. Gusfield, "Tradition and Modernity: Misplaced Polarities in the Study of Social Change," *American Journal of Sociology,* 72 (1967), 351-362.

party system, thereby encouraging coups d'état. Conversely, if the two elites overlap to a degree, the party system is likely to be strengthened and political instability to decrease. There are a number of factors which can help us to understand the logic behind this double-barreled proposition. But before taking them up, a few brief comments must be made on the nature of party elites in Latin America, a much misunderstood phenomenon.

It is widely believed that Latin American countries are run by an "oligarchy" or "power elite." In this view, a small, homogeneous, and cohesive group of men have inherited monopolistic power over both the political and economic realms; and this power is invariably exercised for their own exclusive benefit, at the expense of others. The belief in the existence of this group is prevalent not only among North Americans,[35] who may be inclined to draw comparisons on the basis of C. Wright Mills' "power elite," but among Latin Americans as well.[36] The point to be emphasized, however, is that these beliefs are somewhat exaggerated. While there are fewer participants and countervailing groups in Latin America than there are, for example, in the United States, there is evidence which suggests that *la oligarquía* is not nearly as homogeneous or ascriptive as popular opinion would lead one to believe. Indeed, there appears to be a traditional separation between political party elites on one hand and the socioeconomic establishment on the other, in many Latin American countries. In effect, several studies have indicated the predominantly middle class background of Latin American political elites.[37] Many political leaders in the area have even worked their way up from lower class origins.[38]

The sharp segregation of political and socioeconomic elites provides fertile ground for the occurrence of *golpes de estado*. First of all, this segregation tends to reduce communication and mutual understanding

[35] See Almond and Powell, *Comparative Politics,* p. 202, and Huntington, *Political Order,* p. 201.

[36] For some pertinent comments, see François Bourricaud, "El Ocaso de las Oligarquías y la Sobrevivencia del Hombre Oligárquico," *Aportes,* Apr., 1967, pp. 4-23.

[37] For Argentina, see de Imaz, *Los que Mandan;* for pre-Castro Cuba, see Solaún, "Democracia en Cuba," and Maurice Zeitlin, "Los Determinantes Sociales de la Democracia Política en Chile," *Revista Latinoamericana de Sociología,* 2 (1966), 223-236; for Peru, see Bourricaud, *Oligarquía en el Perú,* pp. 13-54; for Venezuela, see Gary Hoskin, "Las Pautas del Poder y de la Política en una Ciudad Venezolana: Su Influencia en el Desarrollo de San Cristóbal," *Razón y Fábula,* 16 (1969), 97-116.

[38] See the interesting discussion by Needler, *Political Development in Latin America,* pp. 102-115.

between elites. Under these circumstances, party leaders will try to enhance their support by advocating the cause of redistributionist measures unacceptable to the socioeconomic elite. At times, too, the socioeconomic elite may misperceive the reformist intentions of the party as being more threatening than they really are. At any rate, escalated interclass conflict — a frequent source of coups in the area — is a likely consequence in situations of acute elite bifurcation. This appears to have been a factor, for example, in the Peruvian and Venezuelan coups of 1948. If on the other hand there is some overlap between the elites, communication is enhanced, along with mutual cooperation. Greater aggregation of diverse points of view is facilitated, and the likelihood of interclass conflict will probably diminish as a result of the improved rapprochement.

The logic behind these propositions is relatively simple. In the absence of a degree of overlap between the socioeconomic and party elites, each will probably possess a very narrow conception of its own interests. Big businessmen seek to maximize their profits; large landowners, their acreage; politicians, their votes. In this situation, politicians will be most receptive to popular demands, given their desire for maximum support. The businessmen, following the maximum-profit criterion, will militantly oppose reformist tendencies involving such things as progressive taxation and redistribution of wealth, as will the large estate holders. The seeds of sharp interclass conflict are clearly present. With overlapping elites, on the other hand, the socioeconomic and party elites will gain an increased appreciation of each other's divergent needs. Politicians will become more sensitive to the "needs" of the established interests and less likely to manifest radical left-wing political styles. At the same time, members of the socioeconomic establishment active in the party will serve to "educate" the established interests as to the need for a measure of reform. In the final analysis, greater aggregation of the diverse interests of the elite and popular sectors can be achieved through common participation in political parties, and the pressures making for interclass conflict will be reduced. Party systems that have a measure of socioeconomic elite participation will tend to produce governments that are more effective than those that suffer from the sharp separation of elites. Pressures for coup d'état are reduced accordingly.

It might appear odd to suggest that socioeconomic elite participation in the parties reduces the likelihood of *golpes*. It might be argued, for example, that this participation militates against the promotion of socioeconomic reforms, which tend to reduce pressures working toward political breakdown. In this context, it must be admitted that the domination of party systems by the socioeconomic elite can transform them into narrow, highly partisan, and nonaggregative institutions. Still the complete absence of the elite from the parties serves to undermine the civic-mindedness of the upper class, which may therefore come to exert an "irresponsible" influence over the country's destiny, for which it cannot possibly be held politically accountable if it does not participate in the party cadres.[39] In other words, this isolation from the party system produces a situation in which the rich will not feel sufficiently committed to the country, and their actions may come to reflect this lack of commitment. If the American experience is any indication, direct participation in the party system by members of the socioeconomic elite promotes a sense of civic responsibility and institutional development, and it thereby enhances the probability of political stability. In Latin America, on the other hand, the excessive bifurcation or compartmentalization of the party and socioeconomic elites has militated against socioeconomic reforms, by virtue of its stultifying effects on those who control most of the essential material resources and by encouraging conservative *golpes*. In other words, socioeconomic reform and its subsequent salutary effects on political stability may be advanced by encouraging a degree of socioeconomic elite participation in the political parties.

The crucial question, of course, is how much participation? In precise terms, we cannot say what the "optimal composition" of party elites is. In this context each country must be treated separately. In general terms, however, we can suggest a few guidelines. First, socioeconomic elite participation in the party system must be adequate to prevent governments from espousing policies too radical for the elite to accept without feeling gravely threatened. At the same time, this participation must not become dominance, for then the party system would lose its ability to aggregate mass support, and the leavening necessary for the cultivation of the civic-minded sentiments that encourage flexibility vis-à-vis reform would be absent. Only when elements from the popular sector have a substantial measure of representation will salutary reform measures be likely to be implemented. Finally, a measure of participation by members of the socioeconomic elite in the political parties tends to strengthen the parties in yet another way: the political weight of the establishment added to the administrative skills that the elite possess

[39] This point has been suggested by Bourricaud, *Oligarquía en el Perú.*

cannot help but increase party effectiveness. By increasing party effectiveness in this way, the probability of coup activity is diminished.[40]

The preceding arguments pertaining to the background of Latin American party elites can be summarized in these terms. The party system can be strengthened and the frequency of *golpes* diminished if the socioeconomic elite will join with other social strata in manning the political parties. The probability of civilian rule is enhanced when there is a measure of overlap between the party and socioeconomic elites, as the establishment adopts the mode of seeking representation through civilian, as opposed to military, channels.

The relationship among party strength, political stability, and the overlap of party and socioeconomic elites can be illustrated by examples from both Colombia and pre-Castro Cuba. In Colombia, the strength of the party system and the political fabric as a whole has been enhanced by the overlap of elites. This overlap contributed to the survival of the party system and civilian rule through the years of the Great Depression and the transition toward greater working-class participation in the 1930s, when many other Latin American countries were suffering breakdown. The welfarist measures introduced at the time, which reduced interclass tensions and the coup pressures to which they give rise, were initiated by the Liberal party elite, which was well integrated with the socioeconomic establishment. As a matter of fact, the Liberals, the country's more progressive party, had relatively more members from the establishment than did the Conservatives. Apparently, participation by the socioeconomic elite had a liberalizing effect on the group as a whole.[41] This is precisely the point made earlier — a degree of overlap between party and socioeconomic elites does not necessarily block reform.

The opposite case is exemplified in pre-Castro Cuba. During the 1930s the country experienced a series of *golpes*. In this case, the young politicians seeking to ease the country through this transitional period by implementing reforms did not enjoy the fortifying effect that socioeconomic elite participation can lend to party organization. The most

[40] Low levels of administrative effectiveness of political parties is sometimes pointed to as a cause of coups in underdeveloped countries. See, for example, Lucian W. Pye, "Armies in Political Modernization."

[41] This finding is presented in the senior author's forthcoming study of Colombian political parties. In this context, it is enlightening to consider that the Liberals' ideology during the 1930s and 1940s was quite similar to that of the middle class, Aprista-type parties, such as Venezuela's AD and Peru's APRA, both of which were excluded from power in the 1940s by coups because of their "extremism."

important party of the time, the *Partido Revolucionario Cubano,* did not have a significant foothold in the establishment, and this is one reason why it was incapable of aggregating interests effectively during the transitional period.

Examples from other countries could also be mentioned. For instance, according to Imaz, all the leaders of the Argentine Radical party during the Peronist era were sons of nonestablishment immigrants![42] Moreover, the background of party elites — the presence of a measure of socioeconomic elite representation — is not strictly determined by levels of socioeconomic development, as static analysis would suggest. In Table 3 both Colombia and Argentina belong to the group of relatively developed countries, yet the latter suffered from the sharp bifurcation of elites while the former did not; and this factor might help to account in part for Colombia's superior record of political stability during the 1943-67 period. Argentina suffered seven *golpes;* Colombia had only two.

To recapitulate, we have discussed three different factors related to the strength of party systems and, by indirection, political stability which are not strictly determined by levels of socioeconomic development: revolution, traditional party identification, and a measure of participation by members of the socioeconomic establishment in the parties. The importance of these party-related factors is well exemplified by those countries which experienced substantial political instability, Argentina and pre-Castro Cuba. Neither had experienced a social revolution or a significant level of traditional identification with political parties. Moreover, both have been characterized by a more or less acute separation between socioeconomic and political elites. Based on these considerations, one would expect to find weak parties and relatively high levels of political instability in both countries. We have seen this to be the case. On the other hand, those countries which have achieved relatively high levels of political institutionalization despite lower levels of socioeconomic development, Mexico and Colombia, show themselves favorably with respect to at least two of the three variables related to party strength. Mexico underwent a social revolution and seems to enjoy moderately high levels of traditional identification with

---

[42] de Imaz, *Los que Mandan,* pp. 194-195. As suggested by a reading of de Imaz' tenth chapter, the beginning of Argentine militarism in the 1930s appears to have coincided with a process of increasing segregation between party and socioeconomic elites. The old leaders of the displaced Radical party, who had been closely tied to the socioeconomic establishment, were unable to pass this tradition on to the younger generation of leaders.

its official party. Although its effects have been mixed, Colombia also has had high levels of identification with its two parties. In addition, significant numbers from its socioeconomic elite have participated in both parties. Both countries, as we would expect on the basis of these comments, have had relatively strong, flexible party systems, and both have enjoyed relatively low levels of military intervention.

In this section and the one immediately preceding, we have emphasized certain factors relating to the strength of political structures which show a degree of independence from the level of socioeconomic development achieved by society. For this reason, it may be concluded that levels of achieved socioeconomic development do not wholly determine the frequency of coups. At the same time, this is not to deny the significant impact which achieved levels of socioeconomic development appear to exercise over the probability that coups will occur in any given society. It must be remembered that Latin America's less developed countries experienced twice as many coups between 1943 and 1967 as did its more developed countries. Even with respect to the factors discussed in this section, one can still detect a certain element of socioeconomic determinism. First, of the three social revolutions that were discussed, only in the case of the least developed country, Bolivia, was there an eventual return to the pattern of military intervention. Second, if we contrast those Latin American countries which enjoy a substantial degree of traditional identification with their parties, which for purposes of illustration can be evidenced by the long-term survival of a two-party system, it appears that those countries at higher levels of socioeconomic development tend to experience fewer *golpes*. Both Uruguay and Colombia manifest long-lived, two-party systems.[43] But the more developed country, Uruguay, has experienced no coups, while Colombia has had two coups between 1943 and 1967. Finally, although Colombia has had a significant degree of overlap between its socioeconomic and political elites, this has still not enabled it to overcome wholly the destabilizing consequences of what is still a comparatively low level of socioeconomic development.

For all of these reasons, one must conclude that if static approaches to the interpretation of coup activity in Latin America do not enable one to account fully for the frequency of coups in all societies, these approaches still give a good indication of what to expect. With qualifications, levels of achieved socioeconomic development remain an im-

[43] With Uruguay's recent economic and political difficulties, new party structures appear to have gained a foothold. Yet the recent presidential elections suggest that the two traditional parties are still quite strong.

portant conditioner of the frequency of coups. As indicated by the positioning of the coup-free countries in Table 3, relatively high levels of socioeconomic development appear to have been a necessary, though not sufficient, condition for the absence of coups d'état during the 1943-67 time period. Also, high levels of socioeconomic development were necessary for the institutionalization of relatively democratic, strong party systems in the Latin American context. As noted previously, and in comparison with all other regimes in the Latin American setting, these strong party systems have endured for the longest periods of time without experiencing breakdown.

Dynamic Analyses

In this section we will focus on the contribution of dynamic analyses of socioeconomic factors to an understanding of the observed high frequency of coups d'état in Latin America. Specifically, we will be dealing here with modes of analysis which emphasize short-run economic crises as well as those which stress the effects of rates of industrialization and urbanization over middle-term periods of time. In both cases we are interested in the consequences of socioeconomic change for the incidence of *golpes* in Latin American countries.

First of all, the variable consequences of short-run economic crises vis-à-vis *golpes* might lead one to the conclusion that such crises were neither a necessary nor sufficient condition for the occurrence of coups in Latin America. In some cases, economic crisis appears to have played a role in coups, as in Argentina in September, 1955, and in Brazil in 1964. In Argentina, an acute deterioration in the balance of trade and international monetary reserves preceded the *golpe*.[44] In Brazil, a slowdown in national production, an adverse balance of trade, and spiraling inflation figured significantly as factors leading to the military takeover in April, 1964.[45] In other cases, however, coups have occurred during periods of relative prosperity. For example, Batista's 1952 Cuban coup came after two years of unprecedented expansion in sugar production and national income.[46] In still other instances, such as the recent

[44] For specifics on the economic condition of Argentina during the years in question, see International Monetary Fund, *Annual Report, 1955* (Washington, D.C., 1955), p. 50, and *Annual Report, 1956* (Washington, D.C., 1956), pp. 53-54.

[45] See Skidmore, *Politics in Brazil.*

[46] For the economic data, see reports of pertinent years from the *Memoria del Banco Nacional de Cuba* (Havana). See also José A. Guerra, "La Industria Azucarera, 1932 a 1957," in *Siglo y Cuarto* (Havana, 1957), pp. 98-99.

Uruguayan situation, economic crisis has not resulted in coups.[47] Finally, there have been cases, such as that of Peru in 1968, where coups have taken place after the economic crisis has been overcome.[48] On the basis of these mixed findings it would appear that there is no consistent relationship between economic crisis on the one hand and military intervention on the other.

Still, economic crisis in the short run has frequently accompanied coups in Latin America.[49] In the words of Martin Needler, "... the overthrow of a government is more likely when economic conditions worsen."[50] Economic crises pose political problems that cannot be ignored in that they affect the relative distribution of power, profits, and costs among groups. In so doing, they tend to increase the level of conflict in society. Not only do they lead to the question of distributive justice among social classes — which one should bear the larger burden of the costs of crisis — but they can increase intraelite conflict as well, as evidenced in the confrontation of elites which characterized the Peruvian situation months prior to the 1968 *golpe*. Also, the military's corporate interest in maintaining adequate levels of material benefits may add to military-civilian tensions during these crisis situations. For all of these reasons, economic crises should be considered as an important factor that is capable of precipitating or triggering *golpes de estado*. In our opinion, whether or not a coup materializes in conjunction with such crises will depend on at least two things. First, the intensity of the economic crisis is an important variable, as suggested by the fact that few Latin American governments survived the Great Depression of the 1930s without breakdown. Second, the timing of the crisis is also important.[51] As discussed in the conclusion of Chapter 4, coups can be usefully viewed as the end result of a cumulative process. *Ceteris paribus,* the more numerous the precipitants present at any given time, the greater the likelihood of breakdown. In addition, and

[47] See Carlos Bañales Guimaraens, "Las Fuerzas Armadas en la Crisis Uruguaya," *Aportes,* July, 1968, pp. 26-57.

[48] See *Visión,* 35, no. 7 (1968), 18.

[49] See Warren Dean, "Latin American Golpes and Economic Fluctuations, 1823-1966," *Social Science Quarterly,* 51 (1970), 70-80.

[50] Needler, *Political Development in Latin America,* p. 62.

[51] According to Merkx, 88 percent of the Argentine rebellions between 1870 and 1966 occurred in a year of economic downturn and the first three years of contraction, thus lending support to "Davies' hypothesis that rebellions occur in the first part of an economic downturn." See Gilbert W. Merkx, "Recessions and Rebellions in Argentina" (MS, University of New Mexico, 1969), pp. 5, 11. See also James C. Davies, "Toward a Theory of Revolution," *American Sociological Review,* 27 (1962), 5-19.

as suggested by the contemporary Uruguayan case of economic crisis without breakdown, whether or not a *golpe* occurs will also depend on the presence of predisposing factors toward coups, such as the weakness of civilian political institutions. In this sense, an economic crisis poses a greater or lesser threat to stability depending upon its timing; that is, whether it occurs in conjunction with other factors that encourage *golpes*.

Turning now to an analysis of other socioeconomic factors, we related industrial and urban growth to the frequency of coups during the decade 1950-60 in order to determine the impact of longer-term socioeconomic changes on the frequency of Latin American *golpes*. With this particular mode of analysis, we are concerned with the impact of socioeconomic change over a middle-run duration of time.

As a first step, the countries in the area were ranked in terms of industrial growth rates, which were defined by the rate of growth of the labor force employed in manufacturing and construction. These industrial growth rates were then used for dividing the countries into three groups: those with relatively high growth rates; those with relatively low growth rates; and those in the middle range. Finally, the frequency of coups which occurred in each country during the years in question was added to the data on industrial growth rates. The results are presented in Table 5, along with further details on the procedure followed.

Urban growth rates, defined by the increase in the proportion of the population in towns of 2,000 or more inhabitants, were related to the frequency of coups, using the same general procedure. Table 6 presents the results, along with pertinent details.

Analysis of our data reveals the absence of statistically significant relationships between rates of urban and industrial change and coups in Latin America for the 1950-60 period. However, we find that the group of countries with high rates of industrial growth had a slightly lower tendency toward coups than those in the other two groups. Conversely, the group of countries with the highest urban growth rates had a slightly greater tendency toward coups in comparison with the other two groups. On the basis of these weak directional tendencies, it appears that industrial development might exercise a slight stabilizing influence, while urbanization appears to carry disruptive consequences. Given the relatively high frequency of *golpes* in Latin America, it might be hypothesized that rates of urbanization were outpacing industrial growth throughout much of the area. By synthesizing the data in Tables 5 and 6, we find that this is in fact the case. Table 7 shows that

TABLE 5. Industrial Growth and Coups d'État, ca. 1950-60

	Country	Industrial Growth[52] (in percentages)	Number of Coups
Relatively High Industrial Growth	Mexico	6.4	0
	Panama	6.0	1[a]
	Venezuela[c]	5.5	2[a]
	Brazil[d]	5.2	1[b]
	Costa Rica[e]	4.8	0
			4 (mean: .8)
Middle Range Industrial Growth	El Salvador[c]	4.1	2
	Nicaragua[e]	4.1	0[a]
	Colombia[f]	3.7	2
	Paraguay[g]	3.2	1
	Argentina[h]	2.5	2
			7 (mean: 1.4)
Relatively Low Industrial Growth	Guatemala[f]	2.3	3[a]
	Honduras[e]	2.2	2
	Peru[i]	2.0	1
	Dominican Republic	1.6	0
	Chile[j]	1.5	0
	Ecuador	−0.1	0
			6 (mean: 1.0)

[a] There was also a presidential assassination.
[b] There was also a presidential suicide.
[c] Data for years 1950-61.
[d] Includes increases in some tertiary activities which could not be separated from industrial ones.
[e] Data for years 1950-63.
[f] Data for years 1950-64.
[g] Data for years 1950-62.
[h] Data for years 1947-60.
[i] Data for years 1940-61.
[j] Data for years 1952-60.

[52] Data on industrial growth rates computed from Walter Galenson and Graham Pyatt, *The Quality of Labour and Economic Development in Certain Countries: A Preliminary Study* (Geneva, Switzerland, 1964), pp. 96-97; and International Labour Office, *Yearbook of Labour Statistics, 1952, 1963, 1964, 1965,* and *1966* (Geneva). Data is for the period 1950-60 unless otherwise specified. Growth figures for these years alone could not be found for eleven of the countries in the table; the figures for these countries are as close to the 1950-60 period as possible. Also, four of the twenty Latin American countries are not included in the table because of insufficient data. They are Bolivia, Cuba, Haiti, and Uruguay. In establishing the three categories in the table, the growth rate range of some six points was divided into three nearly equal parts: up to 2.3; 2.5 to 4.1; 4.8 and over. Finally, data on number of coups is taken from Appendix C. The number of coups per country corresponds to the years for which growth data is available.

TABLE 6. Urban Growth and Coups d'État, 1950-60

	Country	Urban Growth[53] (in percentages)	Number of Coups
Relatively High Urban Growth	Costa Rica	9.2	0
	Venezuela	8.7	2[a]
	Dominican Republic	7.4	0
	Honduras	7.4	2
	Guatemala	7.3	2[a]
	Brazil	7.0	1[b]
	Colombia	6.9	2
			9 (mean: 1.29)
Middle Range Urban Growth	Ecuador	6.6	0
	Peru	6.2	0
	Nicaragua	6.1	0[a]
	Haiti	5.9	6
	Mexico	5.9	0
	Panama	5.4	1[a]
	El Salvador	5.4	1
	Paraguay	5.0	1
			9 (mean: 1.13)
Relatively Low Urban Growth	Bolivia	4.2	1[c]
	Cuba	3.9	2[c]
	Chile	3.6	0
	Argentina	2.9	2
	Uruguay	2.0	0
			5 (mean: 1.00)

[a] There was also a presidential assassination.
[b] There was also a presidential suicide.
[c] There was also a revolution.

rates of industrial growth lagged behind urban growth rates in all but two of the sixteen countries for which data was available. This data really adds nothing new to Tables 5 and 6. As expected, the two countries that did not suffer from industrial lag — Mexico and Panama — had fewer coups on the average than did those societies where urban

[53] Data on urban growth rates computed from United Nations, *Provisional Report on World Population* (ST/SOA/SER.R/7), as assessed in 1963; and United Nations, Economic Commission for Latin America, *The Economic Development of Latin America in the Post-War Period,* vol. 2 (E/CN.12/659, Add. 1), Apr. 7, 1963, p. 141. Data on number of coups is taken from Appendix C. In establishing the three categories in the table, the growth range of 7.2 was divided into three equal parts: up to 4.4; 4.5 to 6.8; 6.9 and over.

TABLE 7. Industrial Lag and Coups d'État, 1950-60

	Total Number of Coups	Mean Number per Country
Countries with Lag (14)	16	1.14
Countries without Lag (2)	1	.50
Totals (16)	17	1.06

growth rates outpaced rates of industrial growth. Again, however, the relationship is not statistically significant, even though it is consistent with the relationships that emerged from Tables 5 and 6.

The observation of weak relationships between middle-run rates of socioeconomic change and political breakdown has led some sources to deny the role of social change in creating conditions conducive to political instability.[54] From our point of view, however, one does not have to go this far to acknowledge that the relationships between socioeconomic change and political breakdown are exceedingly complex. In effect, the weakness of the relationships that appear in our tables can be attributed in part to the fact that the connection between socioeconomic change and breakdown is mediated by factors such as achieved levels of socioeconomic development and political structure, variables which act as parameters within which the processes of change operate. As is usually the case, looking at one factor in isolation is no substitute for a multifaceted analysis. Before exploring some of these complexities, however, it would be useful to see if we can discern some reasons for the directional tendencies that do appear in our tables. We will then be in a better position to assess the role of socioeconomic change in producing coups d'état.

It is not difficult to discern a rationale for the tendency of *golpes* to occur in societies experiencing industrial lag. On one hand, the migration from the rural areas to the urban centers tends to produce increased demands that government finds difficult to satisfy. The combination of high aspirations and dislocations typical of the migration process can mobilize the migrant without provision for his assimilation into the mainstream of urban life. This process tends to favor the politicization of the migrant; that is, the urbanization process makes the migrant available for recruitment into new, more active political roles that are held up to him by enterprising politicians of the urban

[54] See, for example, Payne, *Conflict in Colombia*. For the opposite view, see Dix, *Colombia*.

middle sectors.[55] These circumstances produce increased demands for goods and services from government. In countries lacking great accumulated wealth — note, again, the significance of absolute levels of achieved development — these new demands may be virtually impossible to satisfy in anything more than a token way. The overpopulation of the service sector vis-à-vis the industrial sector and the chronic problems of inflation that characterize many Latin American economies are troublesome by-products of the government's futile attempt to provide adequate services in a society where resources are scarce.[56] The government's inability to cope successfully with the mounting level of demands leads to rising tensions, which enhance the probability of violence and political instability. In terms of the approaches employed in Chapter 1, government has a "participation problem" with which it is unable to cope. As a result, government structures strain under the burden; that is, the "organization problem" is aggravated. If the situation becomes acute, military intervention is quite probable.

At the same time that urbanization can be viewed as a mobilizing force that tends to produce disruptive consequences, industrialization can be seen as an assimilating force that decreases the tensions inherent in the former to some extent. For one thing, industrialization brings with it the creation of new and relatively high-paying jobs. In so doing, it helps to absorb some of the tensions arising from the unmet demands associated with the urbanization process. Compared to labor in the overpopulated services sector, the remuneration for industrial labor is superior on the whole. Particularly among blue-collar workers, industrial employment carries "elite" status.[57] In short, the creation of new and productive jobs that comes with industrial growth can contribute to satisfying the so-called "revolution of rising expectations" and the associated frustrations that accompany the urbanization process. In so doing, industrial growth can exert a stabilizing effect.

It appears that the "healthy" effects of industrial growth have been recognized by the Latin American elites. Since World War II, a generalized consensus about the desirability of industrialization has

[55] In this sense see Deutsch, "Social Mobilization," and Di Tella, *Sistema Político Argentino*.

[56] For data on the relatively high weight of tertiary, as opposed to industrial, activity in most Latin American countries, see Víctor L. Urquide, *Viabilidad Económica de América Latina* (Mexico, D.F., 1962), p. 160.

[57] On this point, see Frank Bonilla, "The Urban Worker," in *Continuity and Change in Latin America*, ed. John J. Johnson (Stanford, Calif., 1964), pp. 186-205.

emerged, despite the fact that disagreement still exists over the appropriate means and the relative distribution of costs. On the other hand, industrial stagnation only leads to increasing tensions, as dissatisfaction with the policies of government is likely to be widespread in these circumstances. In this context, it should be noted that Latin American *golpes* are often justified in terms of the need to get the country moving toward the goals of accelerated economic growth. Indeed, political breakdown in Latin America can be understood in part in terms of the difficult-to-satisfy demands for the creation of mass consumption societies with high levels of political participation in an economically underdeveloped setting.[58] In addition, the desire for industrialization forms part of the armed forces' sense of nationalism, which it champions in its role as defender of the country's sovereignty.[59]

The preceding remarks suggest that there is a need to differentiate the violence-inducing from the violence-inhibiting aspects of social change. High rates of industrial growth can encourage political stability and a reduction of coups, while high rates of urban growth can produce the opposite effect, according to the above rationale. At the same time, these relationships are only very weakly supported by our data. There are numerous exceptions in the case of particular countries. Why is this so?

As noted in the previous chapter, the relationship between rates of socioeconomic change and political breakdown is a most complex one. Largely for this reason, we defined the concept of transition in terms of observable political behavior as opposed to rates of socioeconomic change, as is often done. At this point we should point out some of the problems involved in theories that attempt to establish a facile link between rates of socioeconomic change and political breakdown.[60] In so doing, we shall in effect be offering reasons why the findings presented in Tables 5, 6, and 7 do not provide strong support for the rationale described above.

First of all, rates of change are not continually at the "critical point" during any given period of time, as is implied by many sources in the literature that define "transition" in terms of rates of socioeconomic change. Actually, rates of change tend to affect politics through their cumulative impact on the political structure. Moreover, there can be a

---

[58] In this sense see Germani and Silvert, "Military Intervention."

[59] See Pye, "Armies in Political Modernization."

[60] The inability to establish a simple link between social change and political breakdown is acknowledged in the literature. For example, Huntington links revolution to both rapid economic growth and decline. See Huntington, *Political Order*, pp. 51, 56.

lag between the time when a given rate prevails and the time when it will have its alleged effects. For example, high rates of urban growth for the period 1950-60 may not be felt fully until the mid-1960s. Again, the breakdown suffered during the 1950s may reflect rates of growth that prevailed during the 1940s or earlier. On both of these counts, one would have to expect the findings in Tables 5, 6, and 7 to be less clear-cut or forceful than is suggested by the oversimplified theoretical rationale.

A second reason for the weak results produced by our dynamic analysis is that this type of analysis does not take into account the fact that to some degree political processes obey a rhythm and logic of their own. Specifically, this type of socioeconomic analysis overlooks the political factors discussed in this and the preceding chapter, which must be taken into account in the attempt to assess the probabilities for breakdown in a given society. As noted earlier, political variables exercise a certain degree of independence from the socioeconomic ones. For this reason it would be a mistake to expect a strong correspondence between high rates of urban growth over a particular decade, let us say, and a high coup frequency. In effect, there are both static and dynamic political factors affecting coups, factors that are relatively independent of middle-run rates of socioeconomic change. In this chapter we have seen how party strength depends on at least three relatively stable variables which are to some extent independent of levels of socioeconomic development. A similar case can be made for their relative independence from rates of socioeconomic change over a ten-year period. For example, it would obviously be venturesome to assume that a rapid increase in urban population due to migration from rural to urban areas during a particular decade would necessarily destroy traditional party identification over this period. Substantial changes in the party identification factor generally occur in response to a complex set of variables over a relatively long period of time. Furthermore, as suggested in the previous chapter, the dynamics of politics is a somewhat independent force of its own. This can be observed when radical groups are "socialized" by violence and coercion into taking more moderate political positions, no matter what the rates of socioeconomic change over the decade in question.

An example should help to make clear the complexities involved. Urbanization in Colombia during the 1920s and early 1930s resulted in a gradual shift of power from the predominantly rural-based Conservative party to the Liberals, whose main base of support lay in the urban centers.[61] This altered balance of power brought about ideological changes in the Catholic-oriented Conservative party, which began to question the morality of majority rule and to espouse the creation of a corporatist political system based on limited suffrage. These changes in political structure and ideology, induced in part by the cumulative effects of socioeconomic change during the 1920s and early 1930s, set the stage for acute interparty conflict and political breakdown in the 1950s. However, the linkage between socioeconomic change and breakdown was neither immediate nor direct. Indeed, the main precipitants of the 1953 coup — the interparty *violencia* and the continuistic attempt by President Gómez — came many years after the social changes of the 1930s. This case merely demonstrates the exceedingly complex character of the relationships that exist among social change, political structure, and breakdown, and it also suggests a reason for the weakness of the relationships that appear in Tables 5, 6, and 7. Considered in isolation, dynamic socioeconomic analyses cannot provide an adequate understanding of the complex coup phenomenon.

Finally, and in addition to the political structure variable, dynamic socioeconomic analyses leave something to be desired when they ignore the phenomenon which is the subject of static socioeconomic analysis — the levels of socioeconomic development that have been achieved at the time the analysis is undertaken. Thus, high levels of urban growth in a highly urbanized society, such as the United States, may have a lesser impact on the political structure than in a highly rural society, such as Guatemala.[62] In this sense, achieved levels of socioeconomic development are a most important conditioner of coup frequency, and as this static factor is ordinarily ignored by dynamic analyses, one cannot expect much more support for the hypothesized relationships between middle-run rates of socioeconomic change and political breakdown than that which appears in Tables 5, 6, and 7.

Concluding Remarks

In this chapter we began by discussing some relationships between socioeconomic variables and Latin American coups d'état, and this led us to consider the influence of political structure on chances for stability. Both static and dynamic modes of socioeconomic analysis were

[61] For details, see Solaún, "Political Violence in Colombia."

[62] In this respect it is important to differentiate social "change" from "growth," a distinction seldom acknowledged in the literature. The latter can be defined as a quantitative change in social units; the former, in terms of qualita-

investigated. Static analysis assumes that there are relatively fixed or enduring socioeconomic structural characteristics which affect the propensity of societies toward *golpes*. In this context, socioeconomic underdevelopment has been tied to a high coup frequency. Dynamic analysis, on the other hand, links political breakdown to rapid rates of social and economic change over relatively short periods of time. The data in Table 3 indicate that relatively high levels of socioeconomic development were a necessary but not sufficient condition for the complete absence of coups during the 1943-67 period. In contrast, short-run economic crises and rates of urban and industrial growth over the 1950-60 decade were found to be neither necessary nor sufficient conditions for *golpes* in Latin America, although of course they can be significant factors in particular cases.

Relatively high levels of socioeconomic development appear to be necessary for the total absence of coups during the period in question. At the same time, the durability of political institutions is not wholly determined by achieved levels of socioeconomic development. As suggested by cases like Nicaragua under the Somozas, the congruity or "fit" between political and socioeconomic structures is a better determinant of chances for stability than the concepts of political development or socioeconomic development when considered in isolation. In this light, the total absence of coups during the 1943-67 period in Mexico, Chile, and Uruguay can be understood in part as a consequence of congruity between their relatively developed, democratic political structures and their relatively high levels of socioeconomic development. In contrast, the fact that Nicaragua has had only one coup since 1943 can be comprehended in part as a product of congruity between its relatively underdeveloped, patrimonial-authoritarian political structures and its relatively underdeveloped socioeconomic structures.

Another factor suggesting that the strength of political institutions is not wholly determined by achieved levels of socioeconomic development relates to the variable strength of Latin American party systems. Our data indicate that those Latin American party systems that had the strength to avoid *golpes* were characterized by a small number of mass-based parties which were able to prevent attempts at *continuismo* of the leader and to provide an organizational framework for periodic, scheduled changes in the chief executive by elections. As was discussed

tive changes, i.e., the emergence of new kinds of units and new types of relationships between them. As defined here, the process of social change tends to produce transitional politics, thus increasing the probability of political breakdown.

at length, the strength of party systems exhibits a measure of independence from achieved levels of socioeconomic development.

On the whole, our analysis in this chapter indicates that the relatively enduring variables of political structure and achieved levels of socioeconomic development were of far greater importance in inhibiting Latin American coups during the 1943-67 period than were the dynamic socioeconomic factors that we analyzed. Drawing on the distinctions developed in Chapter 3, we can say that both relatively high levels of socioeconomic development and a strong party system appear to be endemic or predisposing factors inhibiting *golpes*. In effect, both of these factors were necessary for relatively high levels of political development and the total absence of *golpes* during the 1943-67 period. In comparison, short-run economic crises and industrial lag over the middle run may be considered precipitating or triggering factors that are neither necessary nor sufficient in themselves for the occurrence of coups, though they may be significant in particular cases, depending on the disposition of the predisposing factors at the time in question.

6

AN INTERPRETATION

The Latin American coup d'état is a highly complex phenomenon subject to a variety of different and contrasting interpretations. For example, the dispute often arises as to whether *golpes* are the product of acute intraelite conflict which does not result in significant political or socioeconomic changes, or whether they are the consequence of escalated interclass conflict which is capable of effecting substantial change in the structures of the polity and the society at large. As discussed in Chapter 1, the former interpretation emphasizes the presence of chronic organizational problems found at the center of the polity, while the latter stresses the participatory problems incurred as a result of the emergence of marginal, lower-class groups during turbulent periods of transition. Employing these analytical perspectives, our data indicate that while interclass conflict has been a more frequent source of political breakdown during the post–World War II period, intraclass conflict has continued to be an important source of *golpes* in contemporary Latin America. At the same time, we have seen that all *golpes* can be viewed as the product of imbalances between the participation and organization dimensions of politics. From this synthetic point of view, the difference between interclass and intraclass coups is primarily one of degree, with disequilibrium between levels of participation and organization relatively greater in cases of interclass conflict.

The point that should be emphasized in this context is that coups must be seen from different perspectives and analyzed in the light of several interpretations. If one fact emerges from our analysis of the thirty *golpes,* it is that no single interpretation can adequately account for the coups. Our analysis, of course, shows that some explanations are more important than others. Still, all coups involve complex processes that manifest more than one cause. For this reason, we have attempted to present the coup phenomenon without excessive over-simplification. A variety of different explanations have been discussed, and their usefulness has been evaluated on the basis of our data.

In this concluding chapter an effort is made to tie together in a more explicit fashion the major points discussed in the preceding chapters. Much of the supporting detail will be ignored, as we shall be concerned with presenting a general framework within which Latin American coups can be better understood. In particular, the framework provides an aid to understanding by distinguishing between immediate or precipitating, as opposed to the more endemic or predisposing, causes of coups. Also, the nature of the *golpe* is clarified by contrasting its causes with ideal-type conditions for long-term political stability. But before plunging into the elaboration of the framework, a few summary statements pertaining to the nature of the coup phenomenon are in order. As suggested in the preface, many analyses of the coups have given little attention to the actual processes that lead up to and define the coup d'état. An appreciation of these processes, however, is essential to an intelligent discussion of the causes of coups.

The Main Processes of Coups d'Etat

A coup d'état is the illegal removal and replacement of the chief executive of a country by a predominantly military force. Usually involving a degree of violence, the *golpe* is the product of escalated political conflict that results in the overthrow and replacement of the highest governmental authority, the president. In effect, the escalated conflict weakens both the governmental and political organization of the society. In the final analysis, the regime is increasingly incapable of regulating or mediating conflict. Formal governmental structures lose their capacity to bear the weight of political competition, and consequently they are reorganized by the coup. In this sense, *golpes* can be interpreted as the joint product of both organizational and participatory problems.

Sectarianism, the tendency to pursue the exercise of power via the total exclusion of countergroups, is the form assumed by escalated political conflict. Sectarian behavior is highly threatening in the context of political competition because it seeks to punish opposing groups. Total dispossession of power, repression, and exile are its characteristic forms. In this atmosphere, countergroups are equated to criminals. In terms of game theory, a sectarian situation in politics is zero-sum:

whatever is won by A must be lost by B. That is to say, one's enemy is a total enemy.

Sectarianism in Latin American politics has two basic modes: *primitive radicalism* and *ideological radicalism*. The primitive radical accuses his opponents of immoral and criminal behavior. As noted in Chapter 4, primitive radicalism generally is found in connection with *golpes* that involve high levels of intraclass or political conflict proper. Ideological radicalism, on the other hand, refers to the type of sectarian behavior ordinarily found in association with coups that involve escalated interclass conflict. Like the primitive radical, the ideological radical views his opponents as thoroughly evil and immoral. But in addition, he also condemns his opponents for holding or exemplifying an evil philosophy or ideology. In terms employed earlier, the opponent of the ideological radical is both sinner and heretic, while the primitive radical's enemies are sinners only. In contrast to the primitive radical, the ideological radical attacks the fundamental values and norms that are at the base of the social order. Not only does he want to restore honesty and morality to government, as does his primitive counterpart, but, more important, he seeks to recast the entire social order. In this sense the similarities that the ideological radical shares in common with his primitive counterpart merely serve to escalate conflict even further in a situation characterized by lack of consensus over fundamental social values and norms.

Both types of radicals tend to undermine the legitimacy of political actors. If your opponents are evil, they are not legitimate participants in the political process. You cannot accept them, least of all have any legitimate dealings with them. In this sense the sectarian behavior of both types of radicals makes compromise difficult to come by, and those compromises which do occur are not considered legitimate. Political institutions tend to lose flexibility, and the probability of violence, repression, and political breakdown increases under these circumstances. In short, you cannot have limited political conflict without a secular orientation that promotes compromise.

The sectarianism of the radicals has a particularly adverse effect on the regime, which is unable to perform its mediating or integrating function with any degree of effectiveness under conditions of escalated conflict. In effect, government is perceived as "belonging to" the incumbents, who are accused of using the offices of government for their own personal benefit, to the exclusion of others. In other words, the differentiation between formal government and political groups breaks down under the impact of the radical's highly charged rhetoric. The formal office and the incumbent become indistinguishable or *structurally fused*. As government is viewed as belonging to a particular clan, party, or class, it is manifestly impossible for government to represent or aggregate diverse interests. From this perspective, governmental illegitimacy occurs with structural fusion, and the subsequent possibility of political breakdown is thereby enhanced.

The sectarian behavior of the radicals, their verbal totalism in particular, is closely related to yet another process which is found in association with many coups — the *diffusion of illegality* syndrome. Within the semi-logical confines of this process, illegal acts against opponents, such as the coup itself, are justified by appeal to the alleged illegality or criminality of the opponents. As the legal system demonstrates little integrative capacity, the theme of self-defense, of legitimate counterviolence, is frequently employed in justifications offered for Latin American *golpes*. Of course, the diffusion of illegality defines a situation marked by the presence of self-fulfilling prophecies. Groups employ violence because countergroups are perceived to act criminally. Conversely, countergroups also tend to opt for violent, illegal methods because they learn to expect criminal acts from their adversaries. In extreme cases, the self-fulfilling prophecy leads to a coup d'état, as the military finds it increasingly difficult to keep from taking sides in conflicts of this variety.

In the highly polarized atmosphere produced by radical rhetoric it becomes very difficult not to take sides. This is particularly true in the case of the armed forces, whose virtual monopoly over the instruments of violence makes them a center of attention when political conflict escalates. If the opposition is able to gain substantial support for its accusations against the government, the military will be inclined to conduct a coup. If it does not it will tend to lose its legitimacy in the eyes of the population for supporting an "immoral" and "criminal" government. In other words, guilt by association will be attached to the military under these conditions of radicalism if it does not act.

Another process making for *golpes* in situations of this kind refers to the so-called "pathology of democracy." The divisive effects of radicalism are likely to find open expression in a relatively democratic context which allows for substantial political freedoms. Under such conditions, the military as well as some sectors of the civilian population begin to question the political arrangements that permit such high levels of agitation and the ascent to power by persons of doubtful moral character. These doubts encourage the formation of beliefs to the effect that a temporary departure from democracy is necessary in order to

cure its "pathology." Under conditions of primitive radicalism, advocates of this "temporary departure" will generally be concerned with
resolving the morale and morality crises induced by the radicals'
rhetoric. When ideological radicalism predominates, it is likely that
remedies for the more inclusive "ills" of society will be sought, in addition to cures for the morality crises that arise in connection with the
staffing of governmental offices. Whatever the particular case, the in-
stallation of an authoritarian regime for the purpose of curing
democracy's "pathology" eventually creates counterpressures working
toward the restoration of democratic rule. Such factors as the absence
of strong ideological support for dictatorship, the questioning of the
golpistas' motives, and the existence of military discipline problems
that tend to come about when the armed forces assume an overtly
political role provide a rationale for the execution of a *golpe* designed
to restore civilian rule. This coup of restoration completes the vicious
circle of the so-called "pathology of democracy," in which weak democratic and authoritarian regimes alternate in a coup-studded, cyclical
pattern.

Beyond these considerations, the illegal character of coups is also
one of their most important features. As suggested in Chapter 1, coups
are illegal acts because they constitute a violation of the constitutional
laws governing executive tenure. In most types of regimes, authoritarian
as well as democratic, the constitution calls for the subordination of the
military to the chief executive; the armed forces are not empowered to
remove the president. Thus coups are a rebellion against constituted
authority.

Golpes violate the law in yet another sense because they produce a
de facto alteration of the public legal system that prescribes spheres
of competence for the various branches of government. Those definitions of coup d'état that emphasize the change of top government personnel as virtually the only coup consequence of any importance tend
to obscure one very significant aspect of the coup phenomenon: coups
alter the regime or the basic formal-legal structure of government. At
the very least, they produce a measure of *structural fusion* when the
military widens its sphere of competence in the coup situation to include determination of the executive. In other words, every coup, at
least temporarily, decreases the structural differentiation of government.[1] The extent of the structural fusion varies from one coup to

---

[1] As noted earlier, although structural fusion always occurs at the moment
of the coup, coups sometimes usher in more differentiated regimes. This is particularly true in the case of those *golpes* that dismantle authoritarian regimes in
favor of democratic ones.

another. At a minimum, the military takes over the executive function for a short time. In this sense, the military and executive structures merge into one and the same unit, thus centralizing power and decreasing the number of differentiated units. In more extreme cases, the armed forces may assume wider governmental functions and dismantle legislative bodies and the higher courts. Whatever the particular case, the important fact is that the basic formal organization of government is altered by *golpes,* and power relations among political groups are also modified to some extent as a result. By emphasizing the breakdown of the regime in our definition of coup d'état, we take into account this significant feature of coups, which is commonly ignored when definition is offered solely in terms of the change of top government personnel.

These remarks suggest that key processes in the coup situation reduce the level of structural differentiation in the polity at the moment of the *golpe.* We have seen, for example, how the rhetoric of radicalism projects the image of a situation in which the group in power "owns" the structures of government, how the regime tends to "melt down" under the intense conflict of the diffusion of illegality syndrome, and how the military establishment becomes fused with the executive institutions of government at the moment of the coup. In addition, it is interesting to note that this process of structural fusion that typifies the coup situation sometimes occurs as a reaction against a disruptive sort of structural differentiation in the polity at large prior to military intervention. At times, the radicalism of the pre-coup situation involves the emergence of differentiated political groups whose radical demands cannot be coordinated effectively by government.[2] As suggested earlier, this sort of uncoordinated political activity can lead to situations of overparticipation and coup d'état. In effect, consolidation of increases in participation and differentiation in the polity at large can be effected only if the regime is flexible enough to absorb and coordinate the increases in political activity by undertaking the necessary adjustment (differentiation) of governmental structures.

In conclusion, all of the above processes — sectarian behavior, the diffusion of illegality, structural fusion — suggest the disruptive character of escalated political conflict in Latin America. But whether or not coups actually take place, these processes begin to appear in all societies experiencing political crisis. Take, for example, the United States at the present time. Sectarianism is apparent in the radical

[2] This is perhaps why Schmitter views structural differentiation as a divisive process. See Schmitter, *Interest Conflict,* p. 3.

rhetoric of the anti-war militants who accuse the President of "murder" in Vietnam, as well as in the case of the black militants who talk of building Black Power for the benefit of "the brothers" to the exclusion of whites. The beginnings of the diffusion of illegality syndrome also are apparent when conflicting groups justify violence as a legitimate means of self-defense. Finally, the politicization of the police in some large cities and the radical definition of government as belonging to the "whites" or the "establishment" exemplifies the beginnings of the structural fusion or partisan transformation of government that comes with the decrease of governmental legitimacy.

When looked at from this point of view, the difference between stable polities like the United States and the unstable ones so common to Latin America is primarily one of degree. In the first place, the processes associated with political crisis tend to be less virulent, generally confined to transitional periods, and more restricted to peripheral groups in the United States than in most Latin American countries. Second, the formal political institutions in the former are better able to withstand conflict than are those in the latter. For both these reasons, the United States is better equipped to absorb increases in participation and endure political crisis than is true of most Latin American countries. The reasons for this will become clear toward the end of the present chapter. For now, we wish only to emphasize that the processes that accompany coups in Latin America are not wholly unknown in stable Western systems.

Factors that Precipitate Coups

To begin with our summary of precipitating factors that have been investigated, some 60 percent of our sampled coups involved escalated interclass conflict as a triggering factor in the coup situation. In this context, it will be recalled that interclass conflict is typically maximized during transitional periods, which are characterized by political pressures for changing relationships among social classes. The clash of philosophies and norms present during these periods lends an ideological cast to *golpes* arising in this context. For these reasons, we were able to frame our two indicators of escalated interclass conflict in terms of the ideological dimension. As indicated in Table 1, roughly 60 percent of the interclass coups were precipitated by opposition to leftist or egalitarian groups, while the remaining 40 percent were triggered by reformist motivations. This last finding may come as a surprise to those who have pictured the Latin American military as a continually reactionary force.

In short, the role of interclass conflict in coups has increased since the 1930s, and it is likely to continue to do so as political pressures for social and economic change continue to manifest themselves throughout the area. On the other hand, it is a mistake to overstate the extent to which escalated intraclass conflict has declined as a precipitant of *golpes* in contemporary Latin America. In effect, we have seen that escalated conflict between "ins" and "outs" touched off coups in 40 percent of the sampled cases.

The debilitating effects of escalated conflict that accompany both inter- and intraclass *golpes* are clearly underlined by the high frequency assumed by the eighth explanation in Table 1. The crises of governmental legitimacy and effectiveness that are encouraged by acute political conflict helped to trigger coup activity in two-thirds of the sampled cases. As measured by indicators 12, 13, and 14, problems of governmental effectiveness and legitimacy furnished the most important source of coup precipitants in Latin America between 1943 and 1967. The occurrence of outbursts of civilian violence and direct action and the formation of overt coalitions between military and civilian factions served to trigger *golpes* with a high frequency, and for this reason they proved to be the most important indicators of legitimacy and effectiveness problems. However, the third indicator, acute presidential-congressional conflict, was found in just four of the thirty coups examined. As suggested earlier, the relatively high propensity toward authoritarian and centralized executive rule which characterizes many Latin American countries tends to reduce congressional autonomy considerably. Acute showdowns between the executive and congress were, therefore, relatively infrequent, and coups were far more likely to be triggered by conflict which found its primary axis outside of the executive-congressional nexus. On the whole it is clear that crises triggered by low levels of governmental effectiveness and legitimacy were a very important precipitant of Latin American *golpes*. The hyperactivity in the civilian sector produced by these crises was a very fertile source of coups.

The importance of forces outside the military organization in processes leading to coups d'état is also attested to by the fact that more than one-half of the sampled coups were precipitated in part by crises of presidential succession, which are characteristic of societies that lack effective formal-legal organizations for the transfer of executive power. Specifically, *golpes* were triggered by continuistic attempts in 40 percent of the cases, whereas they were precipitated by election outcomes in 30 percent. In the former case, the unwillingness of the president to surrender power suggests the inadequacy of electoral mechanisms. In the latter case, disputes centering about the fairness of elections or the acceptability of their results proved decisive as catalysts for coups d'état. Given the weakness of electoral organization throughout much of the area and the fact that pressures for popular participation find a logical outlet through the ballot, electoral crises are likely to remain an important precipitant of *golpes* for some time to come.

In addition to the factors already mentioned, unmet desires for promotion, high levels of turnover of military personnel, and overt physical clashes between military factions are indicative of the importance of military organizational problems in triggering coup activity. In effect, each of these indicators refers to a specific source of organizational cleavage that results from low levels of professionalism in the armed forces. These indicators played a role in precipitating *golpes* in one-half of the coups examined. Significantly, the precariously low levels of cohesion and discipline implied by these three indicators are not solely the result of factors "internal" to the military. Quite frequently, civilian politicians attempt to encourage military intervention, thus discouraging the development of a highly disciplined, professional military. In the words of Víctor Alba, the military officer is often pressured to act politically, thereby becoming "the tool of certain social groups."[3] On the other hand, civilians are by no means solely responsible for military involvement in politics. A rough indication of this fact can be gathered by considering indicators 13 and 14, which suggest that almost one-half of the coups took place in the absence of overt civilian initiatives to overthrow the government, whether in the form of civilian violence or attempts to forge a civilian-military coalition. Whatever the exact figure, increased professionalization should be particularly instrumental in reducing the intramilitary sources of military coups, by virtue of its tendency to promote high levels of internal discipline and *esprit de corps*. Finally, our data indicate that military organizational problems were particularly disruptive during periods of transition. Two-thirds of the coups produced by escalated interclass conflict also involve one or more of the indicators of low levels of military professionalism. This suggests that in the absence of a disciplined military organization, the development of which is encouraged by professionalization, it will be very difficult to achieve socioeconomic reform without a coup d'état.

[3] Víctor Alba, "The Stages of Militarism in Latin America," in *The Role of the Military in Underdeveloped Countries*, ed. John J. Johnson (Princeton, N.J., 1962), p. 165.

In contrast to the causes presented up to this point, threats to military corporate interests appeared to be only moderately important as a precipitant of Latin American *golpes*. In this context we have found that the fear-of-group indicator, present in roughly one-quarter of the cases sampled, provided a more consistent explanation of coup activity than the "material benefits" notion, which interprets coups as selfish military acts designed to increase the armed forces' share of the national budget. Support for the benefit hypothesis was not consistent in that only half of the *golpes* examined fit the hypothesis, while the other half actually led to decreases in the armed forces' share of the national budget. At least until more adequate data can be brought to bear on the benefits hypothesis, therefore, the overall role of military corporate interests in precipitating *golpes* can only be considered moderately important.

Still, the importance of corporate interests in precipitating coups is suggested by the fact that anti-leftist *golpes* were quite often triggered by the fear-of-group indicator; this occurred in 63.6 percent of the cases sampled. In light of this data, it is apparent that there is a need to offer reasonable guarantees to the armed forces that their institutional interests will not be jeopardized by civilian politicians. In particular, civilian groups must refrain from any conduct which would threaten the "integrity" of the armed forces. As indicated by our analysis of coup patterns, the expression of anti-militarist sentiments by civilian groups encourages the emergence of anti-civilian attitudes within the military establishment. Mutual scapegoating and the enhanced probability of military interdiction of the threatening groups is a likely outcome, particularly when these groups happen to be left-wing or egalitarian in character; and one very important consequence of these coups is the repression of reforms. In the absence of efforts to achieve this *modus vivendi*, Latin America can probably expect military corporate interests to provide a continuing threat to political stability in the future.

As compared with the foregoing factors, U.S. interference, as registered by indicator 4 in Table 1, played a relatively unimportant role in triggering those *golpes* which were examined. U.S. personnel offered noticeable encouragement to would-be *golpistas* in just five of the thirty coups. Contrary to the claims of some critics, the United States occasionally even offered strong and explicit opposition to *golpistas*. Peru in 1962 and the Dominican Republic in 1963 are cases in point.[4] At the same time, U.S. interference cannot be ruled out as a possible catalyst

[4] In this sense see Needler, *Political Development in Latin America*, pp. 75-76.

of coup activity in Latin America, particularly when its interests seem threatened by left-wing groups. Indeed, as indicated by Table 2, there was a significant involvement of U.S. personnel in anti-leftist *golpes*.

Of all the potential precipitating causes of *golpes* discussed in Chapter 4, "acute *personalismo*" registered the lowest frequency — 6.7 percent, or two of the thirty coups examined. This suggests that the more blatantly personalistic characteristics that were attributed to coups d'état by earlier studies of violence in the area have declined in importance with the increased bureaucratization of Latin American societies, a process that is associated with rising levels of socioeconomic development. These trends are especially apparent in the post–World War II era. As opposed to those situations in which the interests of the single *caudillo* were clearly dominant, most *golpes* today reflect the "needs" of more broadly based structures which have a set of corporate or group interests. It appears, in short, that the "personality" coup of the "banana republic" has all but disappeared, particularly in the more socioeconomically developed nations.

In addition to the precipitants already discussed, certain socioeconomic changes occurring over middle-run time periods and economic crises taking place in the short run may also trigger coups on occasion. Although we found that industrial lag — a kind of economic stagnation that is defined by the degree to which industrial growth rates lag behind rates of urban growth — was only very weakly related to the propensity for *golpes* to occur during the 1950-60 decade, there are logical reasons which point to a triggering role for this particular variable. For one thing, tensions created by unmet political demands tend to rise in societies where rates of urban growth outpace industrial growth rates, thus tending to weaken political structures. If the lag is large enough, there is an increased probability that coups may be triggered by the rising tension levels. The fact that many coup-emergent authoritarian regimes have justified themselves by referring to the inability of previous governments to produce a high rate of industrial growth suggests that industrial lag is a potential precipitant of coups d'état.

The long-term, cumulative effects of this lag are more important vis-à-vis political stability than one would guess on the basis of its effects over middle-run periods of time, such as a decade. In effect, contrary to the assumptions of "transitional" interpretations, it would be naive to expect rates of lag to be strongly related to the frequency of coups during a particular ten-year period of time, if for no other reason than that political processes to some extent obey a logic all their

own, as illustrated in Chapter 5. At the same time, it would be unwise
to reject totally theories assigning a role to industrial lag based on data
collected over a decade. As previously suggested, the political effects
of rates of socioeconomic change are more important in their cumulative form, particularly in levels of socioeconomic development and in
their long-term effects on the political structure. In brief, industrial lag
over middle-run periods should not be considered necessary or sufficient
for the occurrence of *golpes,* but rather as a potential triggering factor.

Short-run economic crises, such as galloping inflation or currency
devaluation, also are potential precipitants of *golpes.* As with industrial
lag, these crises obviously increase tensions in the society. The destabilizing impact of this type of factor is even more apparent than that produced by industrial lag because it can occur with marked vehemence
during a short period of time. These short-run crises have often accompanied coups in Latin America.

In conclusion, it is apparent that there are many factors capable of
precipitating coups d'état. Indeed, one might even mention a few
others that have not been expressly dealt with in the foregoing. For
example, the Catholic Church, a special kind of political group in
several Latin American countries, is occasionally one of the actors
involved in precipitating coup activity, as was the case in Argentina
in September, 1955. At other times, defeat in a foreign war can enhance
the probability of coups by virtue of the negative impact that such a
defeat will have on military cohesion and discipline. For example, the
Bolivian *golpes* of the immediate post–Chaco War period can be considered in this light.[5]

The main point is clear. *Golpes* have no single precipitating cause.
As previously noted, no single precipitating factor is a necessary or
sufficient condition for *golpes de estado* in the overall Latin American
context. As contrasted with the predisposing factors that we will take
up in the following section, the degree of substitutability among the
precipitating factors is high. Furthermore, coups can be typified in
terms of the different clusters of precipitants that accumulate to
trigger them. In this respect, as our data shows, some precipitants are
more likely to occur in certain types of *golpes* than in others.[6] We have

[5] See Ruth Arrieta, *Bolivia* (Havana, 1965), p. 54. For examples from outside Latin America, see Samuel E. Finer, *The Man on Horseback: The Role of
the Military in Politics* (New York, 1962), pp. 75-76.

[6] Within certain countries, and for certain types of coups, it may be possible
to establish stronger relationships between precipitants and coups. For example,
Stepan suggests that a military-civilian coalition was necessary for the occurrence of *golpes* in Brazil between 1945 and 1964. See Stepan, *Military in*

also seen that precipitants are affected by macrosociological variables such as political structure and the levels of socioeconomic development achieved by given societies. In the light of this evidence, it is possible to question the predictive capacity of the precipitants standing by themselves. Although the triggers cannot be considered in isolation from the predisposing factors of coups, as discussed at the end of Chapter 4, they can provide an awareness of processes that are potentially conducive to *golpes de estado*. Furthermore, the precipitating factors provide a firm basis for future research into coup processes in particular countries, and such detailed, country-by-country research may permit further elaboration and refinement of the basic coup typology presented in Table 2.

Endemic Causes of the Coups

Having begun to fill in our interpretative framework for Latin American coups by enumerating a number of factors which have precipitated or triggered *golpes* throughout the area, we now turn to a consideration of the more fundamental, predisposing, or endemic causes of the coups. An attempt to specify the deeper roots of the coup phenomenon forces one to analyze the enduring cultural and structural characteristics of Latin American societies, elements which normally undergo significant change only over relatively long periods of time. In this section we will deal with those factors that were necessary conditions for the absence of *golpes* during the 1943-67 period. That is, in the absence of these factors potential triggers were inoperative or they were not present at all. For example, the strength of the traditional party system of Uruguay prevented galloping inflation in the 1960s from precipitating a coup. At the same time, this party strength did not allow the manifestation of *continuismo,* another potential trigger of *golpes.* The fundamental question that we must deal with is why some Latin American societies were able to avoid coups by channeling political changes within the legal system while others experienced the breakdown of regimes via coup d'état.

Although there are a number of ways to approach the subject, the

Politics, p. 98. Still, post-1964 events in Brazil indicate that political conditions and coup types (with the conditions that precipitate them) are subject to variation over time. In the case at hand, the political importance of civilian support has diminished considerably since 1964. The 1969 "coup within a coup" that brought Garrastazu Médici to power was conducted without significant civilian collaboration or support. For pertinent details, see Schneider, *Political System of Brazil, 1964-1970,* chap. 8.

endemic causes of Latin American coups are best explored by centering
our discussion upon the forces that have undermined political democracy in these societies. In a very real sense, many coups in Latin America have been the consequence of abortive attempts to institutionalize
democracy under adverse cultural and structural conditions. The history of most Latin American societies has been characterized by a
cycle in which weak democratic and authoritarian regimes have alter-
nated via coups d'état:

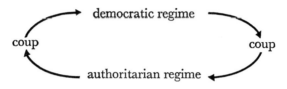

The reader may question our emphasis on the breakdown of democratic regimes. (It should be noted that we have already discussed in
Chapter 2 several factors which account for the high coup propensity
of authoritarian regimes in the Latin American setting.) The reasons
for this emphasis are not simply motivated by an ethnocentric, ideological preference for democracy, as in fact there is evidence that this
type of regime has not been particularly viable in the less socioeconomically developed Latin American countries. In addition, the only
countries that did not experience *golpes* during the post-war period
under investigation had relatively democratic forms of government.
Thus, the democratic perspective is particularly well suited to the
analysis of long-run, predisposing factors inhibiting coup activity.
Finally, democratic breakdown should be emphasized in this context
because many authoritarian regimes in Latin America have justified
themselves as momentary departures from the democratic ideal, unfortunate detours necessary to correct the "pathology of democracy"
syndrome that we have already discussed. It is precisely this weak
ideological support for dictatorial rule which helps to undermine the
long-run legitimacy of authoritarian regimes, thereby leading to a
quasi-democratic, open competition for power which often results in
golpes.[7] Indeed, we have already seen how the highly conflictive processes that typify the events leading up to the coup situation are given
full play by the political freedoms that characterize the relatively democratic setting. For all of these reasons, the discussion of aborted attempts

[7] For a discussion of the ideological weaknesses of authoritarian regimes, see
Linz, "An Authoritarian Regime."

to institutionalize democratic forms lends itself to an exploration of the endemic or predisposing causes of *golpes* in the Latin American context.

Requirements for Stable Democracy

Before exploring the factors which undermine democracy in the Latin American context, it is pertinent to ask what are the basic requirements of stable democracy. In providing answers to this question, we shall at the same time be investigating some of the requirements for the absence of coups in the long run.

We have already discussed in Chapter 2 some of the requirements of democracy, such as high levels of participation and structural differentiation. In this section we present a brief complementary analysis of the conditions underlying democratic equilibrium or stability.[8] The literature on comparative political systems is full of propositions that suggest requirements for equilibrium in the democratic context. These propositions suggest ideal characteristics which no society can ever fully live up to, but at the same time, like the equilibrium framework presented in Chapter 2, they help one to think clearly about the key causes and probabilities of breakdown in actual societies. In a manner of speaking, by describing ideal conditions for "peace," we can increase our understanding of violence. The usefulness of discussing these ideal requirements will become clear, especially by virtue of the contrast they present in comparison with those Latin American societies where coups are quite frequent. In other words, by referring occasionally to the coup processes described in Chapter 4 as we go along, the analytical value of the ideal democratic requirements will become apparent; and the relationship between coups d'état and the failure to institutionalize democratic procedures will also become clear.

To begin with, we should note that democracy is a highly dialectical system in that it requires the institutionalization of political conflict, a point suggested by the electoral competition which typifies all stable democratic systems. The concept of institutionalization suggests regulation. In democratic systems this regulation is supplied by the rule of law, which denotes the existence of a universalistic normative system that serves to limit and integrate the behavior of both political actors and governmental authorities. In the terms employed in Chapter 2,

[8] Our discussion draws mainly from Almond and Powell, *Comparative Politics*, David Easton, *A Systems Analysis of Political Life* (New York, 1965), Huntington, *Political Order*, and Smelser, *Theory of Collective Behavior*.

democracy must strike a balance between the participatory and organizational dimensions by institutionalizing an effective formal-legal
system that is differentiated from the sphere of partisan politics. If this
were not the case, competitive elections would not be possible due to
the fusion that would exist between the incumbent ruling group and
the formal agencies of the state. In other words, democratic equilibrium
is antinomial to the processes of structural fusion and the diffusion of
illegality that characterize the coup situation.

In a democracy the regime — the formal-legal organization of the
polity — plays a primary role in the integration of political behavior
by regulating and mediating partisan conflict. This key characteristic
distinguishes stable democracy as the most formalized type of political
system.[9] This high level of formalization is exemplified by the constitutional continuity — the traditionalized constitutions — that marks the
history of stable democratic systems. In contrast, coup-ridden Latin
American societies are characterized by a "constitutional fetishism," a
strong tendency to tear down and replace the constitutional structure.
According to Blanksten, "the written constitution which lives for more
than a quarter of a century is rare in Latin America."[10] Constitutional
continuity requires adequate support or consensus respecting the fundamental values and norms that constitute the regime. Although it is

[9] That is, in contrast to both the totalitarian and authoritarian system types,
only the democratic system possesses an effectively differentiated formal-legal
structure which is autonomous of the sphere of partisan politics. We should note
here that there has been a tendency in the literature to underestimate the role
of formal-legal factors in producing political integration. This has been the case
even when the positive role of impersonal mechanisms of control in reducing
conflict has been acknowledged in the study of formal-legal organizations. As
noted in Chapter 2, although an essential characteristic of formal bureaucratic
organization is limited authority, the literature has often viewed bureaucracy
as inimical to democracy because of the constraints that it places on participation. It is obvious that all coups involve a breakdown of formal bureaucratic
links between the executive and the military, with the latter losing its functional
specificity. In this context, it is interesting to note that Janowitz suggests the importance of bureaucratic integration in maintaining civilian control of the U.S.
military. According to him, "the effectiveness of civilian political control over the
military is dependent only to a small extent upon the political beliefs held by
the military profession." Finally, the flexibility of formal-legal organization has
been acknowledged in the general literature on this type of organization. For
pertinent comments, see Blau and Scott, *Formal Organizations,* pp. 30, 176-183,
264-265, Janowitz, *Professional Soldier,* p. 253, and Seymour M. Lipset, "Democracy and the Social System," in *Internal War: Problems and Approaches,*
ed. Harry Eckstein (New York, 1964), pp. 267-333.

[10] George I. Blanksten, "Constitutions and the Structure of Power," in *Government and Politics in Latin America,* ed. Harold E. Davis (New York, 1958),
p. 225.

possible to question the degree of consensus required for system maintenance,[11] the ideological radicalism that marks the Latin American experience indicates the need for a substantial degree of ideological consensus among politically relevant groups if democracy is to be institutionalized.

While the dialectic character of democratic stability demands consensus on fundamental political norms and values, its competitive electoral nature requires the presence of some conflict. In theory, democracy is in perfect or stable equilibrium when the conflict is strictly over personnel, that is, when the basic difference between "ins" and "outs" is their mutual claim that each is the most qualified to staff the formal offices of government. This purely political, nonideological conflict over personnel must be contrasted with the escalated brand of political conflict proper that characterizes unstable Latin American polities. As noted in Chapter 4, although primitive radicalism does not involve ideological conflict — with one set of actors espousing democracy, for example, and their opponents Marxist dictatorship — it nonetheless describes a situation of escalated political conflict and lack of consensus with respect to the legality and morality of the actions of political opponents. The primitive radical views his opponent as a criminal, a "sinner." By accusing his opponent of violating those basic norms and values in which they both profess belief, the primitive radical in effect comes to see his adversary as symbolizing counter norms and values. This sort of primitive political conflict undermines consensus, thereby encouraging political breakdown. In addition, primitive radicalism also erodes the regime by increasing the structural fusion in the polity. In other words, the formal structure of government is perceived as belonging to the incumbents. These perceptions result in the diffusion of illegality syndrome in which the regime "melts down" or loses its autonomous and integrative character, and violence (the coup) is justified in self-defense as a necessary means for solving the crisis of the regime. In summary, effectively institutionalized democracies experience periods of relatively nondisruptive political conflict proper which allow the polity to remain close to the 45° equilibrium line described in Chapter 2. In contrast, unstable Latin American democracies often find themselves far from the 45° line because they tend to experience escalated political conflict even during nontransitional periods, when strictly political, nonideological issues take the form of primitive radicalism.

---

[11] See, for instance, Needler, *Political Development in Latin America,* p. 140.

There is another type of conflict that typifies stable democracies: conflict centered at the level of policy formation and implementation. While this type of conflict is characteristic of a more dynamic equilibrium than conflict over personnel in that it may be tied to significant political changes, the fact that the conflict focuses at the policy level rather than at the level of fundamental values or norms permits the absorption of change by the regime. In other words, dynamic democratic equilibrium is achieved when conflict focuses on how to formulate and implement shared fundamental values, not on the desirability of those values. An example can be found in the current opposition to school busing in the United States. The dispute *largely* centers around a specific policy matter, rather than around the ideological issue of the value of racial equality. The centering of conflict at the policy level permits sufficient consensus over fundamental norms contained in the country's Constitution. The busing of school children may be opposed, but the value of the equal-protection clause of the Constitution is not attacked. One can easily imagine how the conflict would escalate if the racial issue were to be mainly focused at the value-constitutional, as opposed to the policy, level. The style of politics in stable democracies is such that it is able to defuse ideologically destructive issues. In contrast to this pragmatic style of partisanship, Latin America's unstable polities frequently experience the ideologization of political conflict in the form of ideological radicalism.

These remarks should not be read to mean that stable democracies never experience ideological conflict and the questioning of basic political norms. As noted in Chapter 2, this sort of conflict is typical of transitional periods such as the one through which the United States is passing at the present time. The pressures for significant changes in the fabric of the polity that such periods portend inevitably involve a measure of ideological and constitutional conflict. Indeed, major change would not be likely to occur in the total absence of escalated conflict. At the same time, effectively institutionalized democracies manage to alleviate the disequilibrating pressures by making only *partial* changes in the constitutional structure and by centering the bulk of the conflict at the level of policy formation and implementation.

This brings us to the cultural characteristics of stable democracies. In addition to high levels of structural differentiation, stable democracies are also defined by cultural secularization.[12] A secular political

[12] For pertinent remarks see Almond and Powell, *Comparative Politics*, pp. 24-25, 57-63.

culture is characterized by a worldly orientation distinguished by pragmatic bargaining over specifics. Political processes are perceived largely as involving exchanges of goods and services. Instrumental and contractual orientations are pervasive in this type of political culture,[13] and they tend to produce a constitutional organization in which "universalism," "specificity," "achievement," and "affective neutrality" are predominant values.[14] As suggested earlier, the rule of law is universalistic in that both government and the citizenry are constrained by it; that is, the constitutional organization is effectively differentiated from the sphere of partisan politics. The specificity of constitutional democracies is exemplified by the high levels of structural differentiation and subsystem autonomy that they manifest, such as the autonomy of the judiciary. The achievement orientation strengthens formal political organization generally and the democratic constitutional requisite of electoral competition in particular.[15] Finally, the affective neutrality of the constitutional structure characteristic of stable democracy is exemplified by the traditional dictum of this type of government, "the rule of law, not of men."

In contrast to the secular orientation supportive of democratic equilibrium, the nonsecular political culture that pervades much of Latin America leads to perceptions of political processes as highly emotional and symbolic confrontations between the forces of Good and Evil; "saints" versus "sinners"; a clash between "truth" and "heresy." Paradoxically, in view of the familistic orientation characteristic of nonsecular cultures, there are low levels of empathy and social trust ("faith in people") in this type of milieu.[16] All of these factors diminish the chances for achieving democratic equilibrium.

[13] These orientations also support formal-legal organizations. See Blau and Scott, *Formal Organizations*, pp. 31, 140. We might add here that the contractual orientation is a product of the belief that mutual gains are possible. In this respect, a contractual orientation is antinomial to a sectarian one.

[14] Of course these value orientations also characterize the ideal type of formal bureaucratic organization. See *ibid.*, pp. 60-62. For a general discussion of these orientations — Talcott Parsons' pattern variables — see Lipset, "Democracy and the Social System."

[15] As suggested by Payne's analysis of political conflict in Colombia, an achievement-task orientation as opposed to a preoccupation with status — the desire to accomplish a task not so much to gain social recognition, but for an inner sense of accomplishment — strengthens formal political organization and reduces conflict in the polity. See Payne, *Conflict in Colombia*.

[16] For a discussion of the numerous attitudes usually considered supportive of democracy, see Kenneth S. Sherill, "The Attitudes of Modernity," *Comparative Politics*, 1 (1969), 184-210.

In summary, the literature has suggested that high levels of structural differentiation and cultural secularization are necessary for stable democracies. In addition, it is also suggested that these two characteristics are predisposing factors that inhibit political breakdown over long periods and even during times of social change.[17] It is not by mere accident that modern institutionalized democracies have experienced greater regime continuity in the face of change than have other types of regimes. In effect, the survival of any regime depends upon: (1) the nature of demands that it must meet, and (2) the strength and flexibility of its institutions. Concerning the first aspect, we have already noted that secularization tends to deideologize conflict by centering it around pragmatic changes in policy, as opposed to changes in the regime itself and in its legitimizing values. Obviously, these nonideological demands can be more easily accommodated by the regime than can ideological ones. As for the second aspect, structural differentiation increases the strength and flexibility of the regime, just as structural fusion produces crises of legitimacy that weaken the regime. Most importantly, structural differentiation permits the institutionalization of conflict and change within the system. Differentiation permits conflict to exist without the implication of regime breakdown. As noted, the differentiation of the regime from the incumbents is necessary for the presence of nonviolent competition for power in the form of free competitive elections. In this respect, flexibility is added to the system, and political changes can be made within the regime itself.

The literature on comparative political systems has often suggested that both democratic institutionalization and the ability of regimes to accommodate changes without breakdown are enhanced by the presence of a decentralized political system characterized by relatively autonomous, countervailing subsystems. Less attention has been given, however, to the relationships between political breakdown and the characteristics of regimes. Specifically, there has been insufficient systematic consideration of the legal and value characteristics of effectively institutionalized democratic regimes. This state of affairs is undesirable because political breakdown via coup d'état involves the unlawful overthrow of regimes. Furthermore, without consideration of these regime characteristics it is difficult to establish the kinds of consensus and conflict that are compatible with regime continuity.

We have already suggested that the survival of democracy depends in part on the level of the political system at which conflict is centered.

---

[17] See, for example, Eisenstadt, *Modernization*.

In this respect, we have indicated that conflict over personnel and the formation and implementation of policy is more negotiable than conflict over fundamental norms and values. To this we can add that overt conflict over some political norms entails a high probability of breakdown, while overt conflict over other norms is not as crucial to regime continuity. For example, a high level of conflict over the method of choosing the executive of a nation is potentially more damaging to regime maintenance than is conflict over the method of choosing the executive of a municipality. In terms of system maintenance, there must be sufficient traditional support for the constitutional organization of the central government. In contrast to the situation of Latin America's unstable polities, changes in the fundamental laws, the constitution, occur infrequently in stable democracies, and when such changes do occur, they usually consist of relatively minor or partial modifications. Changes in stable democratic regimes are more likely to occur at the levels of the legislative statute and the administrative or executive order. Thus, conflict is more pervasive at the lower normative levels, such as at the statutory legal level.[18] This permits changes in the regime and its policies while maintaining its continuity. Actually, in stable democracies change is often justified by reference to the fundamental values (or symbols) reflected in the constitution. Thus, in the famous desegregation ruling of the U.S. Supreme Court, "separate but equal" education was held unconstitutional, an infringement of the equal-protection clause of the Constitution's Fourteenth Amendment. The crucial point here is that significant social change was brought about by reaffirming an important constitutional norm. In other words, at the very moment that the door to change was opened, the fundamental principles which hold the social fabric together, which integrate the polity, were reaffirmed and thereby strengthened. In such cases, stable democracies accommodate the new by reaffirming the old. A case in point is contemporary England, where advanced, welfarist measures are enacted into law by "the Crown in Parliament." A very old, venerable symbolic institution, the monarchy, is used to justify the propagation of new, socially advanced legislation. It is well to bear in mind that a substantial number of stable Western democracies have maintained monarchical forms of government. The old tends to accommodate change and foster its acceptance. In this sense, one might

[18] Although social scientists seldom acknowledge the existence of a hierarchy composed of several normative levels, recognition of such a hierarchy lies at the core of legal training.

say that stable democracies achieve a "positive syncretism" between tradition and demands for change. Obviously, the probability of obtaining changes in the regime while maintaining its continuity is increased with the presence of a hierarchical, differentiated legal structure. Otherwise changes could not be incorporated by making only partial alterations in that structure.

In addition to normative differentiation, the fundamental values that hold stable democracies together are also differentiated to a significant degree. In effect, the secularization of political culture is increased by "cultural differentiation."[19] Differentiation allows for the compartmentalization of values, such that the extent to which they might happen to be mutually exclusive is not crucial. For example, "liberty" and "equality" are actually in a state of tension to some degree. To the degree that this tension is openly activated, conflict is ideologized and consensus over the values that legitimize a regime is reduced. The compartmentalization of contradictory values serves to limit conflict in stable democracies. For example, the fact that Governor George Wallace felt that he could campaign in 1968 and again in 1972 for the virtues of "liberty" without openly saying anything against "equality" illustrates that the two values have been effectively compartmentalized in the minds of many Americans. Rather than opposing "equality," Wallace emphasized traditional American freedoms and campaigned against specific policy matters without which the principle of "equality" would likely go unfulfilled. Wallace's opposition to the busing of school children is a case in point. In this sense, the focusing of conflict at the policy as opposed to the value level reduced the intensity of the conflict by keeping it from becoming overly ideological. An open assault on the principle of "equality" which would have characterized a less "hypocritical" and truly fascist group would undoubtedly have resulted in much greater turmoil during these election campaigns.

Having discussed the need for a hierarchical, differentiated legal system and a differentiated or compartmentalized system of values, we can now summarize these requirements with the aid of Figure 5, which is drawn from legal theory.[20] The survival of a regime requires substantial consensus at the value and moral levels, i.e., low levels of ideological and primitive radicalism among politically significant groups.

[19] See Eisenstadt, *Modernization*, pp. 154, 156.
[20] The reader should note that for the sake of economy we have excluded some aspects of the legal structure, such as court decisions, from Figure 5.

FIGURE 5. Hierarchy of Values and Norms

(1) Value level (collective symbols, values, and ideologies)
(2) Normative level
   (a) Moral norms
   (b) Legal norms
      i. Constitution
      ii. Statutes
      iii. Norms resulting from contracts

Furthermore, there is a particular need for substantial consensus at the upper, constitutional legal level, which establishes parameters for the norms that lie below it. Regime continuity is not as endangered when conflict is centered at the statutory or contractual levels. Although there is some compartmentalization or autonomy between the hierarchical levels, in the long run equilibrium requires consistency between the levels. For example, contracts must not violate the constitution.[21] The regime is in stable equilibrium when top legal norms control those below them. Of course, the measure of compartmentalization or autonomy that exists between hierarchical levels may allow for accommodation of some forms of social change by making lower-level legal changes that do not require significant changes in higher norms. For example, the contractual establishment of new industrial corporations in the United States can occur without significant changes in the nature of contract law. Also, changing social values may find themselves in conflict with legal norms in the short run, thereby creating a stress toward consistency that is reflected by the spread of unlawful conduct in the society. The current campaign to legalize the use of cannabis in the United States is a case in point. The repeal of the Eighteenth Amendment prohibiting the sale and transportation of liquor is another. With these points in mind, the idea that should be stressed here is that the probability of democratic stability is enhanced when pressures for consistency between normative levels take effect gradually and result in partial normative changes. In addition, the chances for democratic equilibrium are maximized when normative changes are effected primarily at lower normative levels.

[21] For example, in the United States no court would uphold a contract the object of which is the sale of a child. In making this point, we are simply restating Durkheim's position that contracts between individuals are governed by higher norms. See the discussion by Neil J. Smelser, *Essays in Sociological Explanation*, p. 250.

The utility of Figure 5 for explaining why some regimes are capable of absorbing change without breakdown is exemplified by the New Deal period. During transitional periods such as this, peripheral labor groups demanding changes in the system attack the constitutional structure and the fundamental ideologies that legitimize the regime. This demonstrates how the ideologization of conflict and the presence of some violence are usually involved in bringing about significant changes in regimes.[22] Yet in the final analysis, stable democracies are flexible enough to incorporate the peripheral groups by making partial adjustments in the hierarchy of values and norms, mostly at the lower levels of statutory law and contract. For example, rather than reorganize the entire constitutional structure, during the New Deal change was absorbed through modification at the lower levels of the hierarchy with the Wagner Act of 1935 and subsequent provisions for collective bargaining arrangements. These changes led to the deideologization of the interclass conflict and to its institutionalization. It is important to note that by the centering of interclass conflict at the contractual level in the form of collective bargaining, strikes lost their initial revolutionary implications and became an integral competitive aspect of the system. Indeed, contractual, nonideological conflict is pervasive in stable democracies. In this respect, one can see how social change in modern democracies is highly dependent upon contractual changes.

In structural terms, the structural fusion characteristic of the pre–New Deal crisis of legitimacy, when government was perceived as being expropriated by "Wall Street," was replaced by an increase in the structural differentiation of the system, as exemplified by the expansion of labor organizations and the establishment of specialized governmental agencies to mediate and represent conflicting interests (the National Labor Relations Board).[23] This incremental pattern of change without breakdown contrasts with the pattern of political decay or stagnation that is characteristic of coup-ridden Latin American polities in which temporary increases in structural differentiation are reversed

[22] As suggested by a reading of Schmitter, the initial impact created by the emergence of radical, structurally differentiated groups is disruptive of the political process. See Schmitter, *Interest Conflict.*

[23] Of course, crises of legitimacy can also be overcome by other formal organizations, such as universities, by increasing structural differentiation. Under conditions of structural fusion, when students perceive that the administration has expropriated the university's formal organization for its exclusive benefit, and when the formerly specialized student role is widened, increased structural differentiation can take the form of the proliferation of student groups and the creation of new administrative units to deal with student-faculty problems. This transition is possible because participants view power as expandable, not zero-sum.

by *golpes*. In these unstable societies, in which violence often "socializes" groups and leads to eventual "compromises," the fact remains that changes in formal-legal political institutions (regimes) occur more frequently than do substantial social changes.[24]

Finally, the high levels of value and normative differentiation and compartmentalization that characterize stable democracies permit the existence of deviance, which would be less tolerated in more monolithic or fused systems. For example, the "hippies" or "freaks" are able to practice an alternate life-style and withdraw from society without producing or seeking regime breakdown. Analogously, new Protestant sects can be established without altering the central structure of the World Council of Churches. The point to be observed in connection with these examples is that in stable democracies change frequently comes about at the level where demands originate without producing changes in the regime. Still, one ought not overstress the autonomy characteristic of groups and subsystems within a stable democracy. As noted, there is a need for substantial consensus and support for the regime and its legitimizing values and symbols among politically active groups. In structural-functional terms, *stable* equilibrium is obtained when the regime and its underlying ideology integrate the polity. Government — the incumbents — must aggregate diverse interests. The party system must provide for the periodic change of the chief executive and it must produce and support governments that represent aggregate interests. This in turn is likely to occur when there is a measure of differentiation between political and socioeconomic systems such that the party subsystem is able to transcend highly divisive social conflicts. In the terms employed in Chapter 2, democratic continuity presupposes a balance between levels of participation on the one hand and levels of organization on the other.[25] The lower the levels of "cultural dif-

---

[24] Anderson, *Latin America*.

[25] With some reformulation of Parsons' four functional problems — goal attainment (G), adaptation (A), integration (I), and pattern maintenance and tension management (also called latency, L) — we might elaborate some of the structural requirements for democratic equilibrium as follows. First, as we have seen, there must be structural differentiation between the sphere of partisan politics (G) and the regime (I). In addition, and as suggested earlier, there must be a measure of structural differentiation between the political sphere (G) and the economy (A). If this were not the case, governments would not be sufficiently aggregative of social or class interests. Finally, the society's socializing mechanisms (L) must gain adherence to these conditions by way of the socialization process. For a succinct description of Parsons' functional problems, and especially their development and usage, see Edward C. Devereux, Jr., "Parsons' Sociological Theory," in *The Social Theories of Talcott Parsons,* ed. Max Black (Englewood Cliffs, N.J., 1961), pp. 1-63.

ferentiation," and the more the party system does not transcend the class structure and thus reflects conflicting ideologies, the greater the need for a relatively centralized regime, i.e., presidential as opposed to parliamentary rule. Yet the Latin American experience indicates that in the face of adverse cultural and socioeconomic characteristics, attempts to institutionalize centralized democratic regimes fail. Put simply, these polities establish a differentiated hierarchy of values and norms only on paper. Structural fusion results from sectarianism and from the diffusion of illegality syndrome in unstable Latin American democracies.

Latin American Culture and Democracy

Having set forth several requisites for democratic stability, our discussion turns in this and the following two sections to a number of predisposing or endemic factors that tend to subvert democratic stability in the Latin American context. While Latin American societies exhibit significant cultural variations, which can be partly explained by their historical and socioeconomic diversity, in the absence of an adequate number of cross-national studies of culture we shall address ourselves here to some of the common characteristics that have been considered descriptive of the traditional Iberian cultural heritage that pervades most of Latin America. In the following section we will consider some of the endemic cultural variations, changeable only over fairly long periods of time.

Gillin has offered a classic analysis of *personalismo,* a fundamental component of the culture.[26] "Although . . . the Rights of Man [are held] in high verbal esteem, the underlying emphasis is upon the inherent uniqueness of each person. The individual is valued precisely because he is not exactly 'like' everyone else."[27] In this Latin American brand of individualism, persons are valued in terms of their uniqueness or "inequality." As the "inner worth" of the person must be carefully guarded, the tendency is toward excessive pride and great concern with honor, dignity, and status.[28] This strong emphasis on personal

[26] We are here considering *personalismo* as a predisposing or endemic cultural factor. It must be differentiated from "acute personalism" — indicator 4, Table 1 — which is an extreme manifestation of this cultural trait and which served to precipitate coups in only two cases of our sample.

[27] Gillin, "Some Signposts for Policy," p. 29.

[28] Payne has employed the term "status" to describe what in fact corresponds to the *personalismo* syndrome. See Payne, *Conflict in Colombia.* For other pertinent analyses, see Bourricaud, "Peruvian Oligarchy," Guillén Martínez, "Estados Unidos," and Jaguaribe, "Brazilian Nationalism."

honor and status is dysfunctional from the point of view of the requirements necessary for the maintenance of democracy. In the personalistic
culture, political competition tends to escalate as it tends to involve
the entire personality. Reaching a compromise on a *point d'honneur*
is difficult. Issues involving the self are not as subject to contractual
agreements as are impersonal ones. When personal sentiments are introduced into the political process, the object of debate centers on the
moral character of the participants, as opposed to more impersonal,
specific policy measures. In effect, Randall has noticed an "excessive"
concern with morality, not only in the political but in the economic
field as well, as evidenced by the prevalence of "moral" as opposed to
"technical" language.[29] In a similar vein, Linz has made reference to
a "loyalty to principles [which gives] a moral value to the intransigence
of leaders."[30]

The personalistic culture is characterized by a rich imagination as to
the personal and affective implications of social action. Within an
openly competitive situation, as must be the case with democratic
politics, this leads to vivid projections of conflicting emotions. In such
a culture persons are highly sensitized to personal passions. Processes
are viewed as part of a great drama in which compromise naturally
plays a lesser role. The point here is that *personalismo* leads to sectarianism, with the highly dramatic style of politics that centers at the
value and moral levels of the normative structure of the regime. In
addition, *personalismo* tends to erode electoral processes by virtue of
the intensely emotional factor that it projects into election campaigns.

Personalismo undermines democracy in yet other ways. As personal
"uniqueness" must prevail, the rule of law is eroded, for the very essence of law lies in its universality. *Personalismo* is essentially particularistic; it orients persons to seek exceptional treatment. It also
undermines formal impersonal organizations,[31] producing structural
fusion in the regime. In effect, the emphasis on gaining privileges leads
to the expropriation of formal governmental organization by the incumbents. This point becomes clearer by introducing two corollaries

[29] Laura Randall, "A Dialogue of the Deaf: The United States and Latin
America," *Dissent*, 9 (1962), 410-417.

[30] Juan Linz, "The Party System of Spain: Past and Future," in *Party Sys-
stems and Voter Alignment,* ed. Seymour M. Lipset and Stein Rokkan (New
York, 1967), p. 243.

[31] For the impact of *personalismo* on the weakening of business formal organization as well, see W. Paul Strassman, "The Industrialist," in *Continuity and
Change in Latin America,* ed. John J. Johnson (Stanford, Calif., 1964), pp.
161-185; and Albert O. Hirschman, *The Strategy of Economic Development*
(New Haven, Conn., 1958), chap. 8.

of *personalismo: familismo* and *amiguismo,* literally "familism" and "friendism." These two traits are characterized by a *fuero* or corporate mentality in which favors are accorded to "family" and "friends." The terms are placed in quotes because the *fuero* mentality carries beyond the extended family and close circle of friends (*hombres de confianza*) to include one's *correligionarios* — all those belonging to the same political group. In this respect, *familismo* and *amiguismo* foster a clannish or sectarian conception of politics.

So far we have seen that the traditional Iberian cultural heritage undermines some of the Parsonian pattern variables that have been considered supportive of democratic constitutional organization. The personalistic culture is particularistic, highly affect-oriented, and diffuse. In addition to this, *personalismo* fosters an ascribed orientation. First, its emphasis on status undermines McClelland's "*n* Achievement."[32] Second, its *fuero* mentality seeks a noncompetitive or permanent privileged position in the society. It is in the light of this orientation that ascription must be viewed. Latin Americans seek to improve their station in life, and as noted in Chapter 4, politics is often viewed as "the road from rags to riches." The point here is that Latins are prone to attribute a static component to success. Social processes are not viewed as a continuous, dynamic competition for success. As indicated by the high propensity to employ professional titles, Latins seek ascribed position in a fashion reminiscent of medieval corporatism.

Of course, this ascriptive orientation contributes to the weakening of electoral processes (*continuismo*), a phenomenon typical of Latin America's weak party systems. Furthermore, when combined with high levels of affectivity, ascription tends to result in the disparagement of the successful. In much of Latin America there is a tendency to presume that success is the result of "favors" or immoral activities. As persons expect a special "familistic" treatment or favors in the process of achieving their goals, success paradoxically tends to be attributed to unmerited factors. The culture leads to perceptions that link success with favors and even immorality or affective disloyalty, thus undermining the legitimacy of the powerful, the government included. However, this does not imply the absence of substantial support for charis-

[32] According to McClelland, "*n* Achievement is a desire to do well, not so much for the sake of social recognition or prestige, but to attain an inner feeling of personal accomplishment." See David C. McClelland, "The Achievement Motive in Economic Growth," in *Industrialization and Society,* ed. Bert F. Hoselitz and Wilbert E. Moore (Paris, 1963), p. 76.

matic leaders, as there are other cultural elements conducive to this phenomenon. Before we consider this messianic dimension a word must be said on the high levels of distrust characteristic of the culture.

Nonsecular cultures are distrustful. Within the Latin American context, the apprehensiveness about the ego, a component of *personalismo*, leads to general distrust.[33] In addition, distrust is also a consequence of *familismo* and *amiguismo*. The tendency to transform secondary relationships into "primary" ones has as a consequence the distrust of "others."[34] Also reinforcing this cultural element is *machismo*, the "he-man" syndrome that stresses sexual prowess. As a crude form of *personalismo*, one of *machismo*'s underlying themes is that the male will try to "get away with murder," while demanding perfect chastity from his women. This double standard fosters distrust of the conduct of others. There is a cunning, picaresque, or "sinful" dimension accompanying *machismo* which has demoralizing effects in that it encourages one to expect "evil" from others and glorifies this type of behavior for oneself. Terms such as *malicia indígena* ("native malice") and *picardía criolla* ("creole picaresque behavior") have been coined to describe this cultural dimension. In political terms, distrust leads to the diffusion of illegality associated with *golpes* and to "generalized beliefs" about the evil nature of the society characteristic of the crises of morality and morale that accompany radicalism.

There is one additional element that pervades Latin American culture that is worthy of comment: the messianic or millenarian dimension. Despite its significance, it seldom receives as much emphasis as does, for example, *personalismo*. In effect, the messianic or millenarian dimension of Latin American culture tends to subvert democratic institutions. The nonsecular character of the culture — the sectarian orientation that conceives of politics as an all-out war between Good and Evil, where bargaining and compromise are not legitimized — creates a set of millenarian or messianic expectations. In this context, the noted Mexican philosopher, Octavio Paz, has asserted that North Americans "consider the world to be something that can be perfected; [Latin Americans] as something that can be redeemed."[35] In a slightly different context, Hirschman has described the propensity of Latin Americans

[33] In this sense, see Scott, "Mexico."

[34] This tendency has led Byars to suggest that the principles guiding small group behavior in the United States can be applied to Latin American macropolitics. See Robert S. Byars, "Small Group Theory and Political Leadership in Brazil: The Case of the Castelo Branco Regime" (unpub. diss., University of Illinois, 1969).

[35] Quoted in Randall, "Dialogue of the Deaf," p. 410.

to seek "total solutions" or a complete reconstructing, as opposed to step-by-step measures.[36] This belief to the effect that no good can come of anything less than "total" action leads to the already noted constitutional fetishism and search for ideologies that characterize many coup situations. As suggested by Bourricaud, the tendency is not to follow the paths of an "input-conversion-output" model, i.e., of operating within an established regime. The propensity toward disequilibrium is high because inputs oscillate between highly specific demands, personalistic in nature, and highly vague, total, and radical ones, "the mere consideration of which [by the government] endangers the existence of the system."[37]

The messianism present in the culture discourages democracy in another way: it fosters the fatalism that undermines the "participant orientation" conducive to democratic equilibrium,[38] and it fosters charismatic rule. At least among the middle sectors, Latin American fatalism consists of the expectation that events beyond one's control can be the source of salvation or redemption. Reinforced by the favoritism implied by *personalismo,* Latins are prone to believe that "luck" or a saving "grace," a *deus ex machina* if you will, will "solve" their problems. Obviously, this cultural orientation is conducive to dictatorial politics in which "saints" and "sinners," "redeemers" and "heretics" struggle for power.

The Catholic Church probably figures importantly in fortifying the nonsecular cultural elements. The Church's spiritual doctrines emphasizing "redemption," "sanctifying grace," and the cult of saints are often carried over into the political sphere, where the search for "pure" doctrines prevails. In addition, the obvious tension between Catholic sexual socialization and *machismo* can be seen as being conducive to rebellion against sacred symbols and authority in general.[39]

We have enumerated several Latin American cultural characteristics — *personalismo, familismo* and *amiguismo,* distrust, *machismo,* messian-

[36] Hirschman, "Out of Phase."

[37] François Bourricaud, "Los Militares: Por Qué y Para Qué?," *Aportes,* Apr., 1970, p. 35.

[38] In this sense, see Gabriel A. Almond and Sidney Verba, *The Civic Culture: Political Attitudes and Democracy in Five Nations* (Boston, 1965), especially chap. 1.

[39] Rebellions against sacred symbols are often quite intense, especially in Spain itself. For example, Spaniards frequently curse using expressions such as *"Me cago en Dios,"* that is, "I shit on God." For an example of the intense rebellion against sacred symbols in Spanish literature, see Pío Baroja, *Camino de Perfección* (New York, 1952), pp. 108-184.

ism-millenarianism, and fatalism — that undermine the requisites of democratic stability. These endemic, traditional cultural orientations are capable of encouraging both interclass and intraclass coups. Some of these characteristics appear to be more related to one type of *golpe* than the other. For example, the ideological radicalism that is generally associated with interclass coups seems to be closely linked to the messianic-millenarian syndrome. On the other hand, the cliquish aspects of *personalismo* seem to be directly related to intraclass *golpes*.[40] Nevertheless, the abstract, somewhat amorphous nature of cultural orientations permits their manifestation in various patterns of social interaction. For instance, the particularistic aspects of *personalismo* can be associated with both relations among persons of the same social class and relations among different classes. Actually, cultural orientations are affected by socioeconomic and political structural characteristics. For example, nonsecular orientations among the establishment are not likely to take the form of beliefs that an inversion in the class structure will produce national "redemption." As discussed in Chapter 5, it appears that the existence of a party system with significant representation of the establishment will reduce the levels of the interclass brand of ideological radicalism in the party system. This can be the case even in societies with widespread messianic orientations.[41] Given the fact that culture is affected by structural characteristics, we will now address ourselves to a discussion of their role in predisposing Latin American societies toward coups d'état.

[40] Both Gillin and Payne seem to suggest that *personalismo* is only related to nonideological escalated conflict. See Gillin, "Some Signposts for Policy," p. 31, and Payne, *Conflict in Colombia*.

[41] Actually, a case can be made that the cultural systems of particular countries are composed of distinct elements which may sometimes be found in a state of tension, and that political processes can be described in part in terms of the interaction between structural variables and these tensions. Colombia offers an example of this sort of interaction or cultural dynamics. The stability of Colombia during the first four decades of this century can be understood in part as a consequence of the predominance of an aristocratic orientation favoring good manners, self-restraint, and legality. The structural conditions that led to the prevalence of this cultural orientation were rooted in the dominant role of the upper class in the party system prior to the mid-1940s. However, the predominance of working-class politics after that time resulted in the decline of this cultural orientation and its replacement by the messianic-millenarian element. This shift of clashing cultural orientations was an important factor underlying *la violencia* which culminated in the coup d'état of 1953. For a treatment of the aristocratic and messianic-millenarian orientations, see José Gutierrez, *De la Pseudo-Aristocracia a la Autenticidad* (Bogotá, 1966). For details of this process of cultural dynamics in Colombia, see Solaún, "Political Violence in Colombia."

Latin American Socioeconomic Development and Democracy

Because levels of socioeconomic development change appreciably only over relatively long-run periods of time, they may be considered as yet another predisposing or endemic factor affecting the occurrence of coups d'état. The socioeconomic structures characteristic of a given level of development can have an effect on politics through their modifying effects on the cultural system and their more direct effects on the political institutions themselves. This is not to suggest that cultural and political structures do not have any effect on socioeconomic development, for they certainly do. Yet given the paucity of empirical cross-national studies of Latin American culture and the compelling effects of socioeconomic development on certain aspects of political structure in the Latin American context, in this section we will adopt the quasi-Marxist interpretation described by the following diagram:

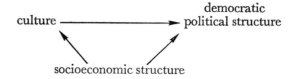

In Chapter 5 we considered relatively high levels of socioeconomic development as a necessary (but not sufficient) condition for democratic stability in Latin America over long periods. Also, Latin American nations with democratic regimes that did not experience *golpes* during the 1943-67 period were found only among the more socioeconomically developed group. Conversely, stability, i.e., the absence of coups during long periods, in the less socioeconomically developed group was likely to be the product of relatively personalistic, quasi-monarchical authoritarian regimes (e.g., Nicaragua under the Somozas). In comparison with the more developed nations, attempts to institutionalize democracy in the less developed group of countries resulted in a higher frequency of *golpes*. Finally, the independent effects of socioeconomic development on democratic stability are suggested by contrasting countries with similar party structure but different levels of socioeconomic development. Both Uruguay and Colombia have had traditional two-party systems, but only the more developed Uruguay avoided breakdown during the 1943-67 period. On the basis of this evidence, it appears that there is a positive static relationship between achieved levels of socioeconomic development and democratic stability.

Although there is no adequate empirical data to test relationships between culture and socioeconomic development in Latin America, the literature has postulated a generally secularizing effect for socioeconomic development. In this respect, development can be seen promoting contractual orientations and undermining magical, messianic-millenarian orientations. By virtue of the increasing educational levels which are a part of socioeconomic development, authoritarianism can also be reduced.[42] Furthermore, socioeconomic development can enhance the possibilities of democratic stability by increasing levels of empathy and trust in the culture [43] and fostering a positive value orientation toward universalism,[44] thus reducing the scope of personalistic-familistic orientations. In the final analysis, consideration of Talcott Parsons' pattern variables suggests that similar cultural orientations support modernity, strong formal organizations, and constitutional democracy as well.[45] For our purposes, it is enough to suggest that socioeconomic development can encourage democratic stability in the long run by fostering the development of these modern cultural orientations, and that *Gemeinschaft* cultural traits do not seem to foster democratic stability in the Latin American context.

High levels of socioeconomic development can also encourage democracy by virtue of their relatively direct impact on political structures. Development tends to increase the level of structural differentiation in the social system, while at the same time increasing the density and strength of formal organizations. As for the political system, the strengthening of these organizations can translate into stronger party systems and governmental bureaucracies, including the military. Contrasting Uruguay with Colombia once again, only in the more developed Uruguay has a civil service system been effectively institutionalized.[46] In addition, strong democratic party systems — those with a substantial

[42] In this sense see Maurice Zeitlin, "Revolutionary Workers and Individual Liberties," *American Journal of Sociology*, 72 (1967), 619-632. However, Putnam only found a negative correlation of .47 between literacy and "military intervention" in his study. See Putnam, "Military Intervention."

[43] In this respect, see Daniel Lerner, *The Passing of Traditional Society: Modernizing the Middle East* (Glencoe, Ill., 1958).

[44] See Philip Selznick, "The Sociology of Law," in *Sociology Today: Problems and Prospects*, ed. Robert K. Merton, Leonard Broom, and Leonard S. Cottrell, Jr. (New York, 1959), pp. 115-127.

[45] In this sense see Bert F. Hoselitz, "Noneconomic Factors in Economic Development," *American Economic Review*, 47 (1957), 28-41; Blau and Scott, *Formal Organizations*, pp. 60-62; and Lipset, "Democracy and the Social System."

[46] Payne, *Conflict in Colombia*, p. 61. In this respect, Uruguay has been more capable of neutralizing the "oversupply of politicians" that Kling sees as undermining stability. See Kling, "Political Instability."

fication, handed down as tradition from one generation to the next, tends to strengthen party organization. Second, an established tradition of participation by members of the establishment in parties can also fortify party structures.[53] Lastly, social revolutions can enhance party effectiveness by building up around the party a stock of enduring, traditional symbols that insure citizen commitment. Strong democratic party systems in Latin America have been characterized by the dominance of relatively few, mass-based parties that managed to provide significant civilian support for governments while preventing attempts at *continuismo* of the leader by enforcing regular changes in the executive through elections.[54]

Strong democratic party systems tend to inhibit *golpes* because: (1) one of their specialized functions is to choose the executive, and therefore the military will not be called upon to fulfill this function; and (2) strong party systems rally sufficient popular support for governments, thereby making military intervention potentially costly and ineffective. By way of contrast, authoritarian regimes do not seek their main base of support in political parties, and they are highly prone to experience *golpes*. The military involvement in politics characteristic of Latin American authoritarian regimes weakens civilian political institutions. As previously discussed, factors such as anti-politician sentiments, a technocratic approach toward problem-solving, and hierarchical-disciplinarian orientations undermine the establishment of official parties by authoritarian regimes. Furthermore, ideological inconsistencies and the need for hierarchical discipline among the military often block the establishment of formal-legal mechanisms to change the executive, thus creating a situation in which uni-personal dictatorships are likely to materialize and in which political crises may lead to a coup d'état. In this respect, the existence of an authoritarian regime practicing *continuismo* is a good predictor that a *golpe* is eventually likely

[53] For comments on the traditional nature of patterns of elite segregation, see Juan Linz and Amando de Miguel, "Within-Nation Differences and Comparisons: The Eight Spains," in *Comparing Nations: The Use of Quantitative Data in Cross-National Research,* ed. Richard L. Merritt and Stein Rokkan (New Haven, Conn., 1966), pp. 267-319.

[54] The reader may wonder if there is not a bit of circularity in our argument for, obviously, if the party systems are able to enforce periodic changes in the executive through elections, then there will be no coups. The point that we are trying to make here is that in these systems the president was willing to allow elections; that is, he did not attempt to rig elections or electoral laws in order to remain in power beyond his legal term in office. These systems were relatively democratic within the Latin American context precisely because they were able to provide, among other things, for the periodic changeover of executives.

to occur. One might even argue that, *ceteris paribus*, the longer an authoritarian regime is in power, the greater the likelihood of a coup d'état.

From the previous arguments we may conclude that a strong democratic party system greatly enhances the probability that coups will be avoided over long periods of time. Our prior comments concerning the ideal conditions for democratic equilibrium, and the contrast that patterns of conflict surrounding *golpes* provide with regard to the requirements for democratic stability, lend additional support to this statement. Indeed, as suggested by their constitutional continuity, civilian rule, adherence to scheduled elections, and record of relatively high respect for political freedoms, the only three Latin American countries that were able to completely avoid coups during the post–World War II period — Mexico, Chile, and Uruguay — were relatively democratic. All of these points suggest the significance of political structure as a variable with some independent influence over chances for political stability in the Latin American context.

At the same time, one cannot gain an adequate understanding of *golpes de estado* by considering political structures in isolation from the broader cultural and socioeconomic context in which they function. In effect, the only Latin American countries which have been able to avoid coups completely since World War II were also among the area's most advanced nations from the perspective of achieved levels of socioeconomic development. As suggested by the decline of the Bolivian MNR in the wake of the 1964 coup conducted in response to President Paz' *continuismo*, it appears that relatively high levels of socioeconomic development have been necessary for both the absence of *golpes* and the institutionalization of a strong democratic party system over long periods. In this respect, one might also argue that the nonsecular, personalistic cultural elements that undermine democratic structures in Latin America have only been abated by the achievement of relatively high levels of socioeconomic development. As already noted, the attempt to institutionalize democratic structures in the area's less socioeconomically developed countries has resulted in a high coup frequency and the pathology of democracy syndrome. In the less developed countries like Nicaragua chances for avoiding *golpes* have been maximized by the imposition of a highly patrimonial, quasi-monarchical form of authoritarian government that harmonizes with the personalistic-familistic political cultures found in these societies.

The relationship between chances for stability and the configuration of party systems provides yet another example of the overriding importance of enduring cultural and socioeconomic factors in the analysis of the Latin American coup phenomenon. As suggested by the cases of Mexico and Colombia, it appears that quasi-democratic, one-party dominance may be functional for stability (i.e., the avoidance of coups) in those countries which have not attained either the very high levels of socioeconomic development characteristic of some stable Western democracies, such as England and the United States, or even the somewhat lower levels of development that typify the most socioeconomically advanced Latin American countries. The nonsecular cultural components that are still much in evidence in both Mexico and Colombia also suggest the functionality of quasi-democratic, one-party rule in these societies.

The experience of twentieth-century Colombia is instructive in this regard. As indicated in Chapter 5, prior to the formation of the *Frente Nacional* in 1958 there were only two instances in this century in which the party controlling the presidency changed, in 1930 and again in 1946. That is, during the fifty-year period between 1901 and 1953 during which Colombia was free of coups, electoral competition for the presidency was usually confined to intraparty politics, and there was a tendency for the dominant party to fuse itself with the regime. When the opposition party finally decided to abandon its traditional practice of electoral abstention in favor of activating sustained two-party electoral competition in the mid-1940s, the *violencia* which finally resulted in the 1953 *golpe* was initiated.[55] It appears that the nonsecular character of party identifications joined with the unfavorable socioeconomic conditions which prevailed at the time to produce a situation in which interparty competition led to substantial increases in violence, thereby encouraging the highly disruptive processes which undermined civilian, quasi-democratic rule. In short, given the socioeconomic and cultural conditions that prevailed in Colombia during much of this century, modified one-party dominance was functional for stability while protracted interparty competition exercised a destabilizing influence. (The point that must be stressed here is that while the outlined ideal type

[55] In this sense see Solaún, "Political Violence in Colombia." We might note here that civilian violence also occurred in conjunction with both the 1930 and 1946 elections. However, the 1946-53 period of violence differed from past experience in that interparty competition was sustained throughout the seven-year period of *violencia*. High points of this period which led to Colombia's first coup in more than half a century were the hotly contested elections of 1947 and 1949 and the assassination of the Liberal party politician, Gaitán, in 1948.

model of stable democracy describes a situation of long-run "perfect" equilibrium, i.e., absence of coups, societies that deviate markedly from this model can only approximate equilibrium over long periods under modified structural political conditions.)

The preceding remarks suggest the complexity of the Latin American coup d'état. In effect, only a complex analytical framework can provide an adequate understanding of the *golpes*. Unitary concepts such as political development, although they may be helpful to some degree, cannot provide the necessary understanding when considered in isolation. When defining political development in terms of levels of political participation and organization, one encounters troublesome exceptions such as the prolonged survival of politically underdeveloped, patrimonial-authoritarian regimes like Trujillo's, which lasted some thirty years.[56] Cases such as this one suggest that if we are to enhance our ability to assess the probabilities of political breakdown in the Latin American context it is necessary to consider political structure in conjunction with cultural and socioeconomic factors; that is, we must view political structure as an "interdependent" variable, as one that is neither wholly dependent nor independent, but one that interacts with the contextual variables of culture and socioeconomic structure. The concept of balanced sociopolitical development satisfies these requirements because it views the questions of long-term political equilibrium and breakdown as a product of the congruity or "fit" (or the absence thereof) between political structure on the one hand and the cultural and socioeconomic dimensions on the other. Employing this perspective, one can better understand why, for example, the emergence of the highly patrimonial and familistic regime of Batista in 1952 in Cuba[57] — a relatively socioeconomically developed country in the 1950s — signaled a high probability of subsequent political breakdown in the short run. (The regime only lasted six years and was followed by revolution.) In contrast to this, as previously noted, the emergence of such a regime in a less socioeconomically developed nation with a relatively nonsecular, personalistic-familistic culture would not necessarily signal political breakdown in the short run. In effect, Latin American countries with low levels of socioeconomic development and nonsecular political cultures have

[56] Using the terms employed in Chapter 2, different types of regimes can avoid coups over several decades because effective institutionalization is not determined by absolute levels of participation and organization, but rather by the relative balance between the two dimensions.

[57] See Solaún, "Democracia en Cuba."

experienced their longest periods without *golpes* under this type of regime.

These comments are not intended to imply that the absolute level of political development is not of some value as an indicator of coup propensity. Actually, in Latin America, politically developed democratic regimes have shown greater endurance than the politically underdeveloped, patrimonial-authoritarian regimes, and this latter regime type has been more enduring than other authoritarian types. At the same time, it is also true that the broader concept of balanced sociopolitical development is necessary if we are to achieve a more comprehensive understanding of Latin American *golpes de estado*.

In this section we have explored the endemic causes of Latin American coups. We first discussed the requirements for democratic stability and contrasted coup patterns to these requirements. The sharp contrast revealed the link between *golpes* and the inability to institutionalize democracy in unstable Latin American polities. Indeed, coup situations were indicative of a "quasi-democratic" brand of politics in which dictatorial rule did not find strong ideological support and in which attempts to institutionalize democracy led to a highly disruptive and fragmented style of politics. We then followed a quasi-Marxist mode of analysis through which we attempted to interpret the higher coup frequency of the socioeconomically less developed nations. We argued that relatively high levels of socioeconomic development could have a salutary impact on political behavior both by eroding the traditional Iberian cultural patterns that work against democracy and by their direct impact on formal political organization.

While levels of socioeconomic development had a compelling impact on the coup phenomenon during the 1943-67 period under investigation, the socioeconomic factor did not fully explain the phenomenon. High levels of socioeconomic development were a necessary but not sufficient condition for the avoidance of *golpes*. In light of this evidence, we proceeded to analyze the characteristics of political structure which, in addition to high levels of socioeconomic development, were necessary for the absence of coups. Strong civilian institutions in general and party systems in particular were necessary for the avoidance of *golpes*. Strong party systems provided a measure of civilian support for governments and prevented *continuismo* of the individual leader. In contrast to this, authoritarian regimes were highly prone to experience coups because of their weak organization both for mobilizing popular support and for ensuring periodic change in the executive.

Three factors were considered conducive to party strength: revolution, a moderately high level of traditional identification with parties, and a measure of participation by the establishment in the party system. Although a nation need not experience every one of the three factors to avoid coups d'état over long periods of time, they were important in some cases. More research needs to be done on the determinants of party system strength in Latin America; elite studies are particularly lacking. In addition to the three outlined factors, there are other possible determinants of party strength. As just one example, one might argue that the nationalistic pride that typifies Chilean political culture, and which encourages them to perceive their democratic political system as more advanced than those of neighboring countries, has been conducive to bargaining, compromise, and system continuity, even under highly stressful conditions. This factor is apparent even in the current situation, with Allende's Marxist government boasting of Chilean "political development" and the uniqueness of the Chilean road toward socialism through constitutional continuity. Unfortunately, the unavailability of case studies has impeded a more systematic analysis of additional factors such as this one in the present study.

Finally, due to the variability of the Latin American coup phenomenon — that is, the occurrence of a high coup frequency in some socioeconomically developed countries along with a low frequency in a few underdeveloped ones during the post-war period — we introduced the concept of balanced sociopolitical development, thereby taking into account the cultural, socioeconomic, and political-structure factors that significantly affect coup probabilities in the Latin American context. By sensitizing our analysis to imbalances and congruities among these endemic factors, we have attempted to provide a useful tool for both understanding post-war problems of political stability and breakdown and for guiding future investigations in the area of Latin American politics.

Final Comments and Paradigm

The study that we are about to conclude has been concerned with explanation of the causes of Latin American coups d'état. Over the course of the study, we have organized the analysis around certain basic analytical frameworks which prove fruitful as guides to clear thinking about the causes of *golpes* and the interrelationships of these causes. We first employed the participation-organization equilibrium framework and then formalized our findings in terms of the distinction between precipitating and predisposing factors. Finally, drawing from legal theory, we established optimal requirements for regime equilibrium in a democratic context, thereby suggesting a set of conditions for the avoidance of political breakdown in the long run.

Throughout our study, we have attempted to adopt an unbiased orientation that would permit us to discuss the coup phenomenon without overemphasizing ideological preferences. For example, our preferences for a democratic political system did not impede us from concluding that this type of system has been particularly unviable in Latin America's socioeconomically less developed nations. In addition to this, we have outlined processes which are likely to produce coups on the assumption that an understanding of the causes of coups suggests ingredients *either* for precipitating or preventing them. However, a systematic empirical analysis of control mechanisms is required in order to obtain a fuller picture of the coup phenomenon, and this we have not been able to do to our satisfaction. The importance of future research on these mechanisms should become apparent with an example: there are some factors that trigger coups, such as purges of military personnel, which can prevent them under different circumstances. Thus, in contrast to those social scientists who criticize the equilibrium implications of structural-functional analysis, we believe that there is much need for studies on both system maintenance and conflict and breakdown. Despite limitations imposed by the scarcity of such studies, we feel that our study offers a set of conceptual formulations that will prove useful in future investigations of coup processes, investigations that are essential if we are to construct interpretive models that are more sophisticated than the one presented in this text.

In this final chapter we have recapitulated the precipitating causes of *golpes de estado* and have discussed their predisposing causes. The predisposing causes set the relatively enduring framework within which the precipitants work. As we have seen, the indicators established for the explanations discussed in Chapters 3 and 4 furnish the majority of the precipitating causes, while the relatively enduring structural and cultural factors discussed in this chapter qualify as predisposing factors. The details are offered in the following paradigm, which first lists the coup precipitants and then presents the cultural and structural factors in juxtaposition with the requirements for democratic stability. By including the requirements for democratic equilibrium in the paradigm we give the reader some idea of the factors that inhibit or prevent the occurrence of *golpes* in the long run.

A. *Precipitating Causes of the Coups.* They are the indicators of our explanations plus items 8 and 9.
   1. Escalation of interclass or intraclass conflict
   2. Problems of governmental ineffectiveness and illegitimacy
   3. Failures of electoral mechanisms
   4. Problems of military cohesion and discipline (low professionalism)
   5. Threats to military corporate interests
   6. U.S. interference
   7. Personal interests of a leader
   8. Short-run economic crises
   9. Industrial lag, a type of middle-term, unbalanced social change defined by higher levels of urban than industrial growth
B. *Predisposing Causes of the Coups.* Democratic requirements discourage coups in the *long run;* anti-democratic configurations encourage them.
   1. Democratic requirements
      (a) Consensus on fundamental political values and norms, as reflected by a constitutional tradition
      (b) Low levels of primitive and ideological radicalism
      (c) Conflict centered on personnel or specific policy issues; pragmatic politics
      (d) Contractual orientations
      (e) Strong formal organizations (formal-legal integration)
      (f) A highly differentiated social system (cultural and structural differentiation)
         i. Of values and legal norms
         ii. Of social structures: between the party subsystem and the state, between the political system and the military, and (to a moderate degree) between the party subsystem and the socioeconomic system
   2. Anti-democratic cultural configuration
      (a) *Personalismo; familismo-amiguismo; machismo*
      (b) High levels of distrust
      (c) Fatalism
      (d) Nonsecularity: highly moralistic and messianic-millenarian orientations
      (e) In terms of Parsons' pattern variables: particularism, diffuseness, affectivity, and ascription
         (These traits run counter to the democratic requirements outlined in 1)

3. Anti-democratic socioeconomic configuration
   (a) Low levels of socioeconomic development (a condition that
       undermines the democratic requirements outlined in 1 by
       fostering an anti-democratic cultural configuration and
       weakening political and formal-legal organizations)
4. Anti-coup political-structural configuration
   (a) Strong party system determining and supporting govern-
       ments and avoiding personalistic *continuismo* (Latin Amer-
       ican party systems have been strengthened by moderately
       strong traditional identification with parties, a measure of
       overlapping of party and socioeconomic elites, and social
       revolution)

As suggested earlier, no single one of the precipitants listed in the
paradigm was either necessary or sufficient for the occurrence of coups
during the post–World War II period in Latin America. The variable
combination of precipitating factors that have triggered coups during
the post-war period indicates the variety of coup types found in the
area. When working with the triggering factors by themselves, we can
suggest little more than that *golpes* are the product of a process in
which, *ceteris paribus,* the accumulation of precipitating factors increases the likelihood of breakdown. Although these characteristics
reduce the predictive capacity of the triggering factors standing by
themselves, the precipitants nevertheless denote critical processes that
can trigger coups. Also, we have seen that some political crises have
been at least temporarily defused by measures designed to check the
emergence of some of the coup-triggering processes investigated in
our study.

In order to enhance our ability to assess coup probabilities in the
Latin American context, the coup precipitants must be considered in
conjunction with the relatively enduring predisposing factors that have
been discussed. As noted, the predisposing factors furnish the context
in which the precipitants work, and the former are necessary for the
occurrence of coups. In other words, if the coup-producing predisposing factors are not present, then coups will be unlikely to occur because
under these conditions the coup precipitants either will not materialize
or their potentially disruptive effects will tend to be neutralized for
relatively long periods of time. This point is best exemplified by considering those twentieth-century Latin American regimes which have
endured for the longest periods of time without experiencing breakdown, i.e., those regimes characterized by a strong, relatively democratic party system operating in the context of fairly high levels of socio-

economic development. Uruguay is a case in point. Although plagued by galloping inflation and terrorism throughout much of the 1960s and early 1970s, Uruguay's relatively high level of socioeconomic development and its traditional party system have managed until now to prevent the emergence of some coup triggers (e.g., *continuismo* of the leader) while neutralizing the disruptive impact of others (e.g., terrorist violence). Of course, this is no guarantee that breakdown can be avoided indefinitely in cases of this kind. The intensity of coup precipitants may eventually become too much for even Uruguay's strong party system to support without drastic change or collapse. Still, the point that must be stressed here is that the absence of coup-inducing predisposing factors tends to impede the coup precipitants from realizing their coup-producing potential. In our opinion, Latin America's effectively institutionalized democratic regimes could be broken by coups only in the presence of prolonged civilian unrest of major proportions and/or the abrogation of electoral processes by the government.

One can also argue the reverse case: in the presence of predisposing factors it becomes increasingly likely that coup precipitants will emerge and realize their coup-inducing potential in a relatively short period of time. This has been the case, for example, with most of Latin America's authoritarian regimes, which have shown themselves highly prone to coups d'état. It has also occurred, however, when attempts have been made to institutionalize democratic forms under the unfavorable conditions described by low levels of socioeconomic development and nonsecular, personalistic cultures (i.e., the pathology of democracy syndrome).

Finally, we have argued that it is necessary to explore carefully the compatibilities or incongruities that may exist among the predisposing factors if one hopes to arrive at an accurate assessment of the probabilities for stability or breakdown in any particular society. The concept of balanced sociopolitical development, which deals with the predisposing factors as interdependent phenomena, is well suited to this purpose. As detailed earlier, the absence (or presence) of coups d'état in any given society can be assessed by exploring the degree of congruity or "fit" (or the lack thereof) that exists between political structures on the one hand and the dimensions of political culture and socioeconomic development on the other. In effect, the concept of balanced sociopolitical development is needed to account for the pathology of democracy syndrome and the existence of exceptional cases like Nicaragua under the Somozas, where stability has been approximated as a result of the congruity that exists between its highly patrimonial, authoritarian regime on the one hand and the highly nonsecular, personalistic-familistic political culture fostered by its low level of socioeconomic development on the other.

The preceding comments have been based, of course, on the historical experience of Latin America. Needless to say, however, the patterns that we have discerned need not be the inexorable image of the future. History is often witness to innovation. The stability that has come to Cuba as a result of Castro's totalitarian experiment is a case in point. Also, two of the most stable Latin American democracies are currently in a state of crisis because of their inability to institutionalize a mass participatory system of extensive social welfare. Pressures for social revolution are being felt throughout Latin America in a situation in which the traditional antagonism between Catholicism and Marxism is being eroded. Although this could possibly increase the probability of a consensual socialist-democratic order in the future, still it is unlikely that most Latin American nations will be able to absorb change without some form of political breakdown.

Even in the face of current pressures for change, a historically oriented study such as ours can suggest some guidelines for the avoidance of coups in the future. Most importantly, a strong party system is becoming increasingly necessary for long-run stability, regardless of the nature of the political system in question. As noted, the only democratic regimes that have been able to avoid breakdown over long periods of time in Latin America during this century have had strong, traditionalized party systems. Totalitarian stability also relies heavily on the strength of the official party. Finally, it even appears that the authoritarian regimes of the future will have to alter their character by cultivating mass-based party support if they hope to overcome the coup-inducing weakness that stems from personalistic *continuismo*. Some of Latin America's authoritarian regimes have been able to maximize their chances for stability by adopting highly patrimonial, quasi-monarchical symbols. However, as revealed by the failure of such symbols among the more socioeconomically developed nations, there is reason to believe that despite recent exceptions, such as the case of Haiti, the pressures for social change that are being felt even in the less developed Latin American countries will progressively erode the effectiveness of quasi-monarchical forms of government in the area. Brazil's 1969 "coup within a coup" also suggests that Latin America's "modernizing" authoritarian regimes — even those exceptional ones which adopt the relatively nonpersonalistic form assumed by the post-1964 Brazilian governments — will have to concern themselves with institutionalization of the strong party systems that have been necessary for the periodic turnover of executive power via elections if they hope to maximize their chances for long-term stability. Thus, if the long-term incidence of *golpes* is to be reduced in Latin America, there is a need to develop strong party systems that will be congruent with the cultural and socioeconomic realities found throughout the area.

APPENDIX A. Coups d'État Studied (by country)

Argentina	1966	El Salvador	1948
Bolivia	1943	El Salvador	1949
Bolivia	1946	Guatemala	1944 (July)
Bolivia	1951	Guatemala	1944 (Oct.)
Bolivia	1964	Haiti	1946
Brazil	1945	Haiti	1950
Brazil	1964	Nicaragua	1947
Colombia	1953	Panama	1949
Colombia	1957	Panama	1951
Cuba	1952	Peru	1948
Dominican Republic	1965	Peru	1962
Ecuador	1944	Venezuela	1945
Ecuador	1947 (Aug.)	Venezuela	1948
Ecuador	1947 (Sept.)	Venezuela	1952
El Salvador	1944 (May)	Venezuela	1958

The thirty coups represent approximately half of the total number of successful coups that occurred in the area during the 1943-67 period. The selected coups include enough of the demographic, cultural, and socioeconomic diversity found in the area to provide an adequate basis for offering the generalizations presented in the text. The thirty coups include at least one example from fourteen of the seventeen countries that experienced coups during the period in question.

APPENDIX B. A Note on the Sources

Both primary and secondary source materials were used in categorizing the thirty coups investigated with respect to the causal indicators presented in Chapters 3 and 4. The listing of secondary sources and an abbreviated recognition of the primary ones may be found in the Bibliography. At this point, however, it would be well to list in somewhat more detail the journalistic or primary sources that are relied upon in helping to reach the judgments recorded in the text. Given their broad coverage and easy accessibility, four journalistic sources provide us with the bulk of our primary data: *Hispanic American Report* (HAR), *Keesing's Contemporary Archives* (KCA), *New York Times* (NYT), and *Time, the Weekly Newsmagazine* (TM).

Coup d'État	*Primary Sources*
Argentina, 1966	KCA, vol. XV, 1965-66
	NYT, May-July, 1966
Bolivia, 1943	KCA, vol. V, 1943-45
	NYT, Dec., 1943
Bolivia, 1946	NYT, June-July, 1946
	TM, vol. XLVIII, nos. 5, 6, 7, 10, July-Sept., 1946
Bolivia, 1951	HAR, vol. IV, no. 6, 1951
	NYT, Mar.-May, 1951
Bolivia, 1964	KCA, vol. XIV, 1963-64
	NYT, Oct.-Dec., 1964
Brazil, 1945	NYT, Sept.-Oct., 1945
	TM, vol. XLVI, nos. 19, 20, 24, 25, Nov.-Dec., 1945
Brazil, 1964	HAR, vol. XVII, nos. 3, 4, 1964
	NYT, Mar.-Apr., 1964
Colombia, 1953	HAR, vol. VI, nos. 5, 6, 1953
	NYT, May-June, 1953
Colombia, 1957	NYT, Jan.-May, 1957
Cuba, 1952	HAR, vol. V, no. 3, 1952
	NYT, Feb.-Mar., 1952

Dominican Republic, 1965   KCA, vol. XV, 1965-66
           NYT, Jan.-June, 1965
Ecuador, 1944   KCA, vol. V, 1943-45
           NYT, May-June, 1944
Ecuador, August, 1947   NYT, Aug., 1947
           TM, vol. L, no. 9, Sept., 1947
Ecuador, September, 1947   NYT, Aug.-Sept., 1947
El Salvador, May, 1944   KCA, vol. V, 1943-45
           NYT, Apr.-May, 1944
El Salvador, 1948   KCA, vol. VII, 1948-50
           NYT, Dec., 1948
El Salvador, 1949   KCA, vol. VII, 1948-50
           NYT, Jan., 1949
Guatemala, July, 1944   KCA, vol. V, 1943-45
           NYT, June-July, 1944
Guatemala, October, 1944   KCA, vol. V, 1943-45
           NYT, Sept.-Oct., 1944
Haiti, 1946   NYT, Jan., 1946
           TM, vol. XLVII, no. 3, Jan., 1946
Haiti, 1950   KCA, vol. VII, 1948-50
           NYT, May, 1950
Nicaragua, 1947   NYT, Apr.-May, 1947
           TM, vol. XLIX, nos. 6, 22, 23, 26, Feb.-June, 1947
Panama, 1949   KCA, vol. VII, 1948-50
           NYT, Nov., 1949
           KCA, vol. VIII, 1950-52
Panama, 1951   NYT, Mar.-May, 1951
Peru, 1948   NYT, Oct.-Nov., 1948
           TM, vols. LI, LII, nos. 20, 23, 3, 15, 16, 19, May-Nov., 1948
Peru, 1962   NYT, June-July, 1962
Venezuela, 1945   NYT, Sept.-Oct., 1945
           TM, vol. XLVI, nos. 18, 20, Oct.-Nov., 1945
Venezuela, 1948   KCA, vol. VII, 1948-50
           NYT, Nov., 1948
Venezuela, 1952   HAR, vol. V, no. 12, 1952
           NYT, Oct.-Dec., 1952
Venezuela, 1958   HAR, vols. X, XI, nos. 10, 11, 1, 1957-58
           NYT, July-Jan., 1957-58

APPENDIX C. Total Coups in Latin America, 1943-67

Argentina	June 4, 1943		July, 1963
	June 6, 1943		Mar., 1966
	Feb., 1944		
7	Sept., 1955	El Salvador	May, 1944
	Nov., 1955		Oct., 1944
	Mar., 1962		Dec., 1948
	June, 1966	6	Jan., 1949
			Oct., 1960
Bolivia	Dec., 1943		Jan., 1961
	July, 1946		
4ª	May, 1951	Guatemala	July, 1944
	Nov., 1964		Oct., 1944
		5ᵉ	June, 1954
Brazil	Oct., 1945		Oct., 1957
3ᵇ	Nov., 1955		Mar., 1963
	Apr., 1964		
		Haiti	Jan., 1946
Chile	None		May, 1950
0			Dec., 1956
		7	Feb., 1957
Colombia	June, 1953		Apr., 1957
2	May, 1957		May, 1957
			June, 1957
Costa Rica	Apr., 1948		
1		Honduras	Dec., 1954
		3	Oct., 1956
Cuba	Mar., 1952		Oct., 1963
2ª	Dec., 1958		
		Mexico	None
Dominican	Jan., 1962	0	
Republic	Sept., 1963		
3ᵉ	Apr., 1965	Nicaragua	May, 1947
		1ᵉ	
Ecuador	May, 1944		
	Aug., 1947	Panama	Nov., 1949
6	Sept., 1947	2ᵉ	May, 1951
	Nov., 1961		

Paraguay	June, 1948	Uruguay	None
	Jan., 1949	0	
5	Feb., 1949		
	Sept., 1949	Venezuela	Oct., 1945
	May, 1954	4[c]	Nov., 1948
			Dec., 1952
Peru	Oct., 1948		Jan., 1958
2	June, 1962		

Total Number of Coups — 63

[a] There was also a revolution.
[b] There was also a presidential suicide.
[c] There was also a presidential assassination.

Main Source: Joseph E. Loftus, *Latin American Defense Expenditures, 1938-1965* (Santa Monica, Calif.: RAND Corporation, 1968).

BIBLIOGRAPHY

Books and Documents

Alexander, Robert J. *The Bolivian National Revolution.* New Brunswick, N.J.: Rutgers University Press, 1958.
————. *Latin-American Politics and Government.* New York: Harper & Row, 1965.
Almond, Gabriel A., and G. Bingham Powell, Jr. *Comparative Politics: A Developmental Approach.* Boston: Little, Brown, 1966.
————, and Sidney Verba. *The Civic Culture: Political Attitudes and Democracy in Five Nations.* Boston: Little, Brown, 1965.
Anderson, Charles W. *Politics and Economic Change in Latin America: The Governing of Restless Nations.* Princeton, N.J.: Van Nostrand, 1967.
Arrieta, Ruth. *Bolivia.* Havana: Casa de Las Américas, 1965.
Banco Nacional de Cuba. *Memoria del Banco Nacional de Cuba, 1950-51.* Havana: Banco Nacional de Cuba, 1951.
Banks, Arthur S., and Robert B. Textor. *A Cross-Polity Survey.* Cambridge, Mass.: M.I.T. Press, 1963.
Baroja, Pío. *Camino de Perfección.* New York: Las Américas Publishing Company, 1952.
Batista y Zaldívar, Fulgencio. *Respuesta.* Mexico, D.F.: Imprenta Manuel León Sánchez, 1960.
Bernstein, Harry. *Venezuela and Colombia.* Englewood Cliffs, N.J.: Prentice-Hall, 1964.
Blau, Peter M., and W. Richard Scott. *Formal Organizations: A Comparative Approach.* San Francisco: Chandler Publishing Co., 1962.
Bourricaud, François, *et al. La Oligarquía en el Perú.* Lima: Moncloa-Campodónico, 1969.
Coleman, James S. *Community Conflict.* Glencoe, Ill.: Free Press, 1957.
Crassweller, Robert D. *Trujillo: The Life and Times of a Caribbean Dictator.* New York: Macmillan, 1966.
Cumberland, Charles C. *Mexico: The Struggle for Modernity.* New York: Oxford University Press, 1968.
de Imaz, José Luis. *Los que Mandan.* Buenos Aires: Editorial Universitaria de Buenos Aires, 1964.
Deutsch, Karl. *The Nerves of Government.* New York: Free Press of Glencoe, 1963.

Di Tella, Torcuato S. *El Sistema Político Argentino y la Clase Obrera*. Buenos Aires: Editorial Universitaria de Buenos Aires, 1964.

Dix, Robert H. *Colombia: The Political Dimensions of Change*. New Haven, Conn.: Yale University Press, 1967.

Downs, Anthony. *An Economic Theory of Democracy*. New York: Harper & Row, 1957.

Easton, David. *A Systems Analysis of Political Life*. New York: Wiley, 1965.

Einaudi, Luigi R. *Peruvian Military Relations with the United States*. Santa Monica, Calif.: RAND Corporation, 1970.

Eisenstadt, S. N. *Modernization: Protest and Change*. Englewood Cliffs, N.J.: Prentice-Hall, 1966.

Fagg, John E. *Cuba, Haiti, & the Dominican Republic*. Englewood Cliffs, N.J.: Prentice-Hall, 1965.

Fals-Borda, Orlando. *Peasant Society in the Colombian Andes: A Sociological Study of Saucío*. Gainesville: University of Florida Press, 1955.

Finer, Samuel E. *The Man on Horseback: The Role of the Military in Politics*. New York: Praeger, 1962.

Fluharty, Vernon L. *Dance of the Millions: Military Rule and the Social Revolution in Colombia, 1930-1956*. Pittsburgh, Pa.: University of Pittsburgh Press, 1957.

Galenson, Walter and Graham Pyatt. *The Quality of Labour and Economic Development in Certain Countries: A Preliminary Study*. Geneva, Switzerland: International Labour Organization, 1964.

Gómez, Laureano. *Comentarios a un Régimen*, 2nd ed. Bogotá: Editorial Central, 1935.

———, and José de la Vega. *El Crimen de la Magdalena*. Bogotá: Editorial Jotade, 1944.

Gutierrez, José. *De la Pseudo-Aristocracia a la Autenticidad*. Bogotá: Ediciones Tercer Mundo, 1966.

Guzmán Campos, Germán, Orlando Fals-Borda, and Eduardo Umaña Luna. *La Violencia en Colombia: Estudio de un Proceso Social*. Bogotá: Ediciones Tercer Mundo, 1964.

Hirschman, Albert O. *The Strategy of Economic Development*. New Haven, Conn.: Yale University Press, 1958.

Horowitz, Irving L. *Three Worlds of Development: The Theory and Practice of International Stratification*. New York: Oxford University Press, 1966.

Huntington, Samuel P. *Political Order in Changing Societies*. New Haven, Conn.: Yale University Press, 1968.

———. *The Soldier and the State: The Theory and Politics of Civil-Military Relations*. Cambridge, Mass.: Belknap Press of Harvard University Press, 1957.

International Labour Organization. *Yearbook of Labour Statistics*, 1952, 1963-66. Geneva, Switzerland.

International Monetary Fund. *Annual Report*, 1955, 1956. Washington, D.C.

Janowitz, Morris. *The Professional Soldier: A Social and Political Portrait*. Glencoe, Ill.: Free Press, 1960.

Johnson, John J. *The Military and Society in Latin America*. Stanford, Calif.: Stanford University Press, 1964.

Lambert, Jacques. *Latin America: Social Structure and Political Institutions,* tr. Helen Katel. Berkeley: University of California Press, 1967.

Lerner, Daniel. *The Passing of Traditional Society: Modernizing the Middle East.* Glencoe, Ill.: Free Press, 1958.

Lieuwen, Edwin. *Arms and Politics in Latin America,* rev. ed. New York: Praeger, 1961.

————. *Generals vs. Presidents: Neomilitarism in Latin America,* rev. ed. New York: Praeger, 1964.

Lipset, Seymour M. *Political Man: The Social Bases of Politics.* Garden City, N.Y.: Doubleday, 1963.

Loftus, Joseph E. *Latin American Defense Expenditures, 1938-1965.* Santa Monica, Calif.: RAND Corporation, 1968.

Martin, John B. *Overtaken by Events: The Dominican Crisis from the Fall of Trujillo to the Civil War.* New York: Doubleday, 1966.

Martz, John D. *Acción Democrática: Evolution of a Modern Political Party in Venezuela.* Princeton, N.J.: Princeton University Press, 1966.

————. *Colombia: A Contemporary Political Survey.* Chapel Hill: University of North Carolina Press, 1962.

Masó Vázquez, Calixto. *Historia de Cuba.* Caracas: Unión de Cubanos en el Exilio, 1963-67.

Merton, Robert K. *Social Theory and Social Structure,* rev. and enl. ed. Glencoe, Ill.: Free Press, 1957.

Morel, Edmar. *O Golpe Começou em Washington.* Rio de Janeiro: Editôra Civilização Brasileira, 1965.

Needler, Martin C. *Political Development in Latin America: Instability, Violence, and Evolutionary Change.* New York: Random House, 1968.

North, Liisa. *Civil-Military Relations in Argentina, Chile and Peru.* Berkeley: University of California Institute of International Studies, 1966.

Payne, James L. *Labor and Politics: The System of Political Bargaining.* New Haven, Conn.: Yale University Press, 1965.

————. *Patterns of Conflict in Colombia.* New Haven, Conn.: Yale University Press, 1968.

Riggs, Fred W. *Administration in Developing Countries: The Theory of Prismatic Society.* Boston: Houghton Mifflin, 1964.

Schmitter, Philippe C. *Interest Conflict and Political Change in Brazil.* Stanford, Calif.: Stanford University Press, 1971.

Schneider, Ronald M. *The Political System of Brazil: Emergence of a "Modernizing" Authoritarian Regime, 1964-1970.* New York: Columbia University Press, 1971.

Scott, Robert E. *Mexican Government in Transition,* rev. ed. Urbana: University of Illinois Press, 1964.

Secretaría General de Gobierno. *Documentos Secretos de la ITT.* Santiago: Empresa Editora Nacional Quimantú Ltda., 1972.

Silvert, Kalman H., ed. *Expectant Peoples: Nationalism and Development.* New York: Random House, 1963.

Skidmore, Thomas E. *Politics in Brazil, 1930-1964: An Experiment in Democracy.* New York: Oxford University Press, 1967.

Smelser, Neil J. *Essays in Sociological Explanation.* Englewood Cliffs, N.J.: Prentice-Hall, 1968.

————. *Theory of Collective Behavior*. New York: Free Press of Glencoe, 1963.

Stepan, Alfred C. *The Military in Politics: Changing Patterns in Brazil.* Princeton, N.J.: Princeton University Press, 1971.

Stokes, William S. *Honduras: An Area Study in Government*. Madison: University of Wisconsin Press, 1950.

United Nations. *Provisional Report on World Population Prospects*. New York. ST/SOA/SER.R/7, 1963.

————, Economic Commission for Latin America. *The Economic Development of Latin America in the Post-War Period*. New York. Vol. 2, E/CN. 12/659, Add. 1, April 7, 1963.

Urquide, Víctor L. *Viabilidad Económica de América Latina*. México, D.F.: Fondo de Cultura Económica, 1962.

Whitaker, Arthur P. *Argentina*. Englewood Cliffs, N.J.: Prentice-Hall, 1964.

Williams, Edward J. *Latin American Christian Democratic Parties*. Knoxville: University of Tennessee Press, 1967.

Essays and Articles

Alba, Víctor. "The Stages of Militarism in Latin America," in *The Role of the Military in Underdeveloped Countries,* ed. John J. Johnson (Princeton, N.J.: Princeton University Press, 1962), pp. 165-183.

Alexander, Robert J. "The Army in Politics," in *Government and Politics in Latin America,* ed. Harold E. Davis (New York: Ronald Press, 1958), pp. 147-165.

Arnade, Kurt C. "The Technique of the Coup d'État in Latin America," in *The Evolution of Latin American Government,* ed. Asher N. Christensen (New York: Holt, 1951), pp. 309-317.

Bañales Guimaraens, Carlos. "Las Fuerzas Armadas en la Crisis Uruguaya," *Aportes,* July, 1968, pp. 26-57.

Blanksten, George I. "Constitutions and the Structure of Power," in *Government and Politics in Latin America,* ed. Harold E. Davis (New York: Ronald Press, 1958), pp. 225-251.

————. "Revolutions," in *Government and Politics in Latin America,* ed. Harold E. Davis (New York: Ronald Press, 1958), pp. 119-146.

Bonilla, Frank. "The Urban Worker," in *Continuity and Change in Latin America,* ed. John J. Johnson (Stanford, Calif.: Stanford University Press, 1964), pp. 186-205.

Bourricaud, François. "Los Militares: Por Qué y Para Qué?," *Aportes,* Apr., 1970, pp. 13-55.

————. "El Ocaso de las Oligarquías y la Sobrevivencia del Hombre Oligárquico," *Aportes,* Apr., 1967, pp. 4-23.

————. "Structure and Function of the Peruvian Oligarchy," *Studies in Comparative International Development,* vol. 2, no. 2. St. Louis: Washington University, Social Science Institute, 1966.

Byars, Robert S. "Small Group Theory and Political Leadership in Brazil: The Case of the Castelo Branco Regime," unpub. diss., University of Illinois, 1969.

Converse, Philip E., and Georges Dupeux. "Politicization of the Electorate in

France and the United States," in *Elections and the Political Order,* ed. Angus Campbell *et al.* (New York: Wiley, 1966), pp. 269-291.

Davies, James C. "Toward a Theory of Revolution," *American Sociological Review,* 27 (1962), 5-19.

Dean, Warren. "Latin American Golpes and Economic Fluctuations, 1823-1966," *Social Science Quarterly,* 51 (1970), 70-80.

Deutsch, Karl. "Social Mobilization and Political Development," *American Political Science Review,* 55 (1961), 493-514.

Devereux, Edward C., Jr. "Parsons' Sociological Theory," in *The Social Theories of Talcott Parsons,* ed. Max Black (Englewood Cliffs, N.J.: Prentice-Hall, 1961), pp. 1-63.

Duncan, W. Raymond. "Education and Political Development: The Latin American Case," *Journal of Developing Areas,* 2 (1968), 187-210.

Fals-Borda, Orlando. "The Ideological Biases of North Americans Studying Latin America." Paper read at a conference organized by the University Christian Movement, Columbia University, December 2, 1966. (Mimeograph.)

Fitzgibbon, Russell H. " 'Continuismo' in Central America and the Caribbean," *Inter-American Quarterly,* July, 1940, pp. 56-74.

————. "Party Potpourri in Latin America," *Western Political Quarterly,* 10 (1957), 3-22.

Germani, Gino and Kalman Silvert. "Politics, Social Structure and Military Intervention in Latin America," *European Journal of Sociology,* 2 (1961), 62-81.

Gil, Federico. "Comments," in "Pathology of Democracy in Latin America: A Symposium," ed. W. W. Pierson, *American Political Science Review,* 44 (1950), 147-149.

Gillin, John P. "Some Signposts for Policy," in *Social Change in Latin America Today: Its Implications for United States Policy,* ed. Richard N. Adams *et al.* (New York: Vintage Books, 1960), pp. 14-62.

Guerra, José A. "La Industria Azucarera, 1932 a 1957," in *Siglo y Cuarto* (Havana: Diario de la Marina, 1957), pp. 98-99.

Guillén Martínez, Fernando. "Los Estados Unidos y América Latina," *Aportes,* Jan., 1968, pp. 4-28.

Gusfield, Joseph R. "Tradition and Modernity: Misplaced Polarities in the Study of Social Change," *American Journal of Sociology,* 72 (1967), 351-362.

Haya de la Torre, Víctor. "Thirty Years of 'Aprismo,' " in *The Ideologies of Developing Nations,* ed. Paul E. Sigmund (New York: Praeger, 1963), pp. 289-299.

Hirschman, Albert O. "Out of Phase," *Encounter,* 25 (1965), 21-23.

Hoselitz, Bert F. "Noneconomic Factors in Economic Development," *American Economic Review,* 47 (1957), 28-41.

Hoskin, Gary. "Las Pautas del Poder y de la Política en una Ciudad Venezolana: Su Influencia en el Desarrollo de San Cristóbal," *Razón y Fábula,* 16 (1969), 97-116.

Huntington, Samuel P. "Political Development and Political Decay," *World Politics,* 17 (1965), 386-430.

Jaguaribe, Hélio. "The Dynamics of Brazilian Nationalism," in *Obstacles to*

Change in Latin America, ed. Claudio Véliz (London: Oxford University Press, 1965), pp. 162-187.

Johnson, John J. "The Political Role of the Latin-American Middle Sectors," *Annals of the American Academy of Political and Social Science,* 334 (1961), 20-29.

Kling, Merle. "Towards a Theory of Power and Political Instability in Latin America," *Western Political Quarterly,* 9 (1956), 21-35.

Landsberger, Henry A. "The Role of Peasant Movements and Revolts in Development," in *Latin American Peasant Movements,* ed. Henry A. Landsberger (Ithaca, N.Y.: Cornell University Press, 1969), pp. 1-61.

Laqueur, Walter. "Revolution," in *International Encyclopedia of the Social Sciences* (New York: Macmillan, 1968), XIII, 501-507.

Linz, Juan. "An Authoritarian Regime: Spain," in *Cleavages, Ideologies and Party Systems: Contributions to Comparative Sociology,* ed. Erik Allardt and Yrjö Littunen (Helsinki: Academic Bookstore, 1964), pp. 291-341.

———. "The Breakdown of Democratic Regimes." Paper prepared for the Seventh World Congress of Sociology, Varna, Bulgaria, September, 1970.

———. "The Party System of Spain: Past and Future," in *Party Systems and Voter Alignment,* ed. Seymour M. Lipset and Stein Rokkan (New York: Free Press of Glencoe, 1967), pp. 197-282.

———, and Amando de Miguel. "Within-Nation Differences and Comparisons: The Eight Spains," in *Comparing Nations: The Use of Quantitative Data in Cross-National Research,* ed. Richard L. Merritt and Stein Rokkan (New Haven, Conn.: Yale University Press, 1966), pp. 267-319.

Lipset, Seymour M. "Democracy and the Social System," in *Internal War: Problems and Approaches,* ed. Harry Eckstein (New York: Free Press of Glencoe, 1964), pp. 267-333.

———. "Some Social Requisites of Democracy: Economic Development and Political Legitimacy," *American Political Science Review,* 53 (1959), 69-105.

McAlister, Lyle N. "Civil-Military Relations in Latin America," *Journal of Inter-American Studies,* 3 (1961), 341-350.

———. "Recent Research and Writings on the Role of the Military in Latin America," *Latin American Research Review,* 2 (1966), 5-36.

McClelland, David C. "The Achievement Motive in Economic Growth," in *Industrialization and Society,* ed. Bert F. Hoselitz and Wilbert E. Moore (Paris: UNESCO-Mouton, 1963), pp. 74-96.

Mendes de Almeida, Cândido. "Sistema Político e Modelos de Poder no Brasil," *Dados,* no. 1, 2nd semester, 1966, 7-41.

Merei, Ferenc. "Group Leadership and Institutionalization," in *Readings in Social Psychology,* 3rd ed., ed. Eleanor E. Maccoby, Theodore M. Newcomb, and Eugene L. Hartley (New York: Holt, 1958), pp. 522-532.

Merelman, Richard M. "Learning and Legitimacy," *American Political Science Review,* 60 (1966), 548-561.

Merkx, Gilbert W. "Recessions and Rebellions in Argentina," MS, University of New Mexico, 1969.

Midlarsky, Manus, and Raymond Tanter. "Toward a Theory of Political Instability in Latin America," *Journal of Peace Research,* 3 (1967), 209-227.

Nahirny, Vladimir C. "Some Observations on Ideological Groups," *American Journal of Sociology*, 67 (1962), 397-405.

Needler, Martin C. "Political Development and Military Intervention in Latin America," *American Political Science Review*, 60 (1966), 616-626.

———. "Political Development and Socioeconomic Development: The Case of Latin America," *American Political Science Review*, 62 (1968), 889-897.

Nun, José. "A Latin American Phenomenon: The Middle-Class Military Coup," in *Latin America: Reform or Revolution?*, ed. James Petras and Maurice Zeitlin (Greenwich, Conn.: Fawcett Publications, 1968), pp. 145-185.

Powell, John Duncan. "Military Assistance and Militarism in Latin America," *Western Political Quarterly*, 18 (1965), 382-392.

Putnam, Robert D. "Toward Explaining Military Intervention in Latin American Politics," *World Politics*, 20 (1967), 83-110.

Pye, Lucian W. "Armies in the Process of Political Modernization," *European Journal of Sociology*, 2 (1961), 82-92.

Randall, Laura. "A Dialogue of the Deaf: The United States and Latin America," *Dissent*, 9 (1962), 410-417.

Ratinoff, Luis A. "Las Clases Medias en América Latina," *Revista Paraguaya de Sociología*, Sept.-Dec. 1965, pp. 5-31.

Scott, Robert E. "Legislatures and Legislation," in *Government and Politics in Latin America*, ed. Harold E. Davis (New York: Ronald Press, 1958), pp. 290-332.

———. "Mexico: The Established Revolution," in *Political Culture and Political Development*, ed. Lucian W. Pye and Sidney Verba (Princeton, N.J.: Princeton University Press, 1965), pp. 330-395.

———. "Political Elites and Political Modernization: The Crisis of Transition," in *Elites in Latin America*, ed. Seymour M. Lipset and Aldo Solari (New York: Oxford University Press, 1967), pp. 117-145.

———. "Political Parties and Policy-Making in Latin America," in *Political Parties and Political Development*, ed. Joseph LaPalombara and Myron Weiner (Princeton, N.J.: Princeton University Press, 1966), pp. 331-367.

Selznick, Philip. "The Sociology of Law," in *Sociology Today: Problems and Prospects*, ed. Robert K. Merton, Leonard Broom, Leonard S. Cottrell, Jr. (New York: Basic Books, 1959), pp. 115-127.

Sherill, Kenneth S. "The Attitudes of Modernity," *Comparative Politics*, 1 (1969), 184-210.

Shils, Edward A. "Authoritarianism: 'Right' and 'Left,'" in *Studies in the Scope and Method of 'The Authoritarian Personality': Continuities in Social Research*, ed. Richard Christie and Marie Jahoda (Glencoe, Ill.: Free Press, 1954), pp. 24-49.

Simpson, David. "Dimensions of World Poverty," *Scientific American*, 219 (1968), 22, 27-35.

Snow, Peter G. "Parties and Politics in Argentina: The Elections of 1962 and 1963," *Midwest Journal of Political Science*, 9 (1965), 1-36.

Solaún, Mauricio. "El Fracaso de la Democracia en Cuba: Un Régimen 'Patrimonial' Autoritario (1952)," *Aportes*, July, 1969, pp. 57-80.

————. "Political Violence in Colombia," unpub. diss., University of Chicago, 1971.

————, and Manuel S. Alguero. "Socialización y Compromiso por Medio de la Violencia," *Razón y Fábula,* 10 (1968), 61-76.

Southwood, Kenneth. "Riot and Revolt: Sociological Theories of Political Violence," *Peace Research Reviews,* no. 3, 1967.

Stokes, William S. "Violence as a Power Factor in Latin American Politics," *Western Political Quarterly,* 5 (1952), 445-468.

Strassman, W. Paul. "The Industrialist," in *Continuity and Change in Latin America,* ed. John J. Johnson (Stanford, Calif.: Stanford University Press, 1964), pp. 161-185.

Whitaker, Arthur P. "Nationalism and Social Change in Latin America," in *Politics of Change in Latin America,* ed. Joseph Maier and Richard W. Weatherhead (New York: Praeger, 1964), pp. 85-100.

Wolf, Charles. "Political Effects of Military Programs: Some Indications from Latin America," *Orbis,* 8 (1965), 871-893.

Wyckoff, Theodore. "The Role of the Military in Latin American Politics," *Western Political Quarterly,* 13 (1960), 745-763.

Zeitlin, Maurice. "Cuba: Revolution without a Blueprint," *Trans-Action,* 6 (1969), 38-42.

————. "Los Determinantes Sociales de la Democracia Política en Chile," *Revista Latinoamericana de Sociología,* 2 (1966), 223-236.

————. "Revolutionary Workers and Individual Liberties," *American Journal of Sociology,* 72 (1967), 619-632.

Newspapers and Periodicals

Alerta (Havana), 1952.
El Siglo (Bogotá), 1950.
Expreso (Panama City), 1968.
Hispanic American Report, vols. 4-17 (1951-64).
Keesing's Contemporary Archives, vols. 5-15 (1943-66).
La Calle (Panama City), 1968.
New York Times, 1943-69.
Time, the Weekly Newsmagazine, vols. 46-52 (1945-48).
Visión, vol. 35 (1968).

INDEX

A Note on the Authors

MAURICIO SOLAÚN is an Assistant Professor, Department of Sociology and Center for Latin American Studies, University of Illinois, Urbana. He received a Doctor of Law degree from the Universidad de Villanueva, Havana, Cuba (1958), M.A. in Economics, Yale University (1959), and Ph.D. in Sociology, University of Chicago (1971).

Mr. Solaún has held a Foreign Area Fellowship, two Fulbright-Hays awards, a fellowship from the Center for Social Organization Studies, University of Chicago, and was Carnegie Fellow of the Committee for the Comparative Study of New Nations at the same university. In addition he has held several grants and has been a consultant for various American and Latin American governmental and private organizations.

MICHAEL A. QUINN is an Assistant Professor and Research Associate, Department of Government and Center for Urban and Environmental Research and Services, Southern Illinois University, Edwardsville. He received his B.A. degree in Political Science from the University of Delaware in 1967 and his M.A. and Ph.D. degrees in Political Science from the University of Illinois, Urbana, in 1969 and 1972, respectively.

Between 1970 and 1972, Mr. Quinn held a Foreign Area Fellowship Program doctoral research grant. Mr. Quinn has also been a Woodrow Wilson Fellow, a National Defense Foreign Language Fellow in Spanish and Portuguese, and a Graduate Intern of the Midwest Universities' Consortium for International Activities.